Communications in Computer and Information Science 2519

Rationale

The CCIS series is devoted to the publication of proceedings of computer science conferences. Its aim is to efficiently disseminate original research results in informatics in printed and electronic form. While the focus is on publication of peer-reviewed full papers presenting mature work, inclusion of reviewed short papers reporting on work in progress is welcome, too. Besides globally relevant meetings with internationally representative program committees guaranteeing a strict peer-reviewing and paper selection process, conferences run by societies or of high regional or national relevance are also considered for publication.

Topics

The topical scope of CCIS spans the entire spectrum of informatics ranging from foundational topics in the theory of computing to information and communications science and technology and a broad variety of interdisciplinary application fields.

Information for Volume Editors and Authors

Publication in CCIS is free of charge. No royalties are paid, however, we offer registered conference participants temporary free access to the online version of the conference proceedings on SpringerLink (http://link.springer.com) by means of an http referrer from the conference website and/or a number of complimentary printed copies, as specified in the official acceptance email of the event.

CCIS proceedings can be published in time for distribution at conferences or as post-proceedings, and delivered in the form of printed books and/or electronically as USBs and/or e-content licenses for accessing proceedings at SpringerLink. Furthermore, CCIS proceedings are included in the CCIS electronic book series hosted in the SpringerLink digital library at http://link.springer.com/bookseries/7899. Conferences publishing in CCIS are allowed to use Online Conference Service (OCS) for managing the whole proceedings lifecycle (from submission and reviewing to preparing for publication) free of charge.

Publication process

The language of publication is exclusively English. Authors publishing in CCIS have to sign the Springer CCIS copyright transfer form, however, they are free to use their material published in CCIS for substantially changed, more elaborate subsequent publications elsewhere. For the preparation of the camera-ready papers/files, authors have to strictly adhere to the Springer CCIS Authors' Instructions and are strongly encouraged to use the CCIS LaTeX style files or templates.

Abstracting/Indexing

CCIS is abstracted/indexed in DBLP, Google Scholar, EI-Compendex, Mathematical Reviews, SCImago, Scopus. CCIS volumes are also submitted for the inclusion in ISI Proceedings.

How to start

To start the evaluation of your proposal for inclusion in the CCIS series, please send an e-mail to ccis@springer.com

Francisco Bellas · Oscar Fontenla-Romero
Editors

AI in Education and Educational Research

First International Workshop, AIEER 2024
Santiago de Compostela, Spain, October 19–20, 2024
Proceedings

Springer

Editors
Francisco Bellas
University of A Coruña
Ferrol, Spain

Oscar Fontenla-Romero
University of A Coruña
Ferrol, Spain

ISSN 1865-0929 ISSN 1865-0937 (electronic)
Communications in Computer and Information Science
ISBN 978-3-031-93408-7 ISBN 978-3-031-93409-4 (eBook)
https://doi.org/10.1007/978-3-031-93409-4

This Springer imprint is published by the registered company Springer Nature Switzerland AG
The registered company address is: Gewerbestrasse 11, 6330 Cham, Switzerland

Preface

This volume includes all the papers accepted and presented in the AIEER 2024 International Workshop on AI in Education and Educational Research. AIEER was part of the 27th European Conference on Artificial Intelligence ECAI 2024.

The scope of the workshop had two distinct foci with the aim of facing the field of AI in education in a wider manner. On one hand a (social science-led) discussion about the real issues in education that AI-enabled applications might help address was carried out. This included the scope of educational and teaching AI, but also social sciences, economics, and humanities, including all subjects such as education and teaching in action, labor market research with a focus on educational needs, history of education and related cultural heritage of education, as well as informative predictions for decision making and behavioral science perspectives. On the one hand, we focused on the connections between AI, education, and society. This includes quantitative and qualitative research, data science methods for analyzing education and labor market data, AI approaches for recommender systems, and digitized learning. On the other hand, we focused on how AI can be used to push the boundaries of the field. This includes developing new methods (including methods using AI), finding and making accessible new data sources, enriching data, and more.

More broadly, we were interested in how AI methods affect all areas of education, as well as businesses and labor markets. This includes approaches to how all sectors of education, from primary to tertiary, are affected by and respond to AI methods. The design of digitalized futures with AI methods raises several questions for education: At the broadest level, legislative and normative questions; at the level of companies, questions about investment decisions and how to maintain productivity and their workforces; at the level of individuals, questions about qualifications and which skills need to be applied and possibly learned anew. Skills and qualifications are thus at the heart of AI in education and educational research.

On the other hand, we saw the need for a (computer science-led) discussion about what AI-enabled applications might be developed (and how) to address the issues raised in the previous part. The use of AI-based systems to support teaching or learning has been under development for more than four decades, but its rise has increased markedly in recent years, due to the increase in the use of e-learning tools during the COVID-19 pandemic and the recent explosion of generative AI. We are at a key moment of development in this field, in which experts in AI and experts in education must join forces to achieve an optimal use of this technology in teaching and learning processes. This workshop aimed to create a space for the presentation of new proposals and reflections on the state of the art in this field of such social relevance. In this part, we were especially interested on the technical aspects of AI, focusing on the specific techniques used for content creation (generative AI), student profiling (machine learning), learning analytics or explainable AI methods for teacher's dashboards. The aim was to provide a clear picture of the type of approach followed in the scope of education, and its particularities.

The workshop had 23 submissions and 16 of them were accepted for presentation after a single-blind peer review process with two reviews per paper. The accepted papers explored various aspects of AI applications in educational settings, particularly emphasizing the integration of Large Language Models (LLMs) and explainable AI (XAI). One prominent area was automated grading, where researchers investigate the practical implications of using AI models such as GPT to evaluate student responses. These studies analysed discrepancies between human and AI graders and assessed their real-world impact on final examination results, offering insights into grading practices and inter-rater variability. Additionally, several submissions demonstrated the use of explainable AI techniques such as Integrated Gradients, for enhancing transparency and robustness in AI-driven tools, specifically in classifying occupational data from online job advertisements for vocational education and training purposes.

Another significant theme was the creation and utilization of datasets and tools aimed at improving the efficiency and accuracy of scientific and educational workflows. Examples include the introduction of the Tex2Py-45K dataset for bidirectional LaTeX-Python conversion, fostering improved computational reproducibility and precision in scientific documentation. Moreover, various contributions highlighted developments in vocational education and training (VET), presenting an overview of digital innovations driven by Germany's INVITE funding initiative. These projects predominantly focus on personalized learning experiences through adaptive learning platforms, recommender systems, and virtual learning assistants, while also identifying current gaps, such as accessibility improvements needed to support diverse learner populations.

March 2024

Francisco Bellas
Oscar Fontenla-Romero

Organization

General Chair

Francisco Bellas	University of A Coruña, Spain

Program Committee Chairs

Francisco Bellas	University of A Coruña, Spain
Oscar Fontenla-Romero	University of A Coruña, Spain
Jens Dörpinghaus	University of Koblenz, Germany
Michael Tiemann	University of Bonn, Germany

Program Committee

Sara Guerreiro-Santalla	University of A Coruña, Spain
Alma Mallo	University of A Coruña, Spain
Alejandro Paz-Lopez	University of A Coruña, Spain
Stefan Udelhofen	Federal Institute for VET, Germany
Laura Getz	Federal Institute for VET, Germany
Beatriz Pérez	University of A Coruña, Spain
Xabier Martínez-Rolán	University of Vigo, Spain
Noelia Sánchez	University of A Coruña, Spain
Laura Morán-Fernández	University of A Coruña, Spain
Peter Peer	University of Ljubljana, Slovenia
Alejandro Catala	University of Santiago de Compostela, Spain
Helen Crompton	Old Dominion University, USA
Dalila Duraes	Universidade do Minho, Portugal
Mortimer Schlieker	Federal Institute for VET, Germany
Richard Fechner	University of Koblenz and Landau, Germany

Contents

Using Explainable AI for Robustness Checks in Requirement Level Classification for German Online Job Advertisements

Kai Krüger(✉)

German Federal Institute for Vocational Education and Training, Bonn, Germany
kai.krueger@bibb.de

Abstract. Online job advertisements (OJAs) have become a significant data source for analyzing labor market dynamics, offering insights into shifts within occupations, industry sectors, skills, and tasks. This paper investigates the cross-lingual and cultural differences in OJAs and their impact on the transferability of Natural Language Processing (NLP) methods and research scope. By analyzing OJAs from Austria, France, Germany, Italy, Spain, the UK, and the US, we point out substantial variations in document length, diversity metrics, syntactic structures, and content features such as salary information. These differences underscore the challenges in applying NLP methods universally across languages and cultures. Our findings emphasize the need for tailored approaches in NLP research and offer a starting point for developing standardized pipelines for analyzing text genres across different languages.

Keywords: Online Job Advertisements · Text Classification · Occupation Classification · Explainable AI · Integrated Gradients

1 Introduction

Online Job Advertisements (OJAs) have become a crucial resource for labor market research, offering detailed information on job requirements, skills, and tasks. These advertisements, typically collected through web scraping, are valuable for analyzing trends and patterns in employment. A key challenge in this domain is accurately classifying job advertisements according to established occupation taxonomies, such as the German *Klassifikation der Berufe 2010* (KldB 2010), which is crucial for stakeholders such as policymakers, educators, and researchers.

Previous methods have primarily focused on matching job titles to occupation taxonomies. However, this approach often leads to inaccuracies due to the ambiguous and inconsistent nature of job titles. Recent research suggests incorporating job descriptions and contextual data to improve classification accuracy. Building on these insights, we propose a supervised text classification model that leverages both job titles and detailed job descriptions to classify OJAs according to the KldB 2010 taxonomy. Our model specifically addresses the requirement

F. Bellas and O. Fontenla-Romero (Eds.): AIEER 2024, CCIS 2519, pp. 1–16, 2025.
https://doi.org/10.1007/978-3-031-93409-4_1

level, a crucial aspect of the taxonomy that indicates the vocational prerequisites needed for a job.

We utilize explainable AI (XAI) techniques, particularly Integrated Gradients, to ensure transparency in our model's decision-making process. This approach helps us understand whether the model bases its classifications on relevant features or statistical artifacts. Our study uses a comprehensive dataset from the German Federal Employment Agency, consisting of approximately 5.5 million job advertisements, to train and evaluate our model.

The main contribution of our study are as follows:

- We derive why it is useful to model occupation taxonomy classification as a supervised text classification problem and why classifying to the KldB 2010 taxonomy specifically should follow a two step procedure.
- We publish[1] three models for classifying German job ads according to the fifth digit of the KldB 2010, which corresponds to the requirement level.
- We employ Integrated Gradients for explainable AI, offering insights into the model's decision-making process and identifying relevant features and potential biases.
- Our study utilizes a large and comprehensive dataset from the German Federal Employment Agency, ensuring robust training and evaluation of our model.
- We provide a detailed analysis of the model's performance and offer recommendations for improving occupation classification systems in labor market research.

2 Background

In recent years, Online Job Advertisements (OJAs) have emerged as a pivotal data source for labor market analysis and subsequent research fields like vocational education or continuous education. Typical analyses extract entities like skills and tasks and correlate them with metadata dimensions such as time, location, and occupation classification. Job advertisements are typically scraped from the internet, during which process metadata can be collected. Among these, the occupation category stands out as particularly important [17]. This is because it is frequently used in labor market research due to its high relevance for various stakeholders and is therefore also helpful for linking research [8]. However, positioning a job advertisement within a taxonomic structure poses a challenge, as the taxonomic position to which a given job advertisement belongs cannot be derived from its source code directly. Therefore, it becomes necessary to employ an algorithm that can accurately assign a job advertisement to a specific position within an occupation taxonomy.

The most relevant [23] German taxonomy for occupations is the *Klassifikation der Berufe 2010* (KldB 2010) [4], which is hierarchically structured, featuring increasingly specialized occupational fields across its first four levels. Uniquely,

[1] https://huggingface.co/KKrueger/oja_reqlevel_de.

the fifth level represents the *Anforderungsniveau (requirement level)* [18], which stands somewhat apart from the hierarchical structure. This level is consistently categorized from 1 to 4, with each number representing the same level of requirement level across different occupations. Table 1 shows the concrete meaning of the four levels.

We now provide a brief overview of recent approaches to classify OJAs according to an occupation taxonomy. [3] pass extracted job titles to a pipeline that includes a BERT based embedding matching between the job titles and KldB labels. To the best of our knowledge, this is currently the only public approach to match OJAs with the KldB. Other work usually classifies OJAs according to the International Standard Classification of Occupations (ISCO), O*NET, or other, mostly custom databases (see [20] for an overview). As [12] point out, most previous methods use job titles as primary features for their classification approaches. They argue that this is insufficient, because job titles often contain ambiguous and inconsistent terms that do not accurately reflect the actual duties or responsibilities, leading to significant classification errors [12]. They recommend incorporating job descriptions and additional contextual data to improve the accuracy of occupation classification systems [12]. The authors then propose a taxonomy-agnostic two-phase unsupervised processing technique. Initially, it creates occupation embeddings from textual descriptions using token-level embeddings averaged to form a foundational reference. In the query phase, it applies a similar embedding process to incoming job descriptions or, using vector similarity searches to match these with the occupation taxonomy.

While conceptually we agree that it is necessary to use more information than job titles only, we argue that unsupervised embedding matching techniques also have inherent limitations. This is because semantic relatedness based on pretrained Large Language Models (LLMs) cannot capture the nuances and rationales that underlie the logic of a taxonomy. [12] show this in their analyses of the taxonomy description embeddings. The inherent problem is that sometimes, occupations can contain two aspects that are unrelated from a taxonomy point of view. Therefore, sometimes a taxonomy can contain partly arbitrary artifacts that are not well captured by LLMs semantic embeddings. In these cases, the job title might actually be a valuable source. Therefore, conceptually an algorithm that classifies job ads according to an occupational taxonomy would take clear mappings from job titles to a certain position within the taxonomy into account and use the content of the ad, such as the tasks or the specified qualifications, to predict the taxonomy position where job titles are unclear, noisy or ambiguous. We hypothesize that given large enough training data, a supervised text classification model can capture these steps sufficiently. As we describe in Sect. 4, we have a large body of training data available, which is why we perform experiments modeling the OJA-to-taxonomy-classification as supervised text classification and perform a XAI technique to gain insight into the models decision making. Our central research question is whether and to what extend the model classifies based on the desired concept described above, or if it merely learned statistical artifacts.

3 Research Method

In this section, we outline the methodologies used to classify job advertisements based on the KldB taxonomy, highlighting our rationale behind classifying the requirement level separately from the other KldB digits and the specific explainable AI (XAI) techniques employed in our analysis.

3.1 Requirement Level Classification

As established in Sect. 2, our objective is to classify job advertisements according to the KldB taxonomy. Since the last digit of the KldB code functions independently from the hierarchy of the initial four digits, we argue against using a single classification function $X \rightarrow Y$. Instead, we argue it is better to employ two separate functions: $f_1 : X \rightarrow Y_1$ for classifying the first four digits and $f_2 : X \rightarrow Y_2$ for the fifth digit. The final classification is obtained by concatenating the results of both stages: $f(x) = f_1(x) \parallel f_2(x)$. This has two major advantages. First, this way the models learning objective is closer to the inherent logic of the taxonomy and how humans would approach this task. Second, it is much easier to construct training and testsets this way, because splitting the classification task allows for more effective use of annotated data. Specifically, by isolating the fifth digit, we can aggregate a larger and more balanced training set for f_2, as this digit often varies within otherwise similar categories. Moreover, separating the first four digits simplifies constructing sufficient and representative training examples for f_1, as it reduces the complexity of the classification space. For the scope of this paper, we only focus on f_2. Table 1 gives an overview over the four requirement levels we differentiate, which correspond to the label space for the following experiments. The classification model developed in this paper can also be seen as a model that assigns a requirement level to an OJA. Consequently, researchers can also use our published model in isolation.

3.2 Explainable AI

The field of Explainable Artificial Intelligence (XAI) has expanded significantly in recent years, driven by the necessity to ensure that AI systems are transparent, understandable, and accountable in their decision-making processes. For space reasons, we do not provide an exhaustive review of the different methods and vast amount of different aspects of XAI (e.g. target audience, popularity, ethics, etc.), but instead reference comprehensive surveys [7,15,16,25]. Our focus is primarily on aspects relevant to our research. We employ a neural transformer-based model for text classification as an instance of AI (Sect. 3.1). Therefore, our XAI goal is to gain insights into the decision making process of the model. Specifically, we aim to determine whether the model's decisions are influenced by the expected key input features-such as job titles, qualification requirements, and tasks-or by statistical artifacts in the data. This aspect of XAI is crucial for enhancing the robustness of the model and building user trust. To formally describe this inquiry: given a text T and a model M, we seek to identify the

Table 1. Levels of Vocational Qualification Requirements [18]

Requirement Level	Normally Required Vocational Qualification
1 - Unskilled or semi-skilled activities	No vocational qualification, or regular one-year vocational training required
2 - Specialist activities	At least two years of vocational training, also graduation from vocational school
3 - Complex specialist activities	Qualification as master craftsman or technician, or equivalent technical school or college graduation, also graduation from a professional academy or university bachelor's degree
4 - Highly complex activities	Completed university studies of at least four years

prediction P made by M on T and discern the influential input features $F \subseteq T$ that impact P, representing a focused local explanation of the model's behavior.

[2] provide a guide on how to choose among the vast options of XAI techniques for text classification and evaluate the usefulness of different methods for this task empirically. Based on their findings and practical aspects of our project, we chose Integrated Gradients (IGs) as our XAI method for this project. Integrated Gradients is a method for attributing the prediction of a neural network to its inputs. Introduced by [22], this technique quantifies the contribution of each input feature to the final prediction by integrating the gradients of the output with respect to the input features along the path from a given baseline to the input. Mathematically, the attribution of an input feature x_i is calculated as:

$$\text{IGs}(x_i) = (x_i - x_i') \times \int_{\alpha=0}^{1} \frac{\partial F(x' + \alpha \cdot (x - x'))}{\partial x_i} \, d\alpha,$$

where x' is the baseline input, x is the actual input, α is the interpolation scalar, and F is the model function. This method satisfies two important axioms: sensitivity and implementation invariance [22], making it a robust tool for explaining model predictions. In NLP models frequently utilize vector embeddings to represent input tokens, which makes selecting a zero vector as the baseline, where each token is represented by a vector of zeros corresponding in dimension to the actual vector embeddings, provides a neutral starting point for the integration, effectively isolating the influence of non-zero elements in the input vectors.

4 Data

4.1 Data Description

Our dataset[2], sourced from the German Federal Employment Agency (Bundesagentur für Arbeit - BA), comprises approximately 5.5 million job advertisements posted between 2013 and 2022 on the BA's job portal. This portal, which

[2] Due to data protection restrictions, we cannot publish our data.

is Germany's single largest source for job postings, records an increasing trend in data volume annually, ranging from 350,000 to 700,000 advertisements.

Advertisements on the BA portal require employers to specify a DKZ number-an eight-digit code representing occupations. Companies are aided by a smart search system during this process. The initial five digits align with the KldB taxonomy, and the remaining three provide further occupation classification. For simplicity, our study focuses on the KldB classification, truncating the last three digits and analyzing data according to the main occupation (MO) and up to two alternatives (AO1 and AO2). Specifically, our analysis targets the prediction of the 'requirement level', the last digit of the KldB code, considering it as a categorical label (ranging from one to four).

Figures 1a, 1b, and 1c illustrate various aspects of the data. Figure 1a indicates a significant imbalance in advertisements across different requirement levels, reflecting, although not mirroring variations in real-world job market demand [5]. Figure 1b shows that approximately 45% of the ads feature at least one alternative occupation. The analysis of 'Alternative Distance' in Fig. 1c reveals that over 1.2 million instances of supposedly different labels for the same advertisement are actually identical, likely due to the derivation of the five-digit KldB number from a more detailed eight-digit DKZ number. This suggests that discrepancies in occupational codes often do not imply different requirement levels. Remarkably, a divergence at the last digit of KldB, indicating a difference solely in requirement level, is the least common type of variation. This implies that alternative labels frequently differ in terms of occupational expertise rather than requirement level, likely reflecting positions that straddle two specializations but share the same level of requirements. However, the method of calculating distances based on the earliest divergence does not preclude the possibility that labels diverging at earlier digits may also differ in requirement level.

4.2 Data Pre-processing

Given the large but unevenly distributed dataset, we used stratified k-fold (k=5) cross-validation to ensure metric robustness. To reduce computing time, we sampled our data to approximately 550,000 ads. Based on other research in text classification in general, and [10] specifically in regards to OJA text classification, we believe that this number should be sufficient to be near the peak of models performance without any more sophisticated data cleaning techniques.

We also test different ways to filter noisy data before running experiments. The precise set-ups listed in Sect. 5.1. When we mention filtering the data, we mean filtering it before the k-fold stratification and train/test split. Therefore, data is not evaluated on the same testset. This is because we assume to filter out noise that exists in the data, which also screws the testsets. Consequently, gain in models performance cannot simply be interpreted as better models based on cleaner input data, because the evaluation task was also simpler due to cleaner test data.

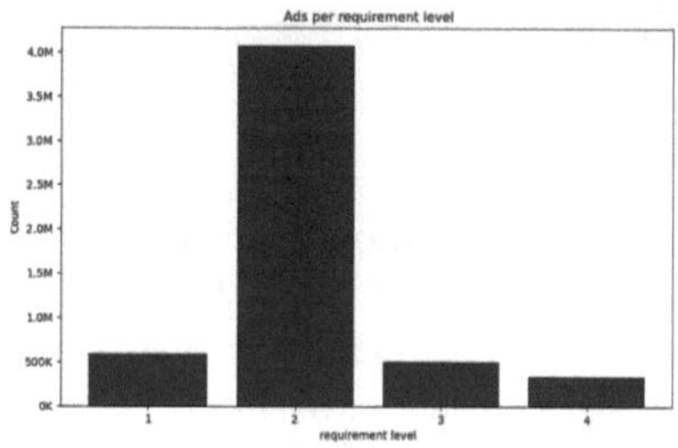

(a) Ads per Requirement Level

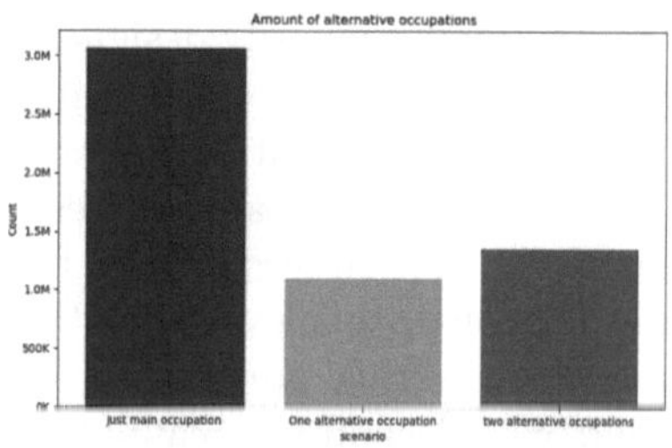

(b) Amount of Alternatives

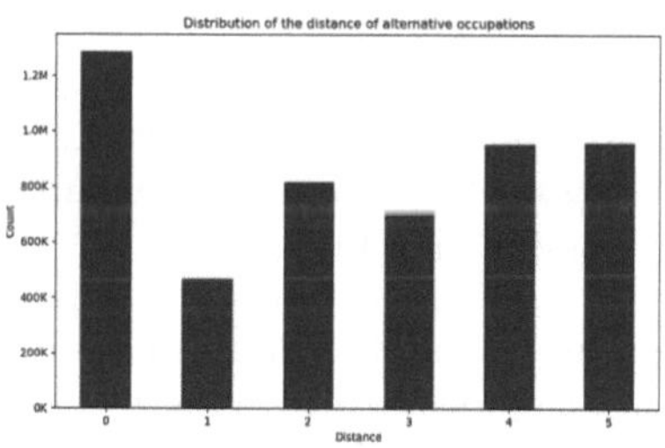

(c) Alternative Distance

Fig. 1. Overview of Data Characteristics. Figure (a) shows the absolute amount of ads per requirement level. Figure (b) displays the number of ads with no, one, or two alternative occupation labels. Figure (c) illustrates the "Alternative Distance", which measures the divergence between alternative labels based on the earliest differing digit. Smaller distances indicate closely related categories, while larger distances signify divergence at higher hierarchical levels. Distance zero means that the alternative labels are actually equal. Distances are calculated between all occupations for one ad, which is why the total amount of distances exceeds the total amount of ads.

5 Experiment Setup

5.1 Model Training

For our experiments, we use a common transformer based fine-tuning setup. We use [10] to derive hyper-parameters that have worked well on similar text classification tasks for OJAs. We also chose a DistilBERT [21] based model for computational efficiency. We ran the experiment pipeline multiple times with different data configurations, explained below.

- **Baseline (BL):** We derive the label solely based on the MO, ignoring possible AOs.
- **NoAppr:** The KldB taxonomy is primarily designed for regular employment roles, rather than for apprenticeships or other positions that primarily serve qualification, complicating the assignment of accurate KldB digits to apprenticeship job postings. Specifically, the challenge lies in mapping these to an appropriate requirement level; apprenticeships are frequently misclassified at level two in our dataset, although this level actually presupposes completed training—thus incorrectly suggesting pre-existing qualification. To address potential data noise and model confusion caused by this misclassification, and given that predicting requirement levels for apprenticeships falls outside the KldB's intended scope, we excluded apprenticeship positions from this training iteration, utilizing dataset metadata for identification and removal.
- **NoApprAlt:** As per the run above, this run also filtered out apprenticeship ads. Furthermore, we only considered ads without any alternative label. The rationale behind this is that it is the easiest way to reduce the number job postings that can be assigned to two different requirement levels in our data, thus streamlining the classification task.

For each configuration, we report the mean and standard deviation of both the F1 score and accuracy across the five folds of our stratified k-fold cross-validation. These metrics provide insights into the consistency and reliability of our model across different subsets of our dataset, illustrating how well the model generalizes under each pre-processing setup.

5.2 Qualitative XAI Analysis

As described in Sect. 3.2 we use IGs[3] to gain insights into what type of input features the model deems relevant to Requirement Level Classification. For comparability, we constructed one dataset of 40 OJAs that we let explain by one model from each run configuration. The model was chosen randomly among the five runs from each configuration, but as the results in Sect. 6 show the deviation of performance was low, such that models should behave similarly in their

[3] We used the transformers-interpret library (available at https://github.com/cdpierse/transformers-interpret) for Integrated Gradients analysis and to generate the visualizations presented in this study.

behavior w.r.t. IG explanations. The dataset was constructed based on BL tests, sampling ten ads for each of the four possible combinations of prediction outcomes and confidence levels: high confidence with correct predictions (True), high confidence with incorrect predictions (False), low confidence with correct predictions (True), and low confidence with incorrect predictions (False). By selecting examples from these distinct groups, we aimed to avoid the potential bias of observing similar behavior by chance, which is particularly important in qualitative analyses where the number of samples is limited. This methodological choice allows us to explore a broad spectrum of the model's performance across different scenarios, providing a more comprehensive understanding of its behavior under varied conditions. For each explanation, we visualized the text with tokens colored w.r.t. their attributions. All images can be accessed in our repository. An example for the images is shown in Fig. 2.

For each ad, we decided which of the models provided the best explanation and in short notes reasoned our choice. The corresponding sheet can be found in our repository. Note, that not always all models predicted the same class. When this was the case, we selected the best model solely based on the explanation for the predicted class rather than the prediction itself (by for example comparing it to the true label). This was mostly the case when even to us it was not clear, which would be the most fitting label, because clues were contradicting. We also considered having a low overall attribution score as good explanation in cases, where there were no real clues in the texts.

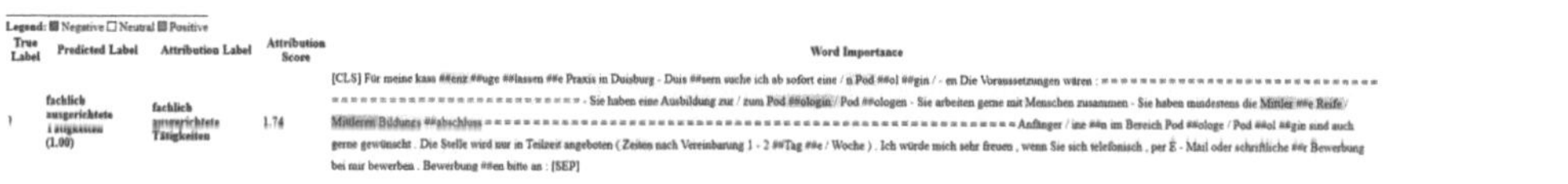

Fig. 2. XAI Example. An example for our XAI images. It shows True Label, Predicted Label, Attribution Label, Attribution Score and the full text with color encoded attributions. Green color means positive contribution for the predicted class, whereas red means negative contribution. Higher saturation means higher contribution.

6 Results

6.1 Training Results

Table 2 presents the outcomes for the three configurations previously discussed. Notably, the standard deviations are consistently low across all configurations and metrics, suggesting minimal impact of data splits on model performance. This stability is expected, considering the rather large amount of training data used. Between the configurations, the Baseline performs substantially worse in terms of F1 than the other two configurations, which show comparable results. The accuracy rates are higher than F1 scores across all configurations, but the discrepancy differs. Baseline has the largest discrepancy with 7% difference, NoApprAlt still has 5% and NoAppr is closest having only 3% difference and also the highest F1 score.

Table 2. Mean and Standard Deviation of F1 Scores and Accuracies for Each Configuration

Config.	Mean F1	SD F1	Mean Acc	SD Acc
Baseline	.84	.001	.91	.001
NoAppr	**.91**	.002	.94	.001
NoApprAlt	.90	.002	**.95**	.001

6.2 XAI Analysis

The qualitative analysis of the IG attributions provides insights into the models' decision making. We divide it into two parts: First, we look at general observations about what type of inputs were used by the models in their classification. In the second part we focus on differences between models from the different configurations described in Sect. 5.1.

General Observations. The type of inputs relevant to the models' decisions is diverse, frequently including expected input feature types such as occupational titles and formal requirements like certificates. For example, the finished apprenticeship to a podiatrist was a significant feature in the example shown in Fig. 2. Skills and tasks typical for certain occupations within the respective requirement level are also sometimes consulted. For instance, leading a team was associated with a level three prediction, whereas leadership qualities negatively influenced a level two prediction. Hard skills were observed to have a more frequent influence compared to soft skills.

On the other hand, several undesired influence patterns were also identified. Below, we list these observations. In Sects. 7 and 8, we interpret and reflect on them further.

- **Company names:** Large companies' names, like 'Deutsche Bahn', influenced model predictions, likely due to their frequent representation in the dataset.
- **Company description:** Descriptions and industry sectors sometimes influenced predictions, with, for example, IT or Law contributing to higher requirement levels and restaurants to lower ones.
- **Locations:** Information such as regions, cities, or street names also influenced model predictions.
- **Punctuation:** Punctuation marks were regularly attributed positively or negatively.

- **Contradictions:** The same tokens within a single ad were attributed both negatively and positively. An example for this can be seen in Fig. 2 where the occupational title "Podologe" was once attributed highly positive, once moderately negative and once relative neutral. The contextual embeddings of the transformer architecture makes it possible for the model to treat different instances of the same word differently, which is a major benefit of these models. Here however, we specifically refer to instances, where this is unexpected behavior, like in the example above, where the different instances of "Podologe" should all be treated the same from a human perspective.
- **Random factors:** There are several words or tokens marked with high attributions that do neither seem plausible nor belong to a group of input features like the ones above. This includes function words including determiners ("einer") or prepositions ("für") or unrelated content words like "Deutschland".

Model Variance. Table 3 shows how the models explanations performed against each other. Baseline performed substantially worse compared to NoAppr and NoApprAlt, which performed the best. Summarizing the reasoning behind the choices, we can say that often NoApprAlt had the advantage, because it contained less noise. So the attributions for relevant input features were similar to those of the other models, but less attributions were given to irrelevant features. NoAppr often performed best when the most important clue of an ad was the occupational title, which it seems to be able to match well to a requirement level, whenever possible. Two of the instances labeled as uncertain were because all explanations were deemed unsatisfactory and once when BL and NoApprAlt both provided equally good explanations for different respective class predictions.

There are also some peculiarities w.r.t what types of ads were best explained by which model. Specifically, 15 of the 19 ads, where NoApprAlt had the best explanation came from the ads where the prediction score, i.e. models confidence was low. Consequently, all of BL and most of NoAppr best predictions came from ads where confidence was high.

7 Discussion

The training results indicate several key findings regarding model performance and class distribution. The generally higher accuracy rates compared to F1 scores can likely be attributed to the imbalanced class distribution and consequent over-fitting. The removal of apprenticeships ads, which are likely part of the dominant level two class, is probably the main factor mitigating this imbalance. By removing these ads, the model's ability to recognize and correctly classify instances from minority classes has likely been enhanced. Consequently, this adjustment leads to a notable improvement in the F1 scores for these configurations, reflecting a more balanced and genuinely accurate performance across all classes, rather than an accuracy inflated by bias toward the majority class.

Table 3. Amount of Best Explanations per Model Based on our Qualitative Analysis.

Model	Best Explanations
Baseline	4
NoAppr	14
NoApprAlt	19
Uncertain	3

In general, the performances, especially from NoAppr and NoApprAlt, are very promising. F1 scores above 90% indicate that requirement levels can be detected reliably, underscoring the effectiveness of the modifications made to address class imbalance.

Our XAI analysis to some extend confirms these observations. As outlined before, models generally did frequently identify relevant feature, which is plausible given the rather good performance. It is unlikely that statistical artifacts appear in such a frequency that a model could consistently perform well over so much data, if it only learned patterns that do not correspond to real life factors. The greater influence of hard skills over soft skills is logical in the context of job requirement levels. Most soft skills can be destined valuable regardless of the requirement level of the job position.

However, several undesired influence patterns were observed. The influence of company names, such as 'Deutsche Bahn', and industry-specific terms in company descriptions can be attributed to their frequent occurrence in the dataset, leading to potential biases. For instance, large companies or industries like IT or Law may skew the models towards higher requirement levels, while restaurants contribute to lower levels. This suggests the presence of statistical artifacts that can distort the models' predictions. Location information similarly introduces geographical biases that are not relevant to job requirements. The unexpected influence of punctuation marks indicates possible issues with the self-attention mechanism [24] used by the models, which may not be fully accounted for by the Integrated Gradients (IG) method. Moreover, the contradictory attributions within the same ad and random factors such as function words or unrelated content words highlight noise and inconsistencies in the models' decision-making process. These factors suggest that the models may sometimes rely on irrelevant or misleading features, reducing the reliability of their predictions. This might particularly be the case, when the model predicts the dominant class based on imbalance based over-fitting.

The comparison of model explanations reveals that NoApprAlt consistently provided the clearest and most relevant explanations, largely due to its ability to filter out noise and focus on meaningful input features. It is not easy to interpret why this was the case. One aspect may be that by filtering out ads with alternative labels, we also reduced the amount of ads that were heavily noisy, assuming that those would often have ambigious labels. This assumption, however, would need to be quantified before making conclusions. Also, our analysis presented in Sect. 5.2 does not quantify how much the explanations were apart. Often times, we feel like the difference between NoAppr and NoApprAlt was subtle, which corresponds to their similar performance in F1 and Accuracy. Notably, NoApprAlt excelled in low-confidence scenarios, underscoring its robustness in uncertain situations. In contrast, Baseline and NoAppr models were more effective in high-confidence cases, indicating their reliance on clearer indicators. It is particularly interesting, why NoAppr in some cases was able to much better link the occupational title to a requirement level in these cases, when NoApprAlt did not.

Overall, our comparison confirms the results of the test metrics, showing that NoAppr and NoApprAlt are both strong models to classify OJAs to requirement levels that rely to a large extend on the input features we expect them to. This makes them useful to researchers who need this classification and our further elaboration on their strengths and weaknesses might help to choose when to use which model.

8 Limitations and Outlook

This section outlines the inherent constraints of our study, including the limited scope of experimental techniques employed, the implications of selecting Integrated Gradients as the sole explainable AI method, and the simplifications made in our approach to the classification problem, particularly regarding label uncertainty. Lastly, we discuss some further steps that can be taken to try to improve our models on the basis of our XAI analysis.

Experimental Techniques: Although our results are promising, we did not conduct extensive experiments with various techniques to potentially enhance our model. These techniques range from basic choices such as model selection and hyper-parameter tuning, to more complex methods. Despite evidence from [10] suggesting that many choices in the model training pipeline for a similar OJA text classification problem have minimal impact on performance, thorough testing could likely yield significant improvements in both quantitative performance and qualitative robustness of the model's explanations. The field of text classification is rapidly evolving, with new techniques continuously developed and tested. However, due to the constraints of our study's scope and resources, a comprehensive exploration of these methods was impractical.

Explainable AI Method: Despite choosing IGs as our method of choice based on previous research, there are several limitations. For example, [1] show that IGs, even though perhaps less so than others, are prone to data noise undermining explanation robustness. Our analysis indicated that in some instances, data noise, like special characters used for formatting, and seemingly irrelevant features, such as punctuation, received high attribution scores. This raises concerns about whether these observations are due to poor model robustness or inadequate explanation robustness. Furthermore, our implementation of IGs attributes importance scores to individual tokens, obscuring the importance of the interaction between tokens to some extend [9]. Another major difficulty of choosing IGs are their computational cost, which made it impractical to "explain" enough models decisions to perform quantitative analysis of the models behavior. Future work in the area of XAI could try to overcome computational costs for large scale IG usage, which would allow using them in a more quantitative manner. For example, by aggregating the important words (based on tokens) for each label and grouping them to relevant categories, like occupational titles, skills, tasks, benefits and other features typical to OJAs, local IG explanations would allow drawing more global conclusions about the models behavior. This would, however, require the use of an automatic classification of the features to these categories.

Another major factor in the qualitative XAI analysis was that we only tested for positive and negative attributions against the predicted class. Therefore, we could not directly relate input features to higher or lower requirement levels. For example, when a feature was attributed negative for a level two prediction, we cannot see whether that is because the feature in the models opinion indicates a lower or higher requirement level. This sometimes can make it difficult to evaluate the explanation of a model, particularly when comparing the explanations of the models against each other. Future work should look into systematically uncover the delimitations of the input features between classes.

Label Uncertainty: We have to a large extend simplified the fact that some ads cannot be classified regarding a requirement level (e.g. apprenticeships), whereas other can have two or more plausible labels. Regarding the first issue, future research should identify characteristics of job ads that make them unsuitable for taxonomy classification, such as inherently training positions. With regard to the second issue, future work should consider ideas from multi label classification [14] and label uncertainty [19] research.

Further Steps: One important question is how we can use the findings of our XAI analysis to further improve our models performance. To overcome the influence of the undesired features, like company names, company descriptions or locations we can either try to use a more explicit sampling of our data where we consider metadata about or ads where these factors can be balanced, if possible. For example, in our dataset we know the city in which the position is located. We can try to create as much balance in terms of city to requirement level ratio as possible. The same goes for company names or industry sectors. Another option would be to use data augmentation [6,11] or synthetic data generation [13] to control a more evenly balanced dataset w.r.t these input features. We can also use data augmentation to try to mitigate the influence of punctuation by creating arbitrary punctuation patterns in our training data, showing the model that punctuation is not a reliable input feature to classify the requirement level of job ads with.

9 Conclusion

This study demonstrates the effectiveness of a supervised text classification model for classifying job advertisements according to the German KldB 2010 taxonomy, with a focus on requirement levels. By integrating job titles and descriptions, our approach overcomes the limitations of methods relying solely on job titles. Using Integrated Gradients for explainable AI gave valuable insights into the model's decision-making process, highlighting relevant features and potential biases. Our model achieved high F1 scores, indicating robust performance in classifying requirement levels. The findings underscore the importance of combining multiple data sources for accurate classification and suggest that addressing class imbalance and data noise can further enhance model performance. Future research should explore advanced techniques in text classification and XAI to build on these results, aiming to refine occupation classification systems and support informed decision-making in the labor market.

References

1. Alvarez-Melis, D., Jaakkola, T.S.: On the robustness of interpretability methods. arXiv preprint arXiv:1806.08049 (2018)
2. Atanasova, P., Simonsen, J.G., Lioma, C., Augenstein, I.: A diagnostic study of explainability techniques for text classification. In: Webber, B., Cohn, T., He, Y., Liu, Y. (eds.) Proceedings of the 2020 Conference on Empirical Methods in Natural Language Processing (EMNLP), pp. 3256–3274. Association for Computational Linguistics, Stroudsburg (2020). https://doi.org/10.18653/v1/2020.emnlp-main.263
3. Baskaran, R., Müller, J.: Classification of German job titles in online job postings using the kldb2010 taxonomy (2023). https://www.and-effect.com/publications/2022-11-21_technical_report_kldb.pdf. Accessed 22 may 2024
4. Bundesagentur für Arbeit: Klassifikation der berufe 2010: Band 1: Systematischer und alphabetischer teil mit erläuterungen
5. Bundesinstitut für Berufsbildung (BIBB): Qualifikations- und Berufsfeldprojektionen (QUBE). Online (2024). https://www.bibb.de/de/qube_datenportal_ergebnisse.php?lang. Accessed 02 May 2024
6. Feng, S.Y., et al.: A survey of data augmentation approaches for NLP. arXiv preprint arXiv:2105.03075 (2021)
7. Guidotti, R., Monreale, A., Ruggieri, S., Turini, F., Giannotti, F., Pedreschi, D.: A survey of methods for explaining black box models. ACM Comput. Surv. (CSUR) **51**(5), 1–42 (2018)
8. Hoffmeyer-Zlotnik, J.H., Warner, U., Hoffmeyer-Zlotnik, J.H., Warner, U.: Harmonisierung demographischer und sozioökonomischer Variablen. Springer (2012)
9. Janizek, J.D., Sturmfels, P., Lee, S.I.: Explaining explanations: axiomatic feature interactions for deep networks. J. Mach. Learn. Res. **22**(104), 1–54 (2021)
10. Krüger, K.: Ausklasser-a classifier for German apprenticeship advertisements. In: Proceedings of the Communication Papers of the 17th Conference on Computer Science and Intelligence Systems, vol. 36. IEEE, Piscataway (2023)
11. Li, B., Hou, Y., Che, W.: Data augmentation approaches in natural language processing: A survey. AI Open **3**, 71–90 (2022)

12. Li, N., Kang, B., de Bie, T.: LLM4Jobs: unsupervised occupation extraction and standardization leveraging large language models (2023). http://arxiv.org/pdf/2309.09708
13. Li, Z., Zhu, H., Lu, Z., Yin, M.: Synthetic data generation with large language models for text classification: potential and limitations. arXiv preprint arXiv:2310.07849 (2023)
14. Liu, W., Wang, H., Shen, X., Tsang, I.W.: The emerging trends of multi-label learning. IEEE Trans. Pattern Anal. Mach. Intell. **44**(11), 7955–7974 (2021)
15. Minh, D., Wang, H.X., Li, Y.F., Nguyen, T.N.: Explainable artificial intelligence: a comprehensive review. Artif. Intell. Rev. 1–66 (2022)
16. Mohseni, S., Zarei, N., Ragan, E.D.: A multidisciplinary survey and framework for design and evaluation of explainable AI systems. ACM Trans. Interact. Intell. Syst. (TiiS) **11**(3–4), 1–45 (2021)
17. Möller, J., Paulus, W.: Perspektiven einer modernen berufsforschung. Berufsforschung für eine moderne Berufsbildung. Stand und Perspektiven, pp. 11–35. Steiner, Stuttgart (2010)
18. Paulus, W., Matthes, B., et al.: The German classification of occupations 2010-structure, coding and conversion table. FDZ-Methodenreport **8**, 2013 (2013)
19. Plank, B.: The "problem" of human label variation: on ground truth in data, modeling and evaluation. In: Proceedings of the 2022 Conference on Empirical Methods in Natural Language Processing, pp. 10671–10682 (2022)
20. Rahhal, I., Carley, K.M., Kassou, I., Ghogho, M.: Two stage job title identification system for online job advertisements. IEEE Access **11**, 19073–19092 (2023). https://doi.org/10.1109/ACCESS.2023.3247866
21. Sanh, V., Debut, L., Chaumond, J., Wolf, T.: DistilBERT, a distilled version of BERT: smaller, faster, cheaper and lighter. arXiv preprint arXiv:1910.01108 (2019)
22. Sundararajan, M., Taly, A., Yan, Q.: Axiomatic attribution for deep networks. In: Precup, D., Teh, Y.W. (eds.) Proceedings of the 34th International Conference on Machine Learning. Proceedings of Machine Learning Research, vol. 70, pp. 3319–3328. PMLR (2017). https://proceedings.mlr.press/v70/sundararajan17a.html
23. Tiemann, M.: Homogenität von Berufen: Arbeit und Beruf im Wandel - ein Blick auf die gesellschaftliche Differenzierung: Zugl.: Köln, Univ., Diss. (2011). Berichte zur beruflichen Bildung, Bertelsmann, Bielefeld (2014)
24. Vaswani, A., et al.: Attention is all you need. In: Advances in Neural Information Processing Systems, vol. 30 (2017)
25. Xu, F., Uszkoreit, H., Du, Y., Fan, W., Zhao, D., Zhu, J.: Explainable AI: a brief survey on history, research areas, approaches and challenges. In: Tang, J., Kan, M.-Y., Zhao, D., Li, S., Zan, H. (eds.) NLPCC 2019. LNCS (LNAI), vol. 11839, pp. 563–574. Springer, Cham (2019). https://doi.org/10.1007/978-3-030-32236-6_51

Enhancing Critical Thinking in Education by Means of a Socratic Chatbot

Lucile Favero[1(✉)], Juan Antonio Pérez-Ortiz[2], Tanja Käser[3], and Nuria Oliver[1]

[1] ELLIS Alicante, Alicante, Spain
{lucile,nuria}@ellisalicante.org
[2] Universitat d'Alacant, San Vicente del Raspeig, Spain
japerez@dlsi.ua.es
[3] École Polytechnique Fédérale de Lausanne, EPFL, Lausanne, Switzerland
tanja.kaeser@epfl.ch

Abstract. While large language models (LLMs) are increasingly playing a pivotal role in education by providing instantaneous, adaptive responses, their potential to promote critical thinking remains understudied. In this paper, we fill such a gap and present an innovative educational chatbot designed to foster critical thinking through Socratic questioning. Unlike traditional intelligent tutoring systems, including educational chatbots, that tend to offer direct answers, the proposed Socratic tutor encourages students to explore various perspectives and engage in self-reflection by posing structured, thought-provoking questions. Our Socratic questioning is implemented by fine and prompt-tuning the open-source pretrained LLM with a specialized dataset that stimulates critical thinking and offers multiple viewpoints. In an effort to democratize access and to protect the students' privacy, the proposed tutor is based on small LLMs (Llama2 7B and 13B-parameter models) that are able to run locally on off-the-shelf hardware. We validate our approach in a battery of experiments consisting of interactions between a simulated student and the chatbot to evaluate its effectiveness in enhancing critical thinking skills. Results indicate that the Socratic tutor supports the development of reflection and critical thinking significantly better than standard chatbots. Our approach opens the door for improving educational outcomes by cultivating active learning and encouraging intellectual autonomy.

Keywords: Critical Thinking · Socratic Chatbot · Education

1 Introduction

Recent advancements in generative artificial intelligence (AI) methods, combined with an almost universal availability of generative AI tools, have expanded the

---

Supplementary Information The online version contains supplementary material available at https://doi.org/10.1007/978-3-031-93409-4_2.

F. Bellas and O. Fontenla-Romero (Eds.): AIEER 2024, CCIS 2519, pp. 17–32, 2025.
https://doi.org/10.1007/978-3-031-93409-4_2

potential to assist people in developing new ways to think, communicate, learn, and solve problems creatively [18]. The integration of large language models (LLMs) in education through interactive chatbots has emerged as a transformative element in the evolving educational technology landscape, opening new avenues for learning and pedagogy [24].

While recent work illustrates the potential positive impact of chatbots in learning [3], their capabilities to support essential aspects of human learning, such as critical thinking and self-regulated learning, are limited [25]. However, addressing such limitations is of paramount importance, as these aspects are widely regarded as fundamental pillars in human learning yet inadequately accomplished with current technologies [26].

In this paper, we focus on tackling these limitations. We present a novel Socratic chatbot designed to align with pedagogical principles by promoting critical thinking, purposeful learning and self-efficacy. We propose the use of Socratic dialogues to enhance learning experiences by having the chatbot ask questions rather than provide immediate answers. Our approach combines the traditional elements of Socratic questioning with the innovative capabilities of AI, aiming to create a personalized, responsive and enjoyable learning experience. Furthermore, we are interested in exploring the capabilities of small, open-source LLMs running locally on the learners' laptops to act as Socratic tutors. Locally run LLMs provide more privacy and contribute to the democratization of education as they do not need a constant internet connection benefiting students in rural or underserved areas.

This paper is organized as follows: the most relevant related literature is presented in Sect. 2, establishing the background and context for our research. Section 3 describes our approach to develop a Socratic chatbot, consisting of (1) fine-tuning an open-source pretrained large language model on a dataset designed to enhance critical thinking skills and (2) prompt-tuning it to create conversations according to the Socratic method. Our experimental evaluation and comparison of the Socratic tutor with two baselines is described in Sect. 4, followed by the result in Sect. 5, a discussion in Sect. 6 and a conclusion and outline of future lines of research in Sect. 7. Furthermore, a discussion about the ethical implications and challenges is provided in the supplementary material.

2 Related Work

In this section, we first provide an overview of the most relevant previous works in critical thinking and Socratic questioning, both from an educational and technological perspective.

2.1 Educational Chatbots

For the past fifteen years, scholars have explored several facets of integrating chatbots into educational settings, examining their effectiveness, benefits, and challenges [34]. Early work investigated basic interactions and information retrieval tasks [23]. As AI methods improved, studies explored the role of chatbots in personalized learning [37], student engagement [14], and language learning [13]. Recently, the use of LLM-based chatbots in education has gained significant research attention and societal adoption with the emergence of numerous EdTech startups devoted to this topic [35]. Yet, there is a lack of educational chatbots to support critical thinking and self-regulated learning.

2.2 Critical Thinking

Definition in education. Critical thinking (CT) is a complex cognitive process involving the evaluation, analysis, and synthesis of information to form reasoned judgments [2,5,33]. Essential across all educational levels and disciplines, CT empowers students to think independently, solve problems, and make informed decisions. Several strategies are effective in promoting CT skills [2], such as: (1) engaging students in structured dialogues to explore various perspectives; (2) exposing students to real-world scenarios requires them to actively apply their CT skills; and (3) providing personalized mentoring to support the development of CT capabilities.

However, assessing CT skills presents difficulties due to a lack of a standardized evaluation framework, complicating efforts to further integrate and enhance CT training in educational environments [5].

Chatbots for Critical Thinking. Incorporating chatbot technology into educational settings offers substantial benefits for enhancing CT [32]. Indeed, chatbots can effectively employ the three previously mentioned strategies by facilitating guided dialogues focused on specific, concrete problems. Although research in this area is still emerging, some progress has been reported in the past two years. For example, the AI-IESLS chatbot enhances the students' learning experiences and critical thinking in higher education through the use of concept mapping and probability distribution analysis [29]. Moreover, a chatbot designed according to cognitive styles has been proven effective in advancing science concepts and critical thinking skills among preparatory school students [8]. Finally, the online education nonprofit Khan Academy has recently developed Khanmigo, an AI-powered tutor and teaching assistant hand-crafted by their learning experts. It aims to promote critical thinking by guiding students through interactive problem-solving[1].

2.3 Socratic Questioning

Definition in Education. Named after the classical Greek philosopher Socrates, Socratic questioning is a structured way of asking questions to explore complex ideas, reveal underlying assumptions, and discern what is known from what is not [33].

[1] https://www.khanmigo.ai.

Socratic questioning is part of the scaffolding theory of learning, a process in which a learner achieves a goal through guided efforts [40]. Students are prompted with questions that guide them towards the solution by solving problems beyond their zone of proximal development [39].

Its primary purpose in education is to test and deepen the students' understanding, encourage them to ask profound questions, help them think critically about complex topics, and foster an understanding of different viewpoints [33]. Socratic questioning has been shown to promote critical thinking, improve the student's understanding and encourage a culture of inquiry and reflection, essential for reasoning through complex issues and understanding diverse perspectives [11,19,41].

However, the effectiveness of the Socratic method varies among learners because it depends on their ability to abstract and generalize knowledge [15]. Thus, this method should be adapted to individual differences in cognitive processing, prior knowledge, or learning styles [33].

Chatbots for Socratic Questioning. Chatbots can support the Socratic method of questioning by engaging users in a guided dialogue, consisting of probing, open-ended questions that encourage critical thinking and deep reflection [5,36].

To the best of our knowledge, we are unaware of any fully implemented chatbot designed to leverage the Socratic questioning method to enhance critical thinking in human learning. Nonetheless, recent advancements have applied machine learning techniques (like zero-shot prompt tuning and reinforcement learning) to automatically generate relevant Socratic questions in diverse contexts: math word problems [36], debugging code [4], physics [16], and cognitive behavioral therapy [22].

Furthermore, Ang et al. [6] introduced *SocratiQ*, a dataset consisting of approximately 110,000 Socratic question-context pairs curated from the subreddit *r/changemyview*[2]. The authors employed a transformer-based encoder to classify each question-context pair into specific Socratic question types as detailed in Table 2, in the supplementary material. Subsequently, for each identified type of Socratic question, a decoder-like language model was trained to generate new questions corresponding to that specific type from a given context. Both automated and human evaluation studies demonstrated that these models successfully produce type-sensitive, relevant, and human-like Socratic questions.

Filling the existing gap in the literature, our Socratic tutor's core design principle is the use of Socratic questioning to guide the student's learning process, changing the focus from providing answers to formulating questions that would support the learner's critical thinking. In our approach, we leverage the *SocratiQ* annotated dataset of question-context pairs to fine-tune an open-source, pretrained LLM to generate specific types of Socratic questions.

2.4 Contributions

Given the existing literature, the contributions of our paper are five-fold:

[2] https://www.reddit.com/r/changemyview/.

1. We develop an LLM model focused on critical thinking by fine and prompt-tuning open-source, pretrained small LLMs (Llama2 7B- and 13B-parameter models) to create a Socratic tutor that poses a variety of Socratic questions in a computationally efficient manner;
2. We propose an approach for generating tutoring dialogues by means of an LLM-based dual-agent (tutor-learner) setup;
3. We introduce an extrinsic evaluation method that assesses the quality of the questions by comparing the learner's responses to the ideal responses based on the problem description;
4. We implement an automatic evaluation mechanism using an LLM that is designed to replicate human evaluative behaviors; and
5. We validate our approach on a Theory of Knowledge task and compare it with two baselines.

3 Socratic Tutor Implementation

In this section, we describe the fine and prompt-tuning approach that we adopted to build our Socratic tutor. We experiment with two open-source, pretrained large language models: Llama2 Instruct with 7B parameters and Llama2 Instruct with 13B parameters [38] which are fine-tuned on Google Colab with a L4 GPU. The fine-tuned models are then run on an Apple M1 Pro laptop with 32 GB RAM. This approach of using small models on a local computer is chosen to enable students to operate the chatbot independently on their personal computers, with the aim of democratizing education and protecting privacy. A key challenge in this regard lies in optimizing the chatbot's performance to ensure it operates efficiently on local machines without excessive resource consumption.

3.1 Socratic Fine-Tuning

To fine-tune the open-source, pretrained LLMs we applied parameter-efficient fine-tuning (PEFT) techniques: Low-Rank Adaptation (LoRA) [20] and Quantized Low-Rank Adaptation (QLoRA) [12]. They offer a way to effectively adapt LLMs to specific tasks without the need to retrain or alter the entire pre-trained model. LoRA focuses on modifying a small number of additional parameters that act upon the pre-trained weights of the model. This approach is especially valuable due to its efficiency and the reduced computational overhead it introduces. Building upon LoRA, QLoRA incorporates quantization into the fine-tuning process (4-bit quantization in our case). It reduces the precision of the low-rank parameters to further decrease memory usage and computational demands.

Hyperparameters. LLMs were fine-tuned on a single GPU, using mini-batches of size 4. We adopted a learning rate of 2×10^{-4} and used the AdamW optimizer ($\beta_1 = 0.9$, $\beta_2 = 0.999$) in 32-bit precision and a cosine-based scheduler with a step ratio for linear warmup of 0.03. A weight decay of 0.001 was applied to all weights except biases and normalization layer parameters. Regarding QLoRA, the rank of LoRA modules, r is 64, the LoRA scaling factor, α is 16 with 0.1 dropout and 4-bit quantization.

Fine-Tuning Dataset. The fine-tuning process requires a specialized dataset. In our case, we used the *SocratiQ* dataset [6] which collects contentious viewpoints and the questions challenging these viewpoints from Reddit (Subreddit channel called *subreddit r/changemyview*). This channel corresponds to an active community specifically designed as "*a place to post an opinion you acknowledge may be flawed, in an effort to understand other perspectives on the issue*". Discussions often revolve around controversial topics, such as politics, media, and culture. Members are encouraged to approach these discussions with an openness to dialogue rather than debate. Due to its foundational goal of encouraging users to "change their view", comments frequently include questions that promote introspection and reflection.

Ang et al. [6] classified the context-question pairs of this Subreddit into the Socratic categories devised by Paul and Elder [33]. The question types along with definitions and examples can be found in Table 2. These categories address intellectual standards to enhance the rigor of Socratic dialogues [33].

The fine-tuning was performed with a subset of 600 context-question types of questions from *SocratiQ* that had been annotated through the Amazon Mechanical Turk crowdsourcing platform [10]. Given a context and a specific type of question, the LLMs are fine-tuned to generate Socratic questions of this kind.

3.2 Socratic Prompt-Tuning

In addition, we prompt-tuned the fine-tuned LLMs. Prompt-tuning is a method of fine-tuning a language model on specific tasks by adjusting its input prompts without altering the underlying model. We prompt-tuned three different types of LLM-based tutors: the Socratic tutor and two baselines (described in Sect. 4.3) which correspond to a basic tutor, and a random tutor. The prompts provided to the Socratic tutor are composed of the items listed below[3] and reflected in the first row of Table 3, in the supplementary material:

- **Role.** In the first part of the prompt, we inform the LLM of its role. In the case of the Socratic tutor, it is instructed to be a philosopher who follows Socratic methods, which involves asking probing questions to encourage deep thinking and challenge assumptions.
- **Goal.** The second part contains the goal of the interaction, namely to help a student think about a question (*Theory of Knowledge or ToK question*).
- **Resources.** Then, the prompt imposes the restriction of using only the provided dialogue history (*history*) and the student's latest response (*input*). These elements serve as the context and content from which the LLM must derive its question, underscoring that the tutor should not teach or introduce new material, but instead focus on exploring the students' thoughts and facilitating their reflection, consistent with the principles of Socratic dialectic [33].

[3] We direct the reader to the supplementary material for a description of the prompt engineering performed in this paper.

- **Expected outcome.** Finally, the prompt specifies the expected outcome. The question asked should logically continue the ongoing conversation and must be designed to lead the student to explore their thoughts and ideas further rather than providing direct answers.

Table 4, in the supplementary material, provides an example of a simulated conversation with our *Socratic tutor*.

4 Automatic Evaluation

To evaluate the effectiveness of the proposed Socratic tutor in fostering critical thinking, we simulate a dialogue between our Socratic tutor and an LLM-based simulated learner whose task is to respond to a specific Theory of Knowledge (ToK, see below) question. While an empirical evaluation with human subjects would be ideal and it is planned as a next step, simulated evaluations are necessary for several reasons. First, they enable a preliminary assessment of the functionality, efficiency, and safety of the approach. Second, they allow for the creation of benchmark data for comparison against human interaction. Finally, they enable running numerous simulated conversations to gather data and refine the chatbot's behavior without the logistical challenges associated with human participants.

4.1 Domain: Theory of Knowledge (ToK)

The *Theory of Knowledge* (ToK) course is part of the International Baccalaureate (IB) Diploma Programme[4]. It aims to develop critical thinking by exploring the process of knowing rather than teaching specific knowledge[5]. The course's main goals include linking knowledge construction to academic disciplines and the real world, fostering awareness of diverse cultural perspectives, and encouraging personal reflection on beliefs and assumptions.

However, ToK courses and assessments, do not fully capture the depth of critical thinking skills intended, raising concerns about their validity [21]. To enhance its effectiveness, the course could benefit from a broader inclusion of critical thinking skills, particularly in creative and active thinking, and adjustments to its assessment strategies to better align with these skills [21]. A chatbot designed to promote critical thinking could engage and support students in diverse and complex questioning, encouraging them to explore and evaluate multiple perspectives and scenarios actively. Specifically, the final assessment for this course comprises two main components: an exhibition and an essay. The latter, limited to 1,600 words, addresses a theoretical question within ToK. It typically prompts students to analyze and discuss claims about the nature of knowledge

[4] https://www.ibo.org/.

[5] https://www.ibo.org/programmes/diploma-programme/curriculum/dp-core/theory-of-knowledge/what-is-tok/.

production. An example essay topic might require students to explore the assertion that the methods employed in generating knowledge are influenced by the intended application of that knowledge (see footnote 5). Table 7, in the supplementary material, includes examples of ToK questions from the International Baccalaureate curriculum[6].

Our approach is to use our Socratic chatbot to help a learner think about these ToK questions to help them develop and articulate logically their ideas to complete the essay.

4.2 Generation of Synthetic Conversations Using LLMs

In order to empirically evaluate the proposed Socratic tutor we generate synthetic dialogues using two LLM-based agents that engage in a conversation with each other, as has been recently done in the literature with the purpose of assisting users in building linear programming models [1]. In our case, we create an LLM-based conversational student that generates the learner's responses by prompt-tuning a small LLM (Llama2 7B-parameter model) with the following prompt: "ANSWER to the question <input> IN ONE SENTENCE. DO NOT USE COMPLEX WORDS OR IDEAS".

4.3 Baselines: Non-socratic Tutors

To evaluate the effectiveness of the proposed Socratic tutor, we benchmark it against two non-Socratic LLM-based tutoring methods: (1) A *basic tutor* which engages learners in discussions about the Theory of Knowledge questions without a specific intention to help them; and (2) a *random tutor* which produces arbitrary responses and serves as a control in our study. We create these two tutors by prompt-tuning the open-source, pretrained Llama2 7B-parameter model according to the prompts described in Table 3, in the supplementary material. As a result, we create three different tutors (Socratic, basic and random).

Additional results comparing the Socratic tutor and a baseline tutor that had not been neither fine- nor prompt-tuned can be found in the supplementary material.

We test each of these tutors on 5 different ToK questions displayed in Table 7 in the supplementary material. For each tutor and question, we perform 20 conversations of 5 turns each. Given that the topic of the conversations is cognitively demanding and thought-provoking, our Socratic chatbot should enable students to successfully respond to the task within a limited number of interactions. Thus, we set the number of turns to 5. We also include results corresponding to longer conversations with 20 turns in Fig. 6 in the supplementary material.

[6] https://ibtokessaytutor.com/ibtokessaytopics/May2023/ib-tok-essay-titles-May-2023.shtml.

4.4 Evaluation Metrics

We compare the performance of the three types of chatbots by means of an extrinsic evaluation approach [1]. We assess the quality of the questions generated by the tutors by analyzing the responses provided by the simulated learners. This evaluation operates under a key hypothesis: if the learner delivers accurate responses, this suggests that the tutor has posed effective questions that led the learner to generate such answers. Thus, we measure the effectiveness of the questions by comparing the concatenated learner's responses to a summary of the essential points that are expected in the responses to each of the 5 ToK questions. Tables 8, 9 and 10 in the supplementary material, include examples of the ToK questions used with a summary of the information that should be included in the answer to the questions.

We use standard n-gram-based metrics—BLEU [28,31], ROUGE-L [27] and METEOR [7]— to evaluate the quality of the responses provided by the learners [30]. However these commonly-used measures struggle to accurately assess paraphrases that, while different in wording, are equally valid interpretations of the reference questions. Thus, we use the BERTScore [42] to overcome these limitations. Metrics leveraging BERT-based models have demonstrated robustness in evaluating text generation tasks, including summarization and translation, by providing more nuanced assessments of textual similarity [17,42]. Finally, we propose a novel evaluation metric by means of an LLM [1] to specifically assess the level of critical thinking in the learner's response. The highest possible value of these metrics is 1. Below is a summary of the advantages and limitations of the BERTScore and LLM-based metrics. See the supplementary material for the other metrics.

- **BERTScore:** Originally, the BERTScore [42] leveraged pre-trained contextual embeddings from BERT to evaluate the similarity between words in candidate and reference sentences using cosine similarity. This metric effectively aligns with human judgment, demonstrating strong correlation in both sentence-level and system-level evaluations [42].
  However, *DeBERTa* [17] enhances both the BERT and RoBERTa architectures by incorporating disentangled attention mechanisms and an improved mask decoder. With 80 GB of training data, DeBERTa surpasses both BERT and RoBERTa on the majority of natural language understanding tasks, thereby demonstrating superior performance across a broad range of evaluations.
- **LLM-score:** Previous metrics primarily assessed the similarity between the learner's response and a summary of potential answers to the formulated question. To more directly evaluate critical thinking, we introduce a score generated by a pretrained Llama2 7B-parameter LLM [38] which is specifically prompted to assess the level of critical thinking in the learner's response. The evaluation prompt is composed of the following elements: (1) *role*, provided in the first part of the prompt where it specifies that the LLM should act as an AI evaluator specialized in assessing critical thinking in discourse; (2)

definition of critical thinking as per [9]; (3) *goal*, which is expressed as the evaluation of the use of critical thinking in the learner's response to a specific ToK question; and (4) *outcome*, which is a score ranging from 0 to 5, reflecting the degree of critical thinking evident in the responses. This score should be accompanied by an explanation, employing the chain-of-thought prompting technique. Ultimately, the LLM-score is normalized to a scale between 0 and 1 to be comparable to the rest of scores. Table 11, in the supplementary material, provides a summary of the prompt used to generate the LLM-score.

The code to create the LLM-based tutors and learner, and to run the experiments described in this paper can be found here: https://github.com/lucilefavero/ECAI_2024.

5 Results

Tables 4, 5 and 6, in the supplementary material, provide examples of simulated conversations with the *Socratic tutor*, the *basic tutor*, and the *random tutor*, respectively, all generated with the Llama2 7B-parameter LLM. We also create another Socratic tutor using the Llama2 13B-parameter LLM to shed light on the impact of increasing the complexity of the model to achieve the task. The performance of these tutors —quantified using the BLEU, ROUGE-L, METEOR, BERTScore and LLM score– are presented in Table 1, corresponding to the average values of 20 conversations of 5 turns for each 5 of the ToK questions. The differences in performance between the Socratic tutors (indicated with bold font) and the non-Socratic tutors are statistically significant (t-test with p-value < 0.001).

Table 1. Performance of the different types of tutors, averaged over 20 conversations of 5 turns each for each of the 5 ToK questions. The differences between the Socratic tutors (highlighted in bold) and the non-Socratic tutors are statistically significant (t-test, p-value < 0.001). The differences in performance between the two Socratic tutors are not statistically significant.

Tutor type	BLEU	ROUGE-L	METEOR	BERTScore	LLM Score
Socratic Llama2 13B	**3.65**	**0.157**	**0.226**	**0.569**	**0.696**
Socratic Llama2 7B	**3.42**	**0.162**	**0.216**	**0.576**	**0.670**
Basic Llama2 7B	0.494	0.120	0.092	0.535	0.582
Random Llama2 7B	0.210	0.091	0.063	0.444	0.312

Figure 1, Fig. 2, and Fig. 3 depict the performance (METEOR, BERT and LLM scores) of the different types of tutors across 5 turns for 20 conversations for each 5 of the ToK questions. Figure 4 and Fig. 5, in the supplementary material display the performance of the BLEU and ROUGE-L scores. As seen in the figures, for all metrics and the Socratic and basic tutors, the scores increase with the number of turns. Furthermore, the *Socratic tutor* significantly outperforms the other two tutors, demonstrating a more pronounced improvement as the conversation evolves. While the performance of the Socratic tutor implemented with the Llama2 13B-parameter model is superior to that of the Socratic tutor based on the Llama2 7B-parameter model, the differences in performance between these two tutors are not statistically significant.

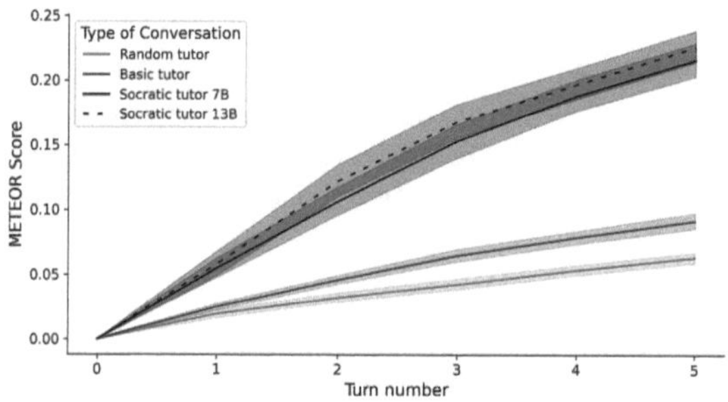

Fig. 1. METEOR scores of the different types of tutors, averaged over 20 conversations of 5 turns each and for each of the 5 ToK questions. The differences between the Socratic tutor and the non-Socratic tutors are statistically significant (t-test, p-value < 0.001). No statistically significant difference is observed in the performance of both Socratic tutors.

6 Discussion

From our study, we draw several implications.

First, our results clearly demonstrate that the Socratic tutor outperformed both the basic and random tutors in assisting students with ToK questions. After only 5 turns of interaction, students engaging with the Socratic tutor showed a significant improvement in their critical thinking abilities compared to those interacting with the baseline chatbots. This superior performance indicates the effectiveness of employing Socratic questioning techniques in guiding students through the process of critical thinking.

Second, by developing educational chatbots based on small LLMs that can be run on personal computers, our methodology lowers the barriers of access to educational resources, democratizing education across different demographics and regions. Thus, our approach contributes to greater educational equity by enabling individuals to independently access and leverage advanced technological tools for learning, regardless of their socio-economic status or geographical location.

Third, as a preliminary evaluation, we assess the effectiveness of our method through dialogues with a simulated learner powered by an LLM. Our experimental methodology contributes to the growing use of LLMs to simulate human

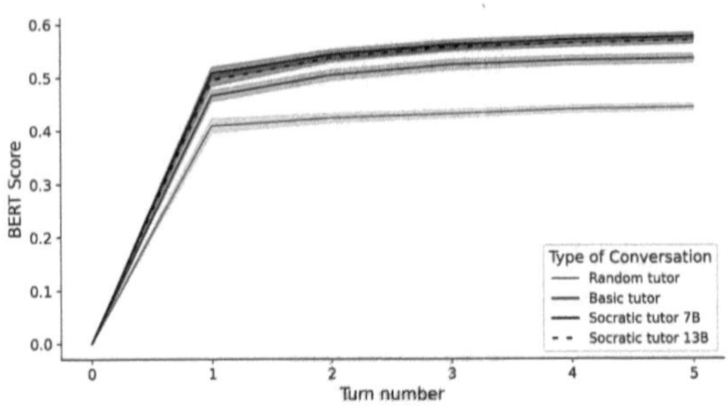

Fig. 2. BERT scores of the different types of tutors, averaged over 20 conversations of 5 turns each and for each of the 5 ToK questions. The differences between the Socratic tutors and the non-Socratic tutors are statistically significant (t-test, p-value < 0.001). No statistically significant difference is observed in the performance of both Socratic tutors.

interactions in data generation tasks. Moving forward, we plan to conduct case studies involving actual students to further validate our method.

Fourth, despite the promising results obtained by leveraging fine and prompt-tuned pre-trained small LLMs for this task, we encountered challenges in prompt-tuning. Designing prompts that effectively elicit critical thinking and guide students through the reasoning process proved to be a complex task. Occasionally, our model would generate dialogues where the tutor both posed questions and provided answers, or indirectly guided the conversation by stating phrases such as *"If I were a Socratic tutor, I would ask..." or "My response to the student is..."*. After extensive empirical work with different types of prompts, we discovered that removing the memory of the dialogue from the learner's prompt substantially enhanced the coherence and logical flow of the conversations, leading to higher-quality interactions.

Fifth, surprisingly, the performance of the Socratic tutor based on the smallest LLM is at par with that of the Socratic tutor built from an LLM with almost twice the number of parameters. These results illustrate the power of even small LLMs to provide educational value even in contexts where resource constraints or computational limitations may be a concern. We leave to future work a more in-depth exploration of how to improve the performance of the Socratic tutor based on the Llama3 8B-parameter model or models of similar complexity.

Sixth, our study's findings have significant implications for education, particularly in the context of online learning and intelligent tutoring systems. Integrating Socratic chatbots into educational platforms can provide students with personalized, interactive, and scaffolded learning experiences that promote the development of critical thinking skills. With our Socratic tutor, educators can augment traditional instruction methods and enhance students' ability to analyze complex issues, evaluate evidence, and construct well-reasoned arguments.

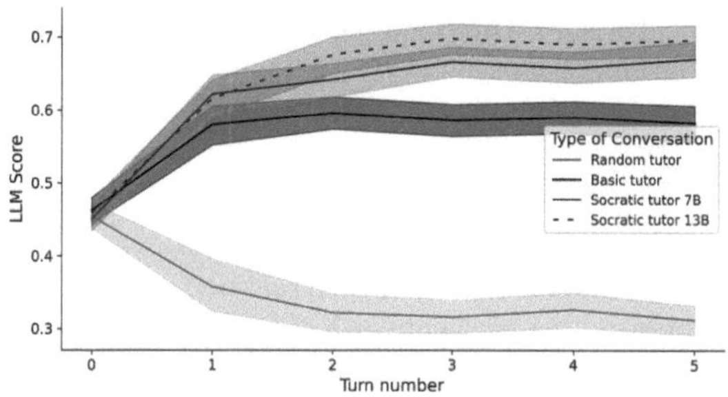

Fig. 3. Critical thinking scores obtained by means of the LLM-score for the different types of tutors. The plots display the average values over 20 conversations of 5 turns for each of the 5 ToK questions. The differences between the Socratic tutor and the non-Socratic tutors are statistically significant (t-test, p-value < 0.001). No statistically significant difference is observed in the performance of both Socratic tutors.

7 Conclusion

Our study contributes to the development of AI-driven tutoring systems by introducing a fine- and prompt-tuned model specifically aimed at generating Socratic questions to enhance critical thinking skills. Our approach enables the creation of a Socratic tutor that surpasses the baselines in delivering effective tutoring conversations to foster critical thinking. The comparison highlights the potential of tailored AI approaches in educational settings.

Looking ahead, we propose several directions for future research. First, further research is needed to continue improving the effectiveness of our Socratic tutor in educational contexts, including the study of sentiment analysis, semantic understanding and reinforcement learning with human feedback to enhance the chatbot's ability to interpret and respond to students' queries more accurately. Second, our approach should be evaluated with human students to measure its effectiveness in real educational settings and gather qualitative feedback on its tutoring capabilities. Third, there is a need to propose more refined evaluation methods that are able to adequately assess critical thinking in the context of automated tutoring conversations. Additionally, investigating the long-term impact of Socratic chatbot interventions on students' critical thinking skills and academic performance would provide valuable insights into the efficacy of this approach. Furthermore, developing a learner model that adapts to individual student responses and learning progress could greatly enhance the personalization and effectiveness of the Socratic tutor. These steps will be crucial in advancing the field of AI-driven educational tools and in creating more effective, responsive and human-centered learning environments.

Acknowledgments. This work has been funded by a nominal grant received at the ELLIS Unit Alicante Foundation from the Regional Government of Valencia in Spain (Convenio Singular signed with Generalitat Valenciana, Conselleria de Innovación,

Industria, Comercio y Turismo, Dirección General de Innovación) and a grant by the Banc Sabadell Foundation.

References

1. Abdullin, Y., Molla-Aliod, D., Ofoghi, B., Yearwood, J., Li, Q.: Synthetic dialogue dataset generation using LLM agents. arXiv preprint arXiv:2401.17461 (2024)
2. Abrami, P.C., Bernard, R.M., Borokhovski, E., Waddington, D.I., Wade, C.A., Persson, T.: Strategies for teaching students to think critically: a meta-analysis. Rev. Educ. Res. **85**(2), 275–314 (2015)
3. Ait Baha, T., El Hajji, M., Es-Saady, Y., Fadili, H.: The impact of educational chatbot on student learning experience. Educ. Inf. Technol. 1–24 (2023)
4. Al-Hossami, E., Bunescu, R., Smith, J., Teehan, R.: Can language models employ the Socratic method? Experiments with code debugging. In: Proceedings of the 55th ACM Technical Symposium on Computer Science Education, vol. 1, pp. 53–59 (2024)
5. Alsaleh, N.J.: Teaching critical thinking skills: literature review. Turk. Online J. Educ. Technol.-TOJET **19**(1), 21–39 (2020)
6. Ang, B.H., Gollapalli, S.D., Ng, S.K.: Socratic question generation: a novel dataset, models, and evaluation. In: Vlachos, A., Augenstein, I. (eds.) Proceedings of the 17th Conference of the European Chapter of the Association for Computational Linguistics, pp. 147–165. Association for Computational Linguistics, Dubrovnik (2023)
7. Banerjee, S., Lavie, A.: METEOR: an automatic metric for MT evaluation with improved correlation with human judgments. In: Proceedings of the ACL Workshop on Intrinsic and Extrinsic Evaluation Measures for Machine Translation and/or Summarization, pp. 65–72. Association for Computational Linguistics, Ann Arbor (2005)
8. Barsoum, S.S., Elnagar, M.S., Awad, B.M.: The effectiveness of using a cognitive style-based chatbot in developing science concepts and critical thinking skills among preparatory school pupils. Eur. Sci. J. ESJ (2022)
9. Black, B., Chislett, J., Thompson, A., Thwaites, G., Thwaites, J.: Critical thinking-a definition and taxonomy for Cambridge assessment (2008)
10. Crowston, K.: Amazon mechanical turk: a research tool for organizations and information systems scholars. In: Shaping the Future of ICT Research. Methods and Approaches: IFIP WG 8.2, Working Conference, Tampa, FL, USA, 13–14 December 2012, Proceedings, pp. 210–221. Springer (2012)
11. Dalim, S.F., Ishak, A.S., Hamzah, L.M.: Promoting students' critical thinking through Socratic method: the views and challenges. Asian J. Univ. Educ. **18**(4), 1034–1047 (2022)
12. Dettmers, T., Pagnoni, A., Holtzman, A., Zettlemoyer, L.: QLoRA: efficient fine-tuning of quantized LLMs. In: Advances in Neural Information Processing Systems, vol. 36 (2024)
13. Fryer, L.K., Ainley, M., Thompson, A., Gibson, A., Sherlock, Z.: Stimulating and sustaining interest in a language course: an experimental comparison of chatbot and human task partners. Comput. Hum. Behav. **75**, 461–468 (2017)
14. Goda, Y., Yamada, M., Matsukawa, H., Hata, K., Yasunami, S.: Conversation with a chatbot before an online EFL group discussion and the effects on critical thinking. J. Inf. Syst. Educ. **13**(1), 1–7 (2014)

15. Goldin, A.P., Pedroncini, O., Sigman, M.: Producing or reproducing reasoning? Socratic dialog is very effective, but only for a few. PLoS ONE **12**(3), e0173584 (2017). https://doi.org/10.1371/journal.pone.0173584
16. Gregorcic, B., Polverini, G., Sarlah, A.: ChatGPT as a tool for honing teachers' Socratic dialogue skills (2024)
17. He, P., Liu, X., Gao, J., Chen, W.: DeBERTa: decoding-enhanced BERT with disentangled attention. In: International Conference on Learning Representations (2021)
18. Henriksen, D., Mishra, P. (eds.): Creative Provocations: Speculations on the Future of Creativity, Technology & Learning, Creativity Theory and Action in Education, vol. 7. Springer, Cham (2022)
19. Ho, Y.R., Chen, B.Y., Li, C.M.: Thinking more wisely: using the socratic method to develop critical thinking skills amongst healthcare students. BMC Med. Educ. **23**(1), 173 (2023)
20. Hu, E.J., et al.: LoRA: low-rank adaptation of large language models. arXiv preprint arXiv:2106.09685 (2021)
21. Hughes, C.: Theory of knowledge aims, objectives and assessment criteria: an analysis of critical thinking descriptors. J. Res. Int. Educ. **13**(1), 30–45 (2014)
22. Izumi, K., et al.: Response generation for cognitive behavioral therapy with large language models: comparative study with Socratic questioning. arXiv preprint arXiv:2401.15966 (2024)
23. Kerlyl, A., Hall, P., Bull, S.: Bringing chatbots into education: towards natural language negotiation of open learner models. In: International Conference on Innovative Techniques and Applications of Artificial Intelligence, pp. 179–192. Springer (2006)
24. Kuhail, M.A., Alturki, N., Alramlawi, S., Alhejori, K.: Interacting with educational chatbots: a systematic review. Educ. Inf. Technol. **28**(1), 973–1018 (2023)
25. Lehmann, T., Hähnlein, I., Ifenthaler, D.: Cognitive, metacognitive and motivational perspectives on preflection in self-regulated online learning. Comput. Hum. Behav. **32**, 313–323 (2014)
26. Liang, Z., Yu, W., Rajpurohit, T., Clark, P., Zhang, X., Kaylan, A.: Let GPT be a math tutor: teaching math word problem solvers with customized exercise generation. arXiv:2305.14386 [cs] (2023)
27. Lin, C.Y.: ROUGE: a package for automatic evaluation of summaries. In: Text Summarization Branches Out, pp. 74–81. Association for Computational Linguistics, Barcelona (2004)
28. Lin, C.Y., Och, F.J.: ORANGE: a method for evaluating automatic evaluation metrics for machine translation. In: COLING 2004: Proceedings of the 20th International Conference on Computational Linguistics, pp. 501–507. COLING, Geneva (2004)
29. Liu, L., Subbareddy, R., Raghavendra, C.G.: AI intelligence chatbot to improve students learning in the higher education platform. J. Interconnect. Networks **22**, 2143032:1–2143032:17 (2022)
30. Pan, L., Lei, W., Chua, T.S., Kan, M.Y.: Recent advances in neural question generation. arXiv preprint arXiv:1905.08949 (2019)
31. Papineni, K., Roukos, S., Ward, T., jing Zhu, W.: BLEU: a method for automatic evaluation of machine translation, pp. 311–318 (2002)
32. Parsakia, K.: The effect of chatbots and AI on the self-efficacy, self-esteem, problem-solving and critical thinking of students. Health Nexus **1**(1), 71–76 (2023)
33. Paul, R., Elder, L.: The Thinker's Guide to Socratic Questioning. Rowman & Littlefield (2019)

34. Pérez, J.Q., Daradoumis, T., Puig, J.: Rediscovering the use of chatbots in education: a systematic literature review. Comput. Appl. Eng. Educ. **28**(6), 1549–1565 (2020)
35. Rudolph, J., Tan, S., Tan, S.: War of the chatbots: bard, Bing Chat, ChatGPT, Ernie and beyond. The new AI gold rush and its impact on higher education. J. Appl. Learn. Teach. **6**(1) (2023)
36. Shridhar, K., Macina, J., El-Assady, M., Sinha, T., Kapur, M., Sachan, M.: Automatic generation of socratic subquestions for teaching math word problems. arXiv:2211.12835 [cs] (2022)
37. Smutny, P., Schreiberova, P.: Chatbots for learning: a review of educational chatbots for the Facebook messenger. Comput. Educ. **151**, 103862 (2020)
38. Touvron, H., et al.: Llama 2: Open foundation and fine-tuned chat models. arXiv preprint arXiv:2307.09288 (2023)
39. Vygotsky, L.S.: Thought and Language. MIT press (2012)
40. Wood, D., Bruner, J.S., Ross, G.: The role of tutoring in problem solving. J. Child Psychol. Psychiatry **17**(2), 89–100 (1976)
41. Zare, P., Mukundan, J.: The use of socratic method as a teaching/learning tool to develop students' critical thinking: a review of literature. Lang. India **15**(6) (2015)
42. Zhang, T., Kishore, V., Wu, F., Weinberger, K.Q., Artzi, Y.: BERTScore: evaluating text generation with BERT. In: International Conference on Learning Representations (2020)

Sentiment Analysis for Academic Interest

Renata Magalhães, Francisco S. Marcondes, Dalila Durães(✉), and Paulo Novais

ALGORITMI Centre/LASI, University of Minho, Braga, Portugal
pg34321@alunos.uminho.pt, francisco.marcondes@algoritmi.uminho.pt, {dad,pjon}@di.uminho.pt

Abstract. School failure and dropout are critical issues affecting students worldwide. Smart schooling uses technology to enhance the educational experience and aims to mitigate these problems. This paper investigates the impact of a conversational agent on student performance by analysing feedback from four sessions. The feedback was overwhelmingly positive, with students expressing increased engagement and improved academic performance by the end of the experiment. The study involved the extraction and analysis of the five most common verbs, nouns and adjectives used in student feedback. This analysis showed that interactions with the conversational agent were well received, demonstrating the potential of such technology to provide personalised support and foster a more engaging learning environment. The project highlights the effectiveness of conversational agents in improving student outcomes and provides insights into the integration of sentiment analysis in educational contexts to support student success.

Keywords: Dropout · Sentiment Analysis · Machine Learning Techniques

1 Introduction

In recent years, smart schooling has gained significant attention as an innovative approach to enhancing the educational experience through the use of digital tools. These technologies aim to make teaching and learning more dynamic and interactive. However, despite the potential benefits, the education system has yet to fully embrace these advancements, particularly in the areas of preventive tools and mandatory schooling [1].

The concept of smart schooling has been emerging in recent years, with the use of digital tools to transform the teaching and learning experience into a dynamic and interactive endeavour, which can be seen through the increasing number of publications on the topic since 2012 [2]. The unexpected pandemic situation of Covid-19 has highlighted the need for smart solutions which have been applied to numerous aspects of life ssuch as transportation, energy, health and governenment [3]. When it comes to the education system, these have not

F. Bellas and O. Fontenla-Romero (Eds.): AIEER 2024, CCIS 2519, pp. 33–43, 2025.
https://doi.org/10.1007/978-3-031-93409-4_3

been fully incorporated. As far as smart education goes, developments have yet to be made, especially regarding mandatory schooling and preventive tools.

Conversational agents, also known as chatbots, have emerged as valuable tools in creating personalized learning experiences and supporting students. Previous research has demonstrated the utility of these agents in higher education, where they have been shown to positively influence student motivation and interaction. Despite their popularity in higher education, there is a need for further exploration of their impact on student motivation and interaction within compulsory education [4].

Previous research has looked into the use of conversational agents in smart schooling and although virtual assistants are popular in higher education, their impact on student motivation and interaction in compulsory education needs more exploration. Initial findings suggest that while some students may find virtual assistants confusing at first, they eventually recognize them as beneficial and motivating. Some students initially find virtual assistants confusing but eventually see them as beneficial and motivating [5]. Positive feedback has also been recorded in elementary education, where both teachers and students have found conversational agents to be user-friendly. However, more research is needed on integrating emotional state data and handling predictive and behavioral issues with digital assistants.

This paper focuses on analyzing student feedback after interacting with a conversational agent designed to support their academic performance. By examining the sentiment expressed in the feedback, we aim to gain insights into the effectiveness of the conversational agent and its potential to improve educational outcomes. Through this study, we seek to contribute to the growing body of knowledge on the use of artificial intelligence in education, particularly in preventing school failure and dropout.

Ethical Statement. Given that the participants are minors, the project and interaction plans were initially presented to their parents. Those parents who provided consent were subsequently asked to sign an informed consent form. The guidelines governing the interactions with the conversational agent were formulated by a collaborative team consisting of educational psychologists, computer science researchers, and a technology company, all of whom are actively involved in the project.

The document is divided into five main sections. Next, the state of the art is presented. Next, the Methods and Methodology section presents the project and the explaination about the methodology. In the Sentiment analysis section, some results are presented, followed by the discussion. Finally, all prior themes are summarized, and the main conclusions are drawn, indicating potential directions for further research.

2 State-of-the-Art

Sentiment Analysis (SA), a significant domain within text mining research, focuses on extracting and categorizing sentiments, emotions, and attitudes conveyed in textual data [6]. This field encompasses summarizing opinions, analyzing reviews, and detecting sarcasm, thereby interpreting emotions in unstructured texts as positive, negative, or neutral, and determining the intensity of these emotions. Techniques from Natural Language Processing (NLP) and Machine Learning (ML) facilitate the identification and examination of emotions in both written and spoken language [7]. SA applications span diverse fields such as healthcare [8], customer feedback analysis [9], social media analysis [10], and education [11].

While terms like opinion mining, opinion extraction, subjectivity analysis, and polarity analysis are often used synonymously with SA, some authors differentiate them. Opinion mining focuses on extracting and analyzing opinions about an entity, whereas sentiment analysis identifies and analyzes the sentiment expressed in a text. Despite these distinctions, both terms, along with the others mentioned, are generally categorized under the broader term SA. Given the textual nature of sentiment extraction and analysis sources, the processes involved are intrinsically related to NLP processes, addressing challenges like dealing with negations, word sense disambiguation, and coreference resolution.

SA operates at three main levels: document-level, sentence-level, and aspect-level [6,12]. Document-level SA evaluates an entire opinion document to determine its overall sentiment about a specific topic. Sentence-level SA classifies individual sentences as subjective or objective and determines the sentiment if subjective. Aspect-level SA, a more fine-grained approach, classifies sentiments based on specific aspects of entities, recognizing that opinions on different aspects of the same entity can vary. This level of detail is crucial in applications such as product reviews, where users may have varied opinions on different features of the same product.

Recent studies highlight the efficacy of SA in various educational contexts. For instance, [13] introduced the SASys architecture, which employs SA to predict student dropouts in e-learning by analyzing text from virtual learning environments and student engagement data. [14] utilized machine learning approaches with the Support Vector Machine (SVM) classifier to classify students' opinions in higher education. Similarly, [15] applied SA to Google app reviews, focusing on university students' behavior, with SVM showing the best performance among the classifiers used. These studies demonstrate the potential of SA in gauging student satisfaction and engagement, aiding in early interventions to reduce dropout rates and improve educational outcomes.

3 Methods and Methodology

Project Description. This project aims to support a public government initiative to prevent school failure and dropout among K-12 students through the development of an advanced educational software platform. Using arisk assessment matrix and artificial intelligence algorithms, the platform focuses on two key areas: the early identification of students at risk of academic failure or dropout, and the promotion of effective study and learning practices. Recommendations are tailored to each student's performance and behavior, categorized into four distinct risk clusters, enabling personalized interventions to foster academic success.

Key features of the platform include an innovative risk assessment matrix that identifies early indicators of school failure, a predictive AI system that detects risk situations, and a conversational agent that guides, motivates, and advises students based on their unique profiles. The platform's development was informed by a pilot study conducted with 845 students from public and private schools in northern regions, using Structural Equation Models to validate predictors of school failure. Following successful testing, the platform was deployed and evaluated in a partner school, demonstrating its potential to improve timely intervention and support for at-risk students.

The goal is to create a technological solution that streamlines data collection and processing, thus freeing up time for educators and psychologists to focus on direct student intervention. The multidisciplinary project team, consisting of educational psychology researchers and computer science experts, collaborates with a technology company to ensure the platform is effectively designed and implemented. This innovative tool aims to mitigate risks associated with school dropout, such as unemployment and mental health issues, by providing a timely, efficient, and personalized approach to educational support.

The proposed solution involves two primary modules, Education Intelligence and Conversational Agent, which interact with three main actors: the class director, students, and the school platform. The Intelligence component processes data from the school platform and students to generate information relevant to the class director and enhance the agent's functionality. Utilizing machine learning techniques, it forecasts students' failure risk. The conversational agent serves as an interactive support system, collecting subjective student feedback and objective school data, such as grades and absences, to provide timely and personalized support.

The Intelligence module employs a risk matrix and student questionnaire data to assess each student's risk level. Machine learning algorithms predict academic standing based on recent grades in core subjects and survey responses. Educational psychologists designed the survey to gather comprehensive academic experience data, which, combined with grades, helps categorize students into risk clusters. The students are grouped into four clusters based on academic performance and engagement, allowing for targeted interventions. This granularity improves the representativeness of the samples and enables proactive support for at-risk students.

Four algorithms were assessed: AdaBoost, DecisionTree, RandomForest, and XGBoost. Results showed that XGBoost provided the highest accuracy in classifying students into their respective risk clusters.

Conversational Agent. Four activities were developed and tested at a partner school with 51 students participating. Activities were designed based on cognitive-behavioral theories to create patterns and set specific objectives, promoting student involvement and effective responses. Activities included closed and open questions, emojis, and images to make the interactions more relatable and engaging.

First Activity: The chatbot introduces itself, asks for a brief student introduction, and presents a questionnaire on study habits, views on education, and family and friends' support. The chatbot discusses hobbies and their academic benefits, demonstrating that school can be fun and integrated into daily activities.

Second Activity: The chatbot greets the student, asks about their week, and tells a joke. It presents a scenario where a classmate is struggling and asks for strategies to improve grades, tailored to the student's assigned risk cluster.

Third Activity: This activity delves deeper into study techniques and their consequences, including a practical exercise where students plan a birthday party using outlined steps. This real-life example helps students understand the benefits of systematic planning for academic success.

Fourth Activity: The chatbot reviews activity 3, discusses students' role models, and compares questionnaire results from the beginning and end of the school year. It concludes with a motivational message.

4 Sentiment Analysis

At the end of the sessions with the chatbot, feedback was firstly collected informally. Students talked to the team of psychologists that was present during the activity, as well as their class director. It was noted that overall the students really enjoyed their interactions with the chatbot, rating the sessions 4 or 5 on a scale of 1 to 5. In addition, there was also an opportunity to hear the students' opinions on suggestions for changes or improvements. Students suggested, for example, adding more or different answer options; more opportunities to write and give their opinion in the chatbot; more jokes; for some students the presentation of the chatbot's messages was too fast, while for others it was too slow; other farewell options.

Student Feedback. Students' feedback was also collected from their answers to the last interaction with the chatbot. This included questions, such as:

- If you had to tell a friend, how would you describe our sessions?
- How did you feel during your participation in these sessions?
- What did you like the least about our conversations?
- Do you think I have helped you improve as a student in any way?
- Would you talk to me regularly if I were available outside the classroom? If so, how long do you think you would talk to me?
- What do you think I could improve in order to help other students?
- Is there anything else you would like to tell me, before we say goodbye?

Since all of the responses to these questions were open-ended, a modest but real amount of textual data was produced. The answers given by the students were taken out and examined.

There were only two negative answers to the questions presented before. One is from a 9th grade student and the other is from a 5th grade student. The 9th grade student said that although interesting, the interactions with the chatbot were too long as it took too long to write. Another criticism is that most answer options are automatized and it would be more fun if students could write more freely. The 5th grade student did not justify his answer, but said he would miss talking to the chabot, which indicates some contradiction.

Feedback was extracted from the students' responses and analyzed as described in this section. Student feedback comprised a total of 1843 words and 11392 characters.

Table 1 shows the extraction of the five most common verbs, nouns and adjectives extracted from the students' feedback.

Table 1. Extraction of most common words.

Verbs	Nouns	Adjectives
like	minute	Interesting
think	day	happy
know	study	good
talk	session	great
improve	joke	funny

Feedback was extracted from the students' responses and analyzed as described in this section. Student feedback comprised a total of 1843 words and 11392 characters.

First, it was necessary to clean the data in order to remove noise, that is, symbols or errant words that do not add any relevant information for sentiment analysis, as well as punctuation.

The next step was the pre-processing of the data, which includes lemmatization, stemming and tokenization. A total of 10825 characters and 1747 words remained.

This analysis was performed using SpaCy, a commonly used library for NLP with python, and NLTK [16]. 141 adjectives, 315 verbs and 442 nouns were extracted and the most common occurences can be seen in 1, in order of frequency. The most common verb within student feedback was the verb "like", which indicates positive affection towards the experience with the conversational agent. This can also be confirmed by the most common adjectives, which are all positive, demonstrating that the students enjoyed the activities, describing them as "interesting" and "funny". The most frequent nouns in the feedback refer to time, as one of the questions asked if the students would talk to the chatbot if it was available outside of the classroom, and how long would they do it for, to which students replied with minutes and days. Less frequent answers also included weeks. "Study" is most frequent on the answer to the question "Do you think I have helped you improve as a student in any way?". Student feedback shows that the chatbot has had a positive effect on students' study habits, helping them improve. This can also be confirmed by the frequent occurrence of the verb "improve". "Session" and "joke" were also amongst the most frequent nouns as it refer to what students enjoyed the most about the interactions with the agent.

Overall, student feedback regarding the contact with the conversational agent was positive. Within the project, student emotion was also calculated and average scores can be seen found in Figs. 1 and 2.

Anxiety	Shame	Boredom	Happiness	Distraction	Optimism	Trust	Interest
0.60	0.55	0.55	0.52	0.52	0.50	0.48	0.46

Fig. 1. Average emotion scores.

It is possible to see that interest was the emotion that showed the lowest scores overall, in contrast to anxiety. This was represented in all school years within the study sample, comprising grades 5 to 9.

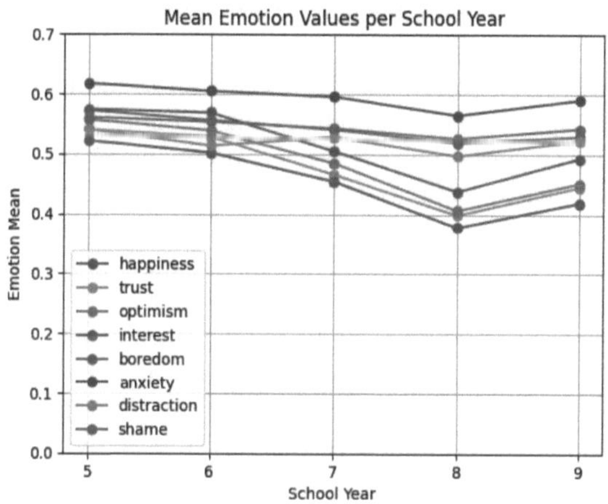

Fig. 2. Average emotion per school year.

At the end of the project, new evaluations and calculations were carried out to determine the students' level of risk. In addition, the number of students willing to talk to the chatbot if it was online was also analyzed. The level of student risk is a key metric for assessing the project's impact on student support and follow-up. This indicator makes it possible to identify vulnerable and in need of intervention. During the project strategies and metrics were adopted to calculate each student's risk level, taking into account factors such as academic record, attendance and behavior. This metric provides an overview of the students' general risk status.

With the activities carried out, overall there has been a 14% improvement in the risk of failure. This improvement is due not only to the improvement in the students' grades, but also to an increase in the different metrics related to engagement.

Other factors such as grade recognition and grade satisfaction increased after the demonstration project.

Students were also asked if they would use the agent if it were online and they could interact with it whenever they wanted. This metric indicates how many students are willing to use the conversational agent as a support tool even after the project has finished. In this case, 78% of the students gave a positive response, which reflects the students' receptiveness to the agent and their perception of its usefulness and benefits.

5 Discussion

The results of this study provide compelling evidence for the efficacy of conversational agents in improving student engagement and academic performance. The overwhelmingly positive feedback from students indicates that these agents can create an enjoyable and supportive learning environment. This finding is significant, considering the global challenge of school failure and dropout, which affects countless students worldwide.

One of the most noteworthy observations from the student feedback is the frequent mention of positive terms such as "like", "interesting", "funny", "happy", and "improve". This suggests that the conversational agent not only captured the students' interest but also contributed positively to their learning experiences. The inclusion of humor and relatable content, such as jokes and discussions about hobbies, likely played a crucial role in making the interactions engaging and enjoyable.

The improvement in students' study habits and academic performance, as indicated by their feedback, highlights the practical benefits of incorporating conversational agents into the educational system. The use of AI to provide personalized support and recommendations based on individual student profiles shows promise in addressing the specific needs of each student, thus fostering a more inclusive and effective learning environment.

Despite these positive outcomes, the study also identified areas for improvement. Some students felt that the interactions were too long or that the answer options were too automated. These insights are valuable for refining the design and functionality of conversational agents to better meet student needs and preferences. Adjusting the pacing of interactions and providing more opportunities for students to input their own responses can enhance the user experience.

The study's use of sentiment analysis to interpret student feedback underscores the importance of understanding students' emotional responses to educational interventions. By analyzing the most common verbs, nouns, and adjectives in the feedback, we gained a deeper understanding of how students perceived their interactions with the conversational agent. This approach can be further developed to include more nuanced emotional state data, which can inform more precise and effective interventions.

Additionally, the findings suggest that conversational agents have the potential to serve as valuable tools for continuous student support beyond the classroom. The willingness of a significant proportion of students to continue using the agent outside school hours indicates that these tools can provide ongoing academic and emotional support, thus contributing to sustained student engagement and success.

While the study focused on a specific group of students, future research should aim to expand the sample size and diversity to include different educational settings and age groups. This will help to generalize the findings and tailor the technology to various educational contexts. Furthermore, exploring the integration of conversational agents with other digital learning tools and platforms can create a more comprehensive smart schooling ecosystem, enhancing the overall educational experience and support system for students.

In conclusion, the study demonstrates the potential of conversational agents to positively impact student engagement and academic performance. By leveraging artificial intelligence and sentiment analysis, educators can create more engaging, personalized, and supportive learning experiences that address the diverse needs of students. Future research should continue to explore the integration of these technologies with emotional state data and predictive tools to further enhance their efficacy and impact in educational settings.

6 Conclusion

This study highlights the significant potential of conversational agents in enhancing the educational experience and addressing the critical issues of school failure and dropout. By analyzing student feedback after interactions with a conversational agent, we observed overwhelmingly positive responses, with students describing the sessions as interesting, enjoyable, and beneficial to their academic performance.

The frequent use of positive terms such as "like", "interesting", "funny", "happy", and "improve" in the feedback underscores the agent's ability to engage students effectively and foster a supportive learning environment. Moreover, the notable improvement in students' academic performance and study habits, as indicated by the feedback, demonstrates the practical benefits of integrating conversational agents into the educational system.

The study's findings suggest that conversational agents can serve as valuable tools for personalized learning, offering tailored support and motivation to students. The positive reception and willingness of students to continue using the agent outside the classroom further validate its usefulness and impact.

Additionally, the study reveals important considerations for optimizing the use of conversational agents in education, such as adjusting the duration and frequency of interactions to better suit students' preferences. The integration of sentiment analysis provided valuable insights into students' emotional states, enabling more precise and effective interventions.

Finally, this research supports the growing body of evidence that conversational agents can play a crucial role in smart schooling. By leveraging artificial intelligence and sentiment analysis, educators can create more engaging, personalized, and supportive learning experiences that address the diverse needs of students, ultimately contributing to reducing school failure and dropout rates. Future research should continue to explore the integration of conversational agents with emotional state data and predictive tools to further enhance their efficacy and impact in educational settings.

Future research should focus on several key areas to further enhance the efficacy and impact of conversational agents in education. Firstly, integrating more sophisticated sentiment analysis techniques and emotional state data can help create even more personalized and responsive interactions. Additionally, exploring the long-term effects of conversational agents on student performance and engagement will provide valuable insights into their sustained impact.

Developing adaptive learning algorithms that adjust the conversational agent's behavior based on real-time feedback and student performance data can also improve the user experience. Furthermore, expanding the study to include diverse educational settings and age groups will help generalize the findings and tailor the technology to various educational contexts.

Lastly, investigating the integration of conversational agents with other digital learning tools and platforms can create a more comprehensive smart schooling ecosystem, enhancing the overall educational experience and support system for students.

Acknowledgements. This work has been supported by Erasmus+ Programme of the European Union - Artificial Intelligence learning modules to adapt VET to labour market needs (AI4VET), AIM@VET - 2022-1ES01-KA220-VET-000089813.

References

1. Pratama, M.P., Sampelolo, R., Lura, H.: Revolutionizing education: harnessing the power of artificial intelligence for personalized learning. Klasikal: J. Educ. Lang. Teach. Sci. **5**(2), 350–357 (2023)
2. Singh, H., Miah, S.J.: Smart education literature: a theoretical analysis. Educ. Inf. Technol. **25**(4), 3299–3328 (2020). https://doi.org/10.1007/s10639-020-10116-4
3. Gracias, J.S., Parnell, G.S., Specking, E., Pohl, E.A., Buchanan, R.: Smart cities-a structured literature review. Smart Cities **6**(4), 1719–1743 (2023)
4. George, A.S., George, A.S.H.: A review of chatGPT AI's impact on several business sectors. Partners Univ. Int. Innov. J. **1**(1), 9–23 (2023)
5. Magalhães, R., Marcondes, F.S., Durães, D., Novais, P.: Emotion extraction from likert-scale questionnaires: –an additional dimension to psychology instruments–. In International Conference on Intelligent Data Engineering and Automated Learning, pp. 166–176. Springer (2023)

6. Medhat, W., Hassan, A., Korashy, H.: Sentiment analysis algorithms and applications: a survey. Ain Shams Eng. J. **5**(4), 1093–1113 (2014)
7. Cui, J., Wang, Z., Ho, S.-B., Cambria, E.: Survey on sentiment analysis: evolution of research methods and topics. Artif. Intell. Rev. **56**(8), 8469–8510 (2023)
8. Milne-Ives, M., et al.: The effectiveness of artificial intelligence conversational agents in health care: systematic review. J. Med. Internet Res. **22**(10), e20346 (2020)
9. Iqbal, A., Amin, R., Iqbal, J., Alroobaea, R., Binmahfoudh, A., Hussain, M.: Sentiment analysis of consumer reviews using deep learning. Sustainability **14**(17), 10844 (2022)
10. Bibi, M., et al.: A novel unsupervised ensemble framework using concept-based linguistic methods and machine learning for twitter sentiment analysis. Pattern Recognit. Lett. **158**, 80–86 (2022)
11. Dake, D.K., Gyimah, E.: Using sentiment analysis to evaluate qualitative students' responses. Educ. Inf. Technol. **28**(4), 4629–4647 (2023)
12. Wankhade, M., Rao, A., Kulkarni, C.: A survey on sentiment analysis methods, applications, and challenges. Artif. Intell. Rev. **55**(7), 5731–5780 (2022)
13. Bóbó, M.L.D.R., Campos, F., Stroele, V., David, J.M.N., Braga, R., Torrent, T.T.: Using sentiment analysis to identify student emotional state to avoid dropout in e-learning. Int. J. Dist. Educ. Technol. (IJDET) **20**(1), 1–24 (2022)
14. Baragash, R.S., Aldowah, H., Umar, I.N.: Students' perceptions of e-learning in Malaysian universities: sentiment analysis based machine learning approach. J. Inf. Technol. Educ. Res. **21**, 439–463 (2022)
15. Ranjan, S., Mishra, S.: Perceiving university students' opinions from google app reviews. Concurr. Comput.: Pract. Exp. **34**(10), e6800 (2022)
16. J NLTK Project. Natural language toolkit

The Interactive Career Atlas - An AI-Based Web Application for Informed Career Decisions

Karoline Schubert[1(✉)], Nina Mader[1,2], Melina S. Welt[1], Björn E. Hommel[1,3], Franz J. M. Wollang[3], and Judith Volmer[4]

[1] Professorship of Work and Organizational Psychology, University of Bamberg, Bamberg, Germany
{karoline.schubert,nina.mader}@uni-leipzig.de
[2] Wilhelm Wundt Institute of Psychology, Leipzig University, Leipzig, Germany
[3] magnolia psychometrics GmbH, Leipzig, Germany
[4] Institute of Psychology, Work and Organizational Psychology, University of Bamberg, Bamberg, Germany
judith.volmer@uni-bamberg.de

Abstract. Navigating through the many options of modern career paths is becoming increasingly opaque for job seekers. With our newly developed AI-based web application "Interactive Career Atlas" we try to counteract this development. The application is simple: users provide information about their current work situation, interests, desires or restrictions in free text format. A fine-tuned language model ("AI") in the background matches the free text with possible jobs, and as a result, users are presented with a map of their individual career landscape. On this map, they see different jobs they could take, filtered by their unique interests, specialties and limitations. The project is supported by scientific research, as findings from work and organizational psychology are integrated into both the development of the application and the design of a planned evaluation study – with the aim of examining the social benefits of the application from a psychological perspective.

Keywords: AI · large language models · career decision · career orientation

1 Introduction

The world of work has changed significantly over the last decades. In the past, jobs were characterized by specific requirements and clearly separated from one another. Today, however, these boundaries are increasingly blurred resulting in a boundarylessness of careers [1, 2]. On the one hand, this development makes successful career orientation for job seekers more and more complex. On the other hand, employers are faced with the challenge of effectively addressing the growing shortage of skilled workers. At its core, this is a matching problem: Employees are looking for professional opportunities that fit their personal life situation and their individual skills. Employers, in turn, must learn to recognize and utilize the potential of applicants beyond the boundaries of rigid job

K. Schubert and N. Mader—Equal contribution.

F. Bellas and O. Fontenla-Romero (Eds.): AIEER 2024, CCIS 2519, pp. 44–51, 2025.
https://doi.org/10.1007/978-3-031-93409-4_4

descriptions. People who are looking for a job, seeking further training or a career change currently have a limited range of career orientation options. Job search engines only provide results for specific search queries and professions. They assume that searchers already know their goal. Career orientation tests are often time-consuming, expensive and disregard the broad range of knowledge, skills, ability and other characteristics that may influence career exploration and decision-making processes. However, focusing on individual needs and expectations is becoming increasingly important in view of the shortage of skilled workers [3].

We address this problem with the Interactive Career Atlas – a newly developed AI-powered web application – by offering job seekers an alternative way to navigate the modern career landscape. With the Interactive Career Atlas, we offer a low-threshold and at the same time individually adapted, informative overview of the possibilities in the career landscape.

Using the latest methods in computational linguistics and results from research in work and organizational psychology, the Interactive Career Atlas offers low-threshold guidance for people who want to align their professional future with their individual skills, experiences, and life situations. As a new career search engine, the Interactive Career Atlas increases the fit between job seekers and employers. A higher fit between person and job is linked to higher job satisfaction and individual performance [4]. In addition, research results from work and organizational psychology clearly show that a good fit is positively related to life satisfaction and therefore positively related to work ability [5, 6]. This results in more effective job filling and higher job satisfaction in times of skilled labor shortages. The societal benefits are evident: the fulfillment of occupational interests and needs is expected to increase job and life satisfaction as work is an important part of people's lives.

In sum, we develop an AI-based web application using the most current knowledge in computer linguistics. We address the gap between job seekers searching for fitting jobs and employers searching for qualified workers with the goal to improve employees' work and life satisfaction.

2 Theoretical Background and Hypotheses

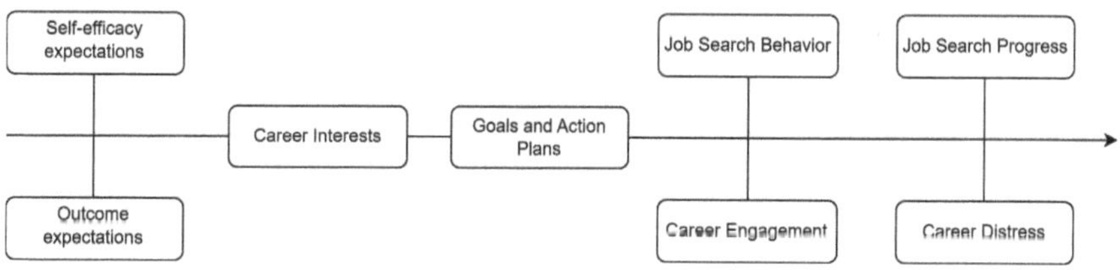

Fig. 1. Schematic representation of the career decision process. Adapted from [7].

We base our assumptions on Social Cognitive Career Theory (SCCT; see Fig. 1, [8–10]) which sheds light on how people develop career-related interests, how career choices are influenced, and on the individual performance exhibited in one's career path. In contrast to other career theories, which mostly ignore environmental factors, the SCCT emphasizes a dynamic interaction between person and environment [9]. Thus, SCCT is more adaptive to personal and environmental changes such as boundarylessness of careers than conservative career theories.

The core factors of SCCT are personal self-efficacy expectations, outcome expectations and personal goals [11]. Personal self-efficacy expectations encompass the subjective judgment of one's own capabilities to pursue goals, thus, the belief in what a person can achieve. Next, outcome expectations reflect the belief about the results of one's behaviors, thus, the expectation of what will happen if one pursues a goal. The interaction of both builds career interests. Finally, personal goals represent the subjective will to achieve something, in other words how much someone wants to achieve a certain goal. Personal goals are influenced by career interests [10, 12].

We expect that using the Interactive Career Atlas influences this consecutive career decision process at different stages. First, we expect, that the Interactive Career Atlas heightens users' self-efficacy expectations as they intuitively and efficiently gather valuable information through the web application. This supports them in coming to informed career-related decisions. Additionally, the web application positively influences users' outcome expectations as next steps in users' careers become clearer, for instance, by encountering requirements for recommended professions. Therefore, we hypothesize higher self-efficacy expectations (Hypothesis 1) and higher knowledge of next steps (Hypothesis 2) after using the web application in comparison to before as has been shown by other career development interventions [13, 14].

Career interests, the next step in the career decision process, are thought to guide persons to make career-related choices [15]. Career interests start developing during early childhood and are influenced by numerous factors, such as parental guidance, education, peers, etc. Moreover, career interests may be guided by the availability of information on certain jobs. The Interactive Career Atlas offers, in a comprehensive way, an abundance of career-related information on which career decisions can be based. Career decision difficulties should, therefore, be reduced [6]. Thus, we hypothesize that the web application will decrease career decision difficulties (Hypothesis 3).

Following career-related choices, people tend to set goals, such as starting a certain training or following a certain career path, and act to fulfill these goals [15–17], for instance by gathering necessary documents or sending out applications. The Interactive Career Atlas can foster these goals and actions as it provides users with information on how to achieve a specific job. Therefore, we hypothesize that planned (Hypothesis 4) and enacted job search behavior (Hypothesis 5), as well as career engagement (i.e., proactive career behaviors; Hypothesis 6), will increase by using the web application.

The outcomes of these job search and proactive behaviors, such as job search progress and career engagement, depend on the earlier steps of the described career development process as well as the ability of the person [15]. As the web application supports every step of the career decision process and, importantly, informs the user about the requirements of the pursued professions, we expect job search progress to be positively influenced using the Interactive Career Atlas. Accordingly, we hypothesize job search progress to be higher after using the web application (Hypothesis 7). On the other hand, encountering difficulties in the career development process can be a stressful experience [18]. As the web application reduces difficulties by providing all the necessary information in a comprehensive and intuitive manner, we hypothesize career distress to be lower after using the web application (Hypothesis 8).

3 Development of the Interactive Career Atlas

The Interactive Career Atlas is a web application that can be used on a PC or mobile phone. The principle is very simple. In the first step, users write a free text with statements about themselves, such as "I was trained as an electrician", "I like being around people", or "I suffer from back pain". Users can then select individual filter options for the results displayed, such as "education only," and so on. A language model ("AI") in the background matches the free text with possible jobs, and as a result, users are presented with a map representing their career landscape. On this map, they see different jobs they could take, filtered by their individual interests, specialties and limitations. Jobs that appear in a person's proximity on the map are more in-line with the person's holistic description of a desirable and suitable career, while jobs that appear further away require additional training or education. Users can explore the career landscape and save jobs that sound interesting to them for later.

The web application gives users a visually appealing and realistic impression of obvious career and training opportunities. In addition to being user-friendly, this visual impression creates a well-sorted overview of training and reorientation opportunities. Figure 2 shows how the final user interface of the web application can look like.

In the background, AI-supported language processing is used to calculate a spatial representation of individuals' positions in the career landscape based on the users' free-text self-description. We use so-called "Sentence Transformer Models" [19] to represent users' textual self-descriptions as numerical vectors. These machine learning methods transform a sequence of characters (e.g., text data) into a numeric representation (i.e., vectors). Vectors can be used to perform mathematical operations, where a comparison between job descriptions and user input text can be calculated using cosine similarity based on mathematical representations. Cosine similarity is a measure of the similarity of two vectors and can be compared conceptually with a correlation (ranges from -1 to 1). This comparison takes place in a high-dimensional representation, often referred to as semantic space. In our case, this space constitutes of 768 dimensions, which is too many for meaningful visual representation. Therefore, the results are projected onto a two-dimensional representation in the form of a graphically appealing landscape using dimension-reducing methods (e. g., UMAP, [20]).

3.1 AI Training Method

We started with a pre-trained Sentence Transformer Model, which was fine-tuned to train the model for our specific application. This was done in two steps following [21] Polarity Calibration and Domain Adjustment. During Polarity Calibration, the model is trained to distinguish between semantically opposed concepts, which is necessary because although cosine similarity ranges from 1 to 1, negative coefficients are rarely

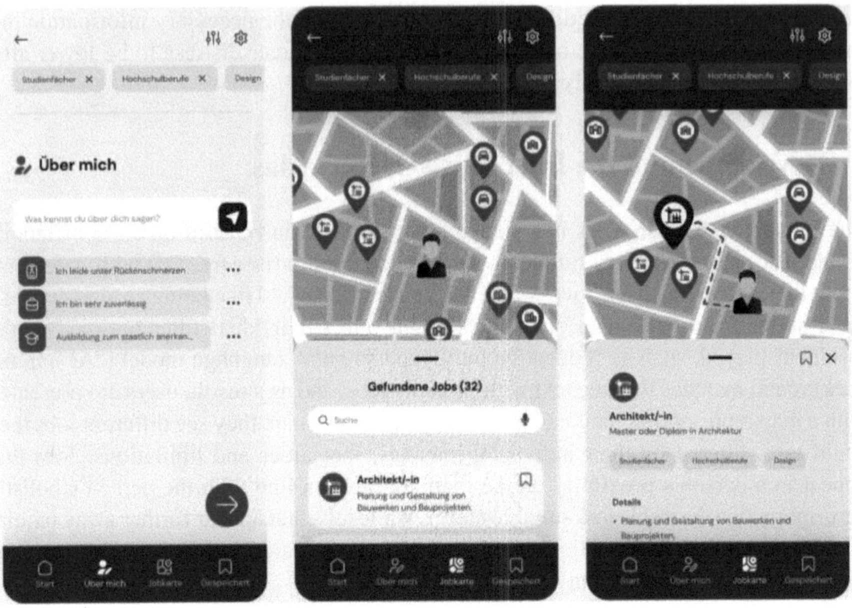

Fig. 2. An example of how the Interactive Career Atlas might look.

produced when comparing vector representations of sentences (see [21]). This limitation arises primarily because the high-dimensional vector representation of sentences encodes a number of abstract linguistic features, many of which tend to be positively correlated across text sequences. The goal of polarity calibration is to maximize the cosine distance between vector representations of opposing concepts. Domain adaptation helps the model focus on text segments that convey relevant information.

Next, we retrieved job-specific descriptors for 3,533 occupations from the BERUFENET website. BERUFENET is a curated and frequently updated ontological database maintained by the German Federal Employment Agency and trained job analysts. It encompasses a wide range of textual data describing the knowledge, skills, abilities, and other characteristics relevant to specific occupations. From this database, we extracted 565 descriptors on average that cover aspects such as personality traits, occupational interests, working conditions, and educational background. The extracted data were encoded using our trained model. Subsequently, the system matches user input data (self-reported descriptors) with occupations based on semantic distance, which is calculated as the cosine similarity between vectors representing both data sources. Occupations exhibiting high cosine similarities are dimensionally reduced and projected onto a two-dimensional surface using Uniform Manifold Approximation and Projection (UMAP; [20]). Finally, this two-dimensional projection is embedded within a procedurally generated landscape [22], with individual occupations retrieved from the semantic search presented as landmarks on the map (illustrated in Fig. 3).

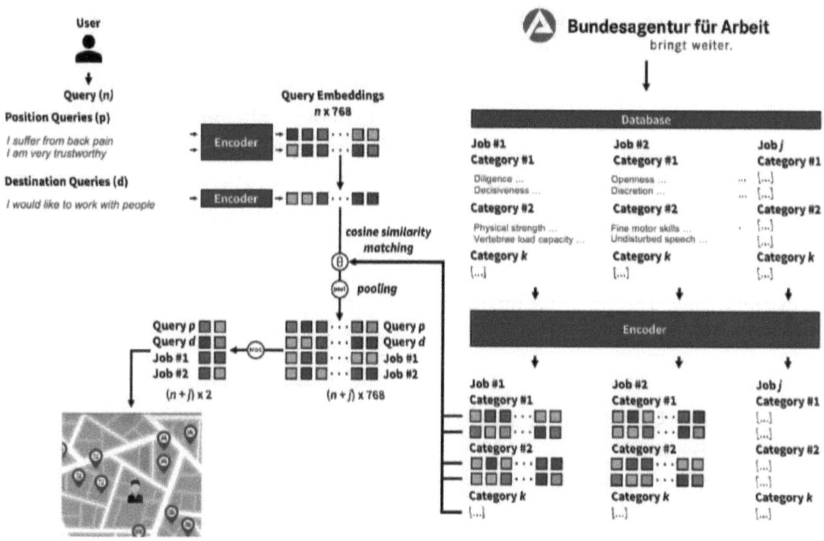

Fig. 3. Schematic depiction of the AI method

4 Evaluation Study of the Interactive Career Atlas

The purpose of the evaluation study is to examine the effectiveness and efficiency of our application and to ensure that it meets the needs of our users. By first analyzing barriers to finding a job and developing a tailored solution, we aim to significantly improve career guidance and development for people at all stages of their lives. The evaluation of the web application is planned in two steps: an evaluation with the first version of the application to check the usability and to find and fix small bugs. Once the usability of the web application is satisfactory, the second step is to evaluate the web application in terms of psychologically relevant concepts.

The methodological design of the evaluation study corresponds to the classical design of an intervention group and a control group. The intervention group will use the Interactive Career Atlas, while the control groups will either not use it, receive traditional job counseling, or receive information about job training from traditional websites. Before and after the intervention, we will collect data on our hypothesized variables and detect changes due to the use of the web application. By collecting and analyzing this data, we aim to provide comprehensive insights into the impact of the Interactive Career Atlas and identify areas for future improvement and expansion.

5 Outlook

In our transdisciplinary research project, we are creating a customized, AI-based, digital career and education guidance service. The AI-based web application is unique in its simplicity of use, where you enter information about yourself in a free text format and receive a personalized visually appealing and realistic impression of obvious career and training opportunities. This is a decisive advantage over traditional career counseling services, which require an intensive exploration of numerous options and a targeted search for suitable career alternatives. This AI-based web application only works with precise fine-tuning of the Sentence Transformer model and a successful evaluation by a scientific team. Once completed, the successful application will be made available to society as widely as possible, whereby working with our project partners gives us the opportunity to reach key audiences head-on. In the long-term, it is planned to integrate more features, such as adding available positions for the jobs to the map.

Acknowledgments. This project is funded by the federal ministry of labor and social affairs and by the funding program "Civic Innovation".

Disclosure of Interests. The authors have no competing interests to declare that are relevant to the content of this article.

References

1. Guan, Y., Arthur, M.B., Khapova, S.N., Hall, R.J., Lord, R.G.: Career boundarylessness and career success: a review, integration and guide to future research. J. Vocat. Behav. **110**, 390–402 (2019). https://doi.org/10.1016/j.jvb.2018.05.013
2. Sullivan, S.E., Arthur, M.B.: The evolution of the boundaryless career concept: examining physical and psychological mobility. J. Vocat. Behav. **69**(1), 19–29 (2006). https://doi.org/10.1016/j.jvb.2005.09.001
3. Hirschi, A.: The fourth industrial revolution: issues and implications for career research and practice. Career Dev. Q. **66**(3), 192–204 (2018). https://doi.org/10.1002/cdq.12142
4. Edwards, J.R., Caplan, R.D., Harrison, R.V.: Person-environment fit theory: conceptual foundations, empirical evidence, and directions for future research. In: Cooper, C.L. (ed.) Theories of Organizational Stress, pp. 28–67. Oxford University Press (1998)
5. Littman-Ovadia, H., Lazar-Butbul, V., Benjamin, B.A.: Strengths-based career counseling. J. Career Assess. **22**(3), 403–419 (2014). https://doi.org/10.1177/1069072713498483
6. Perdrix, S., Stauffer, S., Masdonati, J., Massoudi, K., Rossier, J.: Effectiveness of career counseling: a one-year follow-up. J. Vocat. Behav. **80**(2), 565–578 (2012). https://doi.org/10.1016/j.jvb.2011.08.011
7. Lent, R.W., Brown, S.D., Hackett, G.: Toward a unifying social cognitive theory of career and academic interest, choice, and performance. J. Vocat. Behav. **45**, 79–122 (1994). https://doi.org/10.1006/jvbe.1994.1027
8. Brown, S.D., Lent, R.W.: Social cognitive career theory. In: Walsh, W.B., Flores, L.Y., Hartung, P.J., Leong, F. (eds.) Career Psychology. American Psychological Association, Washington, D. C., pp. 37–57 (2023). https://doi.org/10.1037/0000339-003
9. Lent, R.W., Brown, S.D.: Social cognitive career theory in a diverse world. J. Career Assess. **25**(1), 3–5 (2017). https://doi.org/10.1177/1069072716657811
10. Lent, R.W., Brown, S.D., Hackett, G.: Social cognitive career theory. In: Brown, D. (ed.) Career choice and development, pp. 255–311. Jossey-Bass, San Francisco, CA (2002)
11. Buthelezi, T., Alexander, D., Seabi, J.: Adolescents' perceived career challenges and needs in a disadvantaged context in South Africa from a social cognitive career theoretical perspective. South Af. J. High. Educ. **23**(3) (2010). https://doi.org/10.4314/sajhe.v23i3.51033

12. Wang, D., Liu, X., Deng, H.: The perspectives of social cognitive career theory approach in current times. Front. Psychol. **13**, 1023994 (2022). https://doi.org/10.3389/fpsyg.2022.1023994
13. Osborn, D.S., Sides, R.D., Brown, C.A.: Comparing career development outcomes among undergraduate students in cognitive information processing theory-based versus human relations courses. Career Dev. Q. **68**(1), 32–47 (2020). https://doi.org/10.1002/cdq.12211
14. Whiston, S.C., Li, Y., Goodrich Mitts, N., Wright, L.: Effectiveness of career choice interventions: a meta-analytic replication and extension. J. Voc. Behav. **100**, 175–184 (2017). https://doi.org/10.1016/j.jvb.2017.03.010
15. Lent, R.W., Brown, S.D.: Social cognitive approach to career development: an overview. Career Dev. Q. **44**(4), 310–321 (1996). https://doi.org/10.1002/j.2161-0045.1996.tb00448.x
16. Ajzen, I.: The theory of planned behavior. Organ. Behav. Hum. Decis. Process. **50**(2), 179–211 (1991). https://doi.org/10.1016/0749-5978(91)90020-T
17. Gollwitzer, P.M.: Implementation intentions: Strong effects of simple plans. Am. Psychol. **54**, 493–503 (1999). https://doi.org/10.1037/0003-066X.54.7.493
18. Multon, K.D., Heppner, M.J., Gysbers, N.C., Zook, C., Ellis-Kalton, C.A.: Client psychological distress: an important factor in career counseling. Career Dev. Q. **49**(4), 324–335 (2001). https://doi.org/10.1002/j.2161-0045.2001.tb00960.x
19. Reimers, N., Gurevych, I.: Sentence-BERT: Sentence Embeddings using Siamese BERT-Networks (2019)
20. McInnes, L., Healy, J., Melville, J.: UMAP: uniform manifold approximation and projection for dimension reduction, 9. Februar 2018. Verfügbar unter: http://arxiv.org/pdf/1802.03426
21. Hommel, B.E., Arslan, R.C.: Language models accurately infer correlations between psychological items and scales from text alone. Center Open Sci. (2024). https://doi.org/10.31234/osf.io/kjuce
22. Kelly, G., McCabe, H.: CityGEN: an interactive system for procedural city generation (2007). http://www.citygen.net/files/citygen_gdtw07.pdf

Advancing Student Writing Through Automated Syntax Feedback

Kamyar Zeinalipour, Mehak Mehak(✉), Fatemeh Parsamotamed, Marco Maggini, and Marco Gori

University of Siena, Siena, Italy
kamyar.zeinalipour2@unisi.it, m.mehak@student.unisi.it

Abstract. This study underscores the pivotal role of syntax feedback in augmenting the syntactic proficiency of students. Recognizing the challenges faced by learners in mastering syntactic nuances, we introduce a specialized dataset named `Essay-Syntax-Instruct` designed to enhance the understanding and application of English syntax among these students. Leveraging the capabilities of Large Language Models (LLMs) such as *GPT3.5-Turbo*, *Llama-2-7b-chat-hf*, *Llama-2-13b-chat-hf*, and *Mistral-7B-Instruct-v0.2*, this work embarks on a comprehensive fine-tuning process tailored to the syntax improvement task. Through meticulous evaluation, we demonstrate that the fine-tuned LLMs exhibit a marked improvement in addressing syntax-related challenges, thereby serving as a potent tool for students to identify and rectify their syntactic errors. The findings not only highlight the effectiveness of the proposed dataset in elevating the performance of LLMs for syntax enhancement but also illuminate a promising path for utilizing advanced language models to support language acquisition efforts. This research contributes to the broader field of language learning technology by showcasing the potential of LLMs in facilitating the linguistic development of Students.

1 Introduction

Mastering syntax, which is essentially the set of rules governing how sentences are structured in any given language, stands as a major obstacle in the process of learning English. This challenge is formidable not only for students who are non-native speakers but also for those who have grown up speaking the language. English syntax is notorious for its complexity, with a wide array of rules and numerous exceptions to those rules, making the path to achieving fluency and proficiency a daunting one. Traditional methods of teaching, while valuable in their own right, often do not fully address the unique needs of each learner, leaving gaps in understanding and application of syntactic rules. In the face of these challenges, the burgeoning field of artificial intelligence (AI) and natural language processing (NLP) presents new opportunities for language education. Specifically, the development of Large Language Models (LLMs) has introduced the potential for more personalized, adaptable, and effective learning tools. These models, capable of generating text that closely mimics human writing, represent

F. Bellas and O. Fontenla-Romero (Eds.): AIEER 2024, CCIS 2519, pp. 52–66, 2025.
https://doi.org/10.1007/978-3-031-93409-4_5

a significant breakthrough in approaches to language learning, especially in the intricate area of syntax.

In this study, we present a framework that capitalizes on the most recent Large Language Model (LLM) technology, with a particular focus on models such as *GPT3.5-Turbo*, *Llama-2-7b-chat-hf*, L*Llama-2-13b-chat-hf*, and *Mistral-7B-Instruct-v0.2*. Our objective is to significantly improve English learners' syntactic skills by tackling the challenges they encounter in mastering English syntax. Understanding and applying the complex rules of English syntax is a daunting task for learners, often impeding their progress. The traditional methods of teaching English syntax, despite their benefits, may not fully cater to the varied needs of learners, highlighting the demand for a more personalized and adaptable learning strategy.

Our research leverages these state-of-the-art LLMs to address the intricate challenges associated with learning English syntax. We have developed a specialized dataset aimed at improving both the understanding and application of syntactic rules. This endeavor also involves fine-tuning these LLMs to better serve educational tasks focusing on syntax, thereby making a significant leap in creating tailor-made language learning aids.

We also invite fellow researchers to delve into this unique dataset, thereby setting a new benchmark in language learning technology research. By applying our dataset, these LLMs undergo a meticulous fine-tuning process, specifically designed to bolster syntactic proficiency. This process markedly enhances the models' ability to offer personalized and effective learning experiences. Through our work, we demonstrate a substantial advancement in the use of LLMs for educational purposes, particularly in the domain of syntax learning, offering learners a more intuitive and adaptable means to master the complexities of English syntax.

By detailing the creation of our specialized dataset and the further development of tailor-made LLM-based models, the paper extends its contributions beyond a simple technical discourse. It sets a solid groundwork for additional research, offering a comprehensive framework for assessing the effectiveness of models before and after fine-tuning, using our unique dataset as a reference point. Our holistic approach demonstrates not only the tangible benefits of our intervention in improving the feedback capabilities of LLMs but also provides the academic and educational spheres with a valuable toolkit for addressing the persistent challenges of mastering syntax in language learning. Through these efforts, the study introduces new resources and fine-tuned LLMs to the field of linguistics and paves the way for future exploration into leveraging technology to break down linguistic barriers, showcasing the profound potential of AI and LLMs in transforming language education.

We made the `Essay-Syntax-Instruct` dataset[1] and all models[2] publicly available to contribute to the open-source community, supporting other researchers in using, developing, and extending this type of study. Additionally, it can potentially be used by schools and students to significantly improve English learners' syntactic skills by addressing the challenges they face in mastering English syntax.

The structure of this paper is outlined as follows: Sect. 2 reviews the relevant literature in the field. Our approach is detailed in Sect. 3, followed by a comprehensive analysis of the properties of the generated dataset in Sect. 3.1. The results of our experiments are discussed extensively in Sect. 4, we conclude our findings in Sect. 5.

2 Related Works

The integration of technology in educational assessment has led to significant advancements in Automated Essay Scoring (AES) and Essay Feedback Generation. AES systems utilize machine learning algorithms to evaluate and score written essays with efficiency and consistency, mirroring the grading process traditionally conducted by human educators. Complementing AES, Essay Feedback Generation focuses on the qualitative aspect of writing improvement. Together, these technologies represent pivotal tools in the digital education landscape, facilitating scalable assessment and personalized learning experiences. This section delves into the nuances of AES and Essay Feedback Generation, laying the groundwork for a detailed discussion of each area's contributions, challenges, and potential synergies with our proposed Automatic Syntax Feedback System.

2.1 Automated Essay Scoring

Automated Essay Scoring (AES) represents a vital interdisciplinary field that merges natural language processing (NLP) with educational technology, driving toward the automation of student essay evaluations. Traditional approaches in this domain have followed a dual-step methodology, initiating with the extraction of a broad range of features from texts - spanning statistical to linguistic indicators [2,3] - and followed by the deployment of regression or classification models for predicting essay scores [6–8]. The advent and subsequent rise of deep learning have facilitated the inclusion of more sophisticated techniques such as convolutional neural networks (CNNs), long short-term memory networks (LSTMs), and attention-based models, significantly enhancing the precision of scoring algorithms [9–11].

The AES field has seen further refinement with the integration of pre-trained language learning models (LLMs), leveraging their advanced capabilities to push

[1] https://huggingface.co/datasets/Kamyar-zeinalipour/Essay-Syntax-Instruct.

[2] https://huggingface.co/Kamyar-zeinalipour/Mistral7B-Syntax-Instruct. https://huggingface.co/Kamyar-zeinalipour/Llama2-13B-Syntax-Instruct. https://huggingface.co/Kamyar-zeinalipour/Llama2-7B-Syntax-Instruct.

the boundaries of essay scoring. This integration has been marked by the employment of models like BERT for nuanced essay evaluation strategies [12,13], and the innovation of enhancing BERT's performance through specialized fine-tuning approaches [15,16]. Despite these advancements, efforts to align the latest LLMs, such as GPT, with AES tasks have encountered mixed outcomes. These models, when tuned to specific scoring rubrics, have not consistently surpassed the benchmark set by traditional methodologies or human evaluators in providing accurate scoring [17,19,23].

Leveraging insights from AES developments, our work introduces the "Automatic Syntax Feedback System", a novel solution addressing key challenges within the AES field, such as the lack of expert-annotated, rubric-based datasets and the intricacies of essay scoring. This system emphasizes the syntactic improvement of student essays, offering prompt, constructive feedback, and thus, bridges a crucial gap in AES research. By harnessing deep learning and the precision of modern LLMs, our approach not only supports accurate scoring but also plays a vital role in enhancing students' writing proficiency, marking a significant advancement in AES applications.

2.2 Essay Feedback Generation

The exploration of Language Learning Models (LLMs) in education has recently pivoted towards their potential to revolutionize feedback generation, providing real-time and personalized insights for learners [20,21,29]. Despite the burgeoning interest, there remains a gap in thoroughly investigating how LLMs can be intricately applied to create detailed educational feedback mechanisms. [22] made strides in illustrating how LLMs, when equipped with specific and rich information - termed as "golden knowledge", exhibit significant improvements in areas such as task-oriented dialogue and open-domain question answering. This underscores the value of integrating precise, domain-specific knowledge, like rubric explanations and accurate essay evaluations, into LLMs to enhance their capability to generate more constructive and targeted feedback on student essays.

In this section, we integrate these findings to underscore our research on the "Automatic Syntax Feedback System". By emphasizing the syntactic elements of essays, our system notably leverages the advancements in feedback generation propelled by the enhanced capabilities of modern LLMs. Recognizing the crucial role of detailed, golden knowledge in empowering LLMs, our approach enriches these models with a comprehensive understanding of English syntax and writing pedagogies. This strategic incorporation aims to fine-tune the feedback provided, making it not only immediate but also pedagogically valuable, thereby advancing the realms of automated essay scoring and educational support systems.

3 Methodology

In this study, we developed an Automatic Syntax Feedback Generation system. As a foundational step, we compiled a dataset by utilizing the widely recognized ASAP[3] dataset, which is frequently employed in Automated Essay Scoring (AES) tasks. This foundational dataset comprises essays from students in Grades 7–10, across eight distinct prompts. While the original purpose of the ASAP dataset was for scoring essays, our objective diverged as we aimed to generate automatic syntax feedback from these essays. To adapt this dataset to our needs, we focused on employing essays written by students, alongside leveraging Large Language Models (LLMs) and prompt engineering techniques to produce syntax feedback. Subsequently, the generated feedback was subjected to evaluation by linguistic experts. Based on their insights, we refined our dataset for the final phase of fine-tuning LLMs, including models such as *Llama-2-7b-chat-hf*, *Mistral-7B-Instruct-v0.2*, and *Llama-2-13b-chat-hf*, to specialize in this task.

Figure 1 illustrates the overarching methodology pipeline of this study. Following this, we delve into a discussion centered on the dataset generation process and the specific models we employed to accomplish this task.

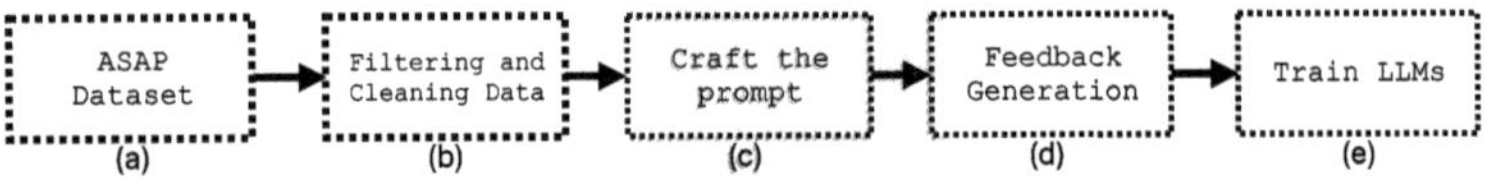

Fig. 1. This figure illustrates the pipeline employed in this study: (a) Acquiring essays authored by humans from the ASAP dataset. (b) Data refinement and filtering to enhance data quality, by the essay placeholder replacement, eliminating excessively short or overly detailed essays. (c) Design of the prompt for generating syntax feedback based on input essay. (d) Exploit of *GPT3.5-Turbo* to generate syntax feedback from the collected data and defined prompts. (e) Fine-tune Large Language Models (LLMs) to enhance their ability to provide syntax feedback.

3.1 `Essay-Syntax-Instruct` Dataset

As we discussed earlier we used the ASAP dataset in the study presented in this paper, a significant and unique data set originating from a competitive environment was employed to scrutinize the automated scoring engine's capability in evaluating written essays. The data set in question encompasses responses to eight distinct essay prompts, resulting in a collection of essays varied in both theme and response length, which runs from an average of 150 to 550 words per essay. These essays were produced by students across a range of academic grades, specifically from Grade 7 to Grade 10. To ensure the credibility and reliability of the scoring, each essay underwent a rigorous evaluation process, being graded by hand and subject to a double-scoring protocol. Reflecting the diverse nature of the essay prompts, the responses exhibit a wide range of characteristics, from dependence on source material to standalone narratives, thus providing a comprehensive test bed for the scoring engines under examination.

[3] https://www.kaggle.com/c/asap-aes.

Place Holder Replacement. In this study, we initially focused on utilizing a dataset intended for Automated Essay Scoring for our Automatic Syntax Feedback System. This involved leveraging essays written by students to generate feedback using Large Language Models (LLMs). A significant challenge we encountered was related to the essays in the ASAP dataset, specifically due to the comprehensive anonymization effort undertaken to protect student privacy. This process involved the use of Stanford's Natural Language Processing group's Named Entity Recognizer (NER) tool, among other techniques, to replace identifiable information (such as names, organizations, locations, dates, times, money, and percent values) with anonymized placeholders (e.g., "@PERSON1"). Although necessary for privacy, this introduced inefficiencies when the LLMs interpreted these placeholders as errors, impacting the quality of the feedback generated.

```
Your task entails identifying and substituting placeholders within the
text.

These placeholders are denoted by an '@' symbol followed by uppercase
letters indicating various categories such as months, percentages,
locations, numbers, person names, and more. It's crucial to ensure that the
replacements seamlessly integrate into the text.

Ensure that all placeholders are detected and replaced with the appropriate
replacements.

To streamline the process, kindly furnish your replacements in JSON format.
The JSON should comprise pairs where each placeholder is associated with
its corresponding replacement word.

Text: {essay}
```

Fig. 2. Place Holder Replacement Prompt.

To address this issue, we employed *GPT3.5-Turbo*, prompting the model to replace placeholders with contextually coherent alternatives that blend seamlessly with the rest of the essay content. This approach significantly improved the LLMs' ability to provide relevant and accurate feedback. We illustrate the prompt used for this task in Fig. 2, showcasing our strategy to overcome the anonymization challenge while maintaining the ethical use of `Essay-Syntax-Instruct` dataset.

Syntax Feedback Generation. After substituting placeholders with suitable replacements, our next objective was to generate syntax feedback for each essay. To achieve this, we utilized *GPT3.5-Turbo*, specifically *GPT3.5-Turbo-0125*, with a temperature setting of 0.3 with a tailored prompt designed to elicit syntax feedback relevant to each essay. This prompt sought to examine various syntax components including misspelled words, conjunctions and linking phrases, modifiers, prepositions, modal verbs, punctuation, and articles. These categories were chosen because they cover the majority of syntax errors found in student essays, allowing for comprehensive and effective feedback that targets the most common issues. Categories of syntax feedback given by real instructors also align with the GPT-generated feedback, except for the grammatical errors category. During our dataset preparation, we noticed that GPT-generated feedback effectively corrected all the errors within a single grammar category. This redundancy led us to omit that one grammar error category, as the other syntax categories were already specified to address those errors. Figure 3 illustrates the prompt utilized for this purpose.

```
Your task is to perform a syntax analysis on an essay, aiming to identify and amend errors across specific syntax categories. Your mission is to
meticulously inspect each category for mistakes, correct them, and elucidate your findings. Concentrate on the following syntax areas:

Syntax Categories to Check:

1. Misspelled Words: Detect and list each misspelling uniquely.
2. Conjunctions and Linking Phrases: Search and list misuse of adverbs or (and, or, but, then, and because) between sentences and paragraphs.
3. Modifiers: Search for improper uses of modifiers.
4. Prepositions: Check for and correct inaccuracies in the use of prepositions.
5. Modal Verbs: Assess modal verbs for their accurate application.
6. Punctuation: Identify and rectify punctuation errors.
7. Articles: Examine the application of "the," "a," and "an," correcting any misuse.

To successfully accomplish this analysis, follow these steps:

1. Begin by systematically searching for syntax errors in the highlighted categories.

2. Ensure that you have thoroughly identified all errors within the specified categories and accurately documented them in your final submission.

3. If no errors are found within a specific category, indicate its absence of errors by writing "N/A" for that category.

4. Document each error found in a structured manner as follows:
   - Syntax Category [Name of Syntax Category]:
     - Error: [found error], Correct version: [appropriate correction]
   Consider that Each error should be mentioned on a separate line for clarity and order.

5. Follow these steps closely to check every part of the syntax carefully. Remember to review and double-check thoroughly for mistakes so that you
don't miss any errors.

ESSAY: {essay}
```

Fig. 3. Syntax Feedback Generation Prompt.

Subsequently, we obtained a dataset comprising essays-devoid of placeholders-written by students, alongside the corresponding feedback generated by the model across the aforementioned syntax categories. To ensure conciseness and relevance, we refined the dataset by excluding essays that were excessively long or short, focusing on those ranging from 100 to 700 words. Following data filtering, we are left with a dataset comprising 8,320 examples of essay and syntax feedback. Additionally, Fig. 4 displays the distribution of tokens within the generated feedback and the essays. For this analysis, we utilized the *Llama-2* tokenizer.

Data Set Quality Evaluation. Due to the lack of a reference corpus specifically for Essay Syntax Feedback, establishing a baseline for comparison of generated Syntax Feedback is challenging. This absence makes it difficult to apply metrics like ROGUE scores to evaluate the effectiveness of educational feedback generation. Consequently, we opted for a qualitative evaluation approach via human assessment. Specifically, we randomly selected a sample of clues and had them evaluated by a panel of experts in linguistics. This method mirrors the approach taken by [24], utilizing a five-tier rating system guided by predetermined criteria:

- `RATING-A`: Feedback is exceptional, systematically identifying every error in the text and clearly mentioning these alongside their accurate corrections. It also enriches the review with substantial suggestions or revised sentences and exhibits a profound comprehension of the content's nuances. The structured approach of this feedback, which methodically points out errors and provides accurate corrections, enhances the overall quality of the review and demonstrates a thorough understanding of the text.

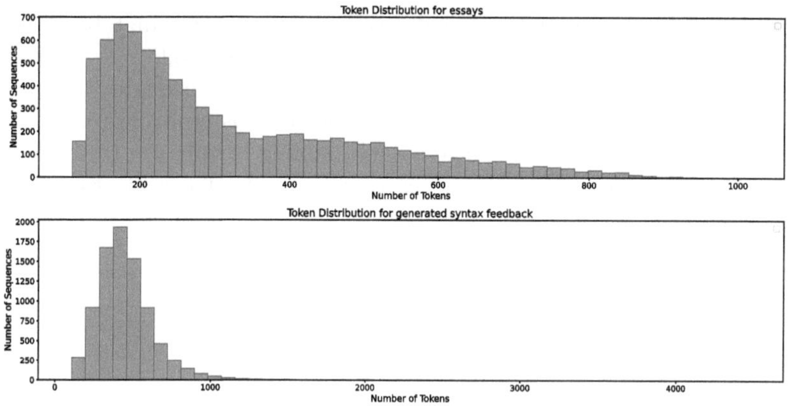

Fig. 4. Token Distribution of essays and generated syntax feedback

- RATING-B: Feedback is robust, pinpointing most errors and correctly articulating them with their respective corrections. It provides constructive criticism but might overlook minor issues. Nonetheless, it demonstrates a high level of engagement with the content's essence. The structured format of this feedback, showcasing a detailed analysis of errors and their corrections, adds value to the review and reflects a strong engagement with the essence of the text.
- RATING-C: Feedback adequately identifies and reports on a considerable amount of errors, offering appropriate corrections. While the suggestions are helpful, they could be more specifically tailored to enhance the text's overall quality and effectiveness. The structure of this feedback, though adequate in identifying errors and providing corrections, could benefit from a more tailored approach to offer specific enhancements for the text's improvement.
- RATING-D: Feedback catches some errors and presents corrections but does so inconsistently. The feedback contains basic suggestions, lacking the depth and detail necessary to facilitate significant improvement in the text. The lack of consistency in the structure of this feedback affects its overall effectiveness in guiding improvements and enhancing the text's quality.
- RATING-E: Feedback is deficient, with little to no identification of the main errors, offering few if any corrections. It fails to provide informative guidance and does not contribute meaningfully to the betterment of the text's accuracy or readability. The absence of a structured approach in this feedback results in a lack of clarity and guidance, hindering its ability to improve the text effectively.

During this human evaluation process, we analyzed 300 examples of essay feedback. The outcomes of this evaluation are depicted in Fig. 5. In the assessment conducted via human evaluation, the feedback generated by GPT-3.5 did not attain 100% accuracy. As depicted in Fig. 5, Rating A is recorded at 29%, while Rating B exhibits a remarkably higher percentage of 63.3%, signifying an exceptional level of quality deemed satisfactory in approximately 80–90% of instances, Rating B notably stands out as exceptionally good.

The results of the human evaluation indicate that the quality of the final `Essay-Syntax-Instruct` dataset is acceptable. In this study, we utilized this dataset to fine-tune several language models, aiming to enhance their ability to perform the task of automatically generating syntax feedback in essays.

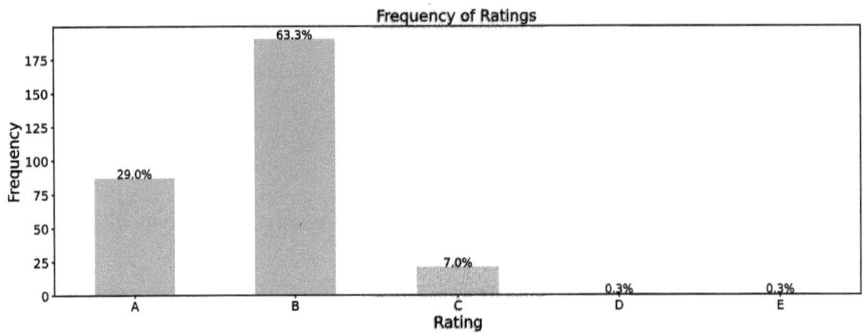

Fig. 5. Assessment results of human evaluations for the syntax feedback produced by `GPT3.5-Turbo`.

3.2 From LLMs to Automatic Syntax Feedback Generation

We developed a system aimed at streamlining the production of Syntax Feedback for essays crafted by students, thereby offering an indispensable resource to educators. This innovation stemmed from a comprehensive process of fine-tuning various Large Language Models (LLMs), including but not limited to the *Llama-2-7b-chat-hf*, *Llama-2-13b-chat-hf* [30], and the *Mistral-7B-Instruct-v0.2* [25]. This refinement process leveraged the rich dataset detailed in Sect. 3.1, ensuring the feedback generated is both relevant and constructive.

By furnishing educators with this system, they are empowered to produce nuanced feedback, which is pivotal in helping students enhance their writing capabilities. Our initiative extends beyond merely developing a tool; it encompasses a thorough examination and assessment of various models. This diligence ensures that the system's underlying language models are optimally selected and tailored to produce feedback that is not only accurate but also pedagogically valuable. Our work places special emphasis on the meticulous evaluation of the chosen LLMs, aiming to refine and perfect the quality of feedback generated.

4 Experiments

We explore how the `Essay-Syntax-Instruct` dataset can be utilized to optimize various families of Large Language Models (LLMs) across multiple dimensions.

4.1 Experimental Setup

Data. We utilized Large Language Models (LLMs) that underwent instruction tuning with `Essay-Syntax-Instruct` dataset. For evaluation purposes, we designated the 300 annotated instances as a testing set and assessed all our models using GPT-3.5 Turbo as a reference point. The training was conducted with the other 8,020 examples.

Baselines. Our examination considers three Large Language Models (LLMs) specifically calibrated for instruction handling: *LLlama-2-chat-hf*, as documented by **(author?)** [30], available in both 7B and 13B configurations; and *Mistral-7B-Instruct-v0.2* introduced by [25], which is offered in the 7B Parameters.

Training Details. Fine-tuning of all models was performed using LORA [28], with specifications of $r = 32$ and $\alpha = 64$ across three training epochs, and a total batch size maintained at 16. The initial learning rate was set to $3 \cdot 10^{-4}$, accompanied by a cosine warm-up with a ratio of 0.1. During inference, model distribution sampling facilitated clue generation, setting the temperature at 0.3. Moreover, the top-p and top-k parameters were adjusted to 0.95 and 50, respectively, following the methodology described by Holtzman et al. (2019). This entire experimental setup was executed on a server outfitted with dual NVIDIA A6000 GPUs, leveraging the capabilities of DeepSpeed [26] and FlashAttention 2 [27].

4.2 Results

To evaluate the results, we implemented an evaluation process that entailed generating data using both the base and fine-tuned models on a test dataset comprised of 300 essays, which were not utilized during the training phase. Subsequently, we conducted two distinct types of evaluations. Firstly, we assessed the generated essays utilizing automatic evaluation metrics, specifically Rouge scores. Secondly, we employed human evaluation to assess the generated feedback in Fig. 6, you can see an example of an essay along with the feedback generated by a fine-tuned model using the proposed dataset. Fine-tuning enhances the model's ability to provide precise and contextually appropriate feedback. We will provide detailed information about this result in the following sections.

Automatic Evaluation. We attempted to calculate the ROUGE scores between the generated feedback from GPT-3.5-Turbo and other models, which we utilized for fine-tuning in two distinct scenarios: the base model before fine-tuning and the fine-tuned model afterward, using the Essay-Syntax-Instruct dataset. The results of these experiments, presented in Table 1, illustrate that after fine-tuning, there was an increase in the ROUGE scores across all models included in this study. Considering that the ROUGE score primarily measures word overlap between the reference and target texts, it may not be highly reliable. This is because the feedback, although potentially insightful, could differ from the

(a) Example of an essay

(b) Example of a feedback generated by a fine-tuned model using the proposed dataset.

Fig. 6. Example of an essay (a) with feedback generated (b) by a fine-tuned model using the proposed dataset.

assessments provided by *GPT3.5-Turbo* While ROUGE can offer some useful ideas, its trustworthiness is limited. To address this issue, we applied human evaluation to achieve a more comprehensive understanding of the efficiency of fine-tuning the models using the fine-tuned versions.

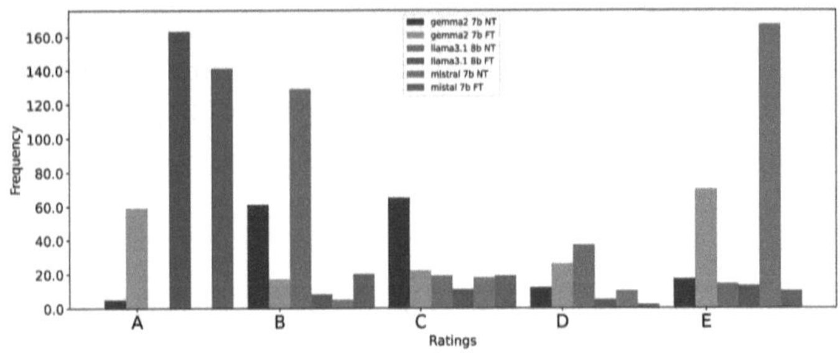

Fig. 7. Human evaluation of syntax feedback generated by the LLMs.

Human Evaluation. For the qualitative evaluation of generated syntax feedback, we employed two human raters who are master's students from the Department of Linguistics. Their advanced academic background and expertise in linguistics ensure that the feedback evaluation is conducted with a high degree of proficiency and reliability. This human assessment complements our quantitative metrics, providing a holistic evaluation of the feedback quality. Our human annotators reviewed the outputs from the fine-tuned language models (LLMs). We focused this comparison on a subset of 300 essays from the test dataset, employing the same guidelines introduced earlier for validating the generated dataset, as discussed in a previous section. The findings of this evaluation are detailed in Fig. 7 and Table 2.

Our analysis revealed that fine-tuning significantly enhances the performance of large language models in generating syntax feedback for essays. The fine-tuned models demonstrate substantial improvements in achieving higher ratings

Table 1. Performance of base LLMs and fine-tuned LLMs using the `Essay-Syntax-Instruct`

model type	model name	# params	ROUGE-1	ROUGE-2	ROUGE-L
Base LLMs	LLAMA2-CHAT	7B	0.351	0.146	0.185
	MISTRAL-INSTRUCT	7B	**0.366**	0.144	0.205
	LLAMA2-CHAT	13B	0.328	**0.148**	**0.214**
Finetuned LLMs	LLAMA2-CHAT	7B	0.477	0.337	0.343
	MISTRAL-INSTRUCT	7B	**0.514**	**0.375**	**0.369**
	LLAMA2-CHAT	13B	0.476	0.340	0.347

Table 2. Assessing the percentage of human evaluation for syntax feedback generated by the LLMs for each rating.

	Llama2 NF	Llama2 F	Llama2 NF	Llama2 F	Mistral NF	Mistral F
# params	7B	7B	13B	13B	7B	7B
Ratings %						
A	1.00	2.67	2.00	4.33	4.00	4.67
B	24.67	44.67	11.00	**60.00**	10.33	**65.67**
C	34.33	**48.00**	**56.00**	24.67	22.67	22.33
D	**39.67**	1.67	24.67	5.67	**43.33**	4.00
E	0.33	3.00	6.33	5.33	19.67	3.33

(A and B), coupled with a notable reduction in poorer ratings (D). This trend is consistent across different model configurations and sizes, affirming that fine-tuning effectively optimizes models for specific tasks, resulting in more accurate and useful feedback in educational contexts. We observed that language models initially produced several errors in syntax feedback, including repeated mistakes across different categories and incorrect highlighting of correct words. However, fine-tuning significantly mitigates these errors, leading to more accurate and constructive feedback.

Llama2 (7 Billion Parameters). Fine-tuning significantly enhanced the capability of the model, resulting in a nearly tripled score for the best feedback (Rating A) from 1.00% to 2.67%. There was also a marked increase in good quality feedback (Rating B) from 24.67% to 44.67% and above-average feedback (Rating C) from 34.33% to 48.00%. Concurrently, there was a dramatic reduction in poorer quality feedback (Rating D) from 39.67% to 1.67%, demonstrating a substantial improvement in feedback quality. The lowest feedback category (Rating E) had only a minimal increase from 0.33% to 3.00%.

Llama2 (13 Billion Parameters). This version showed profound improvements in delivering the best feedback (Rating A), improving from 2.00% to 4.33%, and good feedback (Rating B) from 11.00% to 60.00%. There was a substantial shift towards higher feedback quality with a significant reduction in average feedback (Rating C) from 56.00% to 24.67% and poor feedback (Rating D) from 24.67% to 5.67%. The worst feedback category (Rating E) slightly declined from 6.33% to 5.33%, indicating improved consistency in feedback quality.

Mistral (7 Billion Parameters). Post-fine-tuning, this model slightly improved top-quality feedback (Rating A) from 4.00% These outcomes indicate that fine-tuning improves the alignment of generated content with the anticipated format. Moreover, it also positively influences the overall quality of the generated content, suggesting that fine-tuning not only corrects formatting issues but also enhances the essence of the content.

5 Conclusion

In this research, we have developed an innovative tool, the Automatic Essay Syntax Feedback Generator, which leverages the capabilities of Large Language Models (LLMs) to provide syntax feedback for educational purposes. This cutting-edge system is designed to boost student interaction and enhance the retention of learning material through dynamic engagement.

Furthermore, our study contributes significantly to the expansion of essay syntax feedback resources by introducing `Essay-Syntax-Instruct` dataset. We have compiled a thorough dataset comprising essays written by students alongside the syntax feedback provided. This dataset is indispensable for the development of educational systems and analytical instruments, paving the way for new research and innovation opportunities.

Looking forward, we are dedicated to broadening the scope of our method to encompass more languages, thereby increasing the accessibility of this educational tool. We also aim to refine our syntax feedback methodologies by incorporating more sophisticated LLMs, thereby pushing the boundaries of what's possible in educational technology. In future work, we will conduct real-world case studies to assess the practical impact of automated syntax feedback on student learning outcomes. This will help us determine our findings' applicability to various educational settings. Further research will focus on comparing our system with traditional teaching methods to evaluate its effectiveness. Additionally, We aim to streamline the fine-tuning process of LLMs, making it more efficient and accessible for educational institutions with limited computational resources and expertise.

References

1. Ramesh, D., Sanampudi, S.: An automated essay scoring systems: a systematic literature review. Artif. Intell. Rev. **55**, 2495–2527 (2022)
2. Miltsakaki, E., Kukich, K.: Evaluation of text coherence for electronic essay scoring systems. Nat. Lang. Eng. **10**, 25–55 (2004)

3. Ridley, R., He, L., Dai, X., Huang, S., Chen, J.: Prompt agnostic essay scorer: a domain generalization approach to cross-prompt automated essay scoring. arXiv Preprint arXiv:2008.01441 (2020)
4. Mikolov, T., Chen, K., Corrado, G., Dean, J.: Efficient estimation of word representations in vector space. arXiv Preprint arXiv:1301.3781 (2013)
5. Pennington, J., Socher, R., Manning, C.: Glove: global vectors for word representation. In: Proceedings of the 2014 Conference on Empirical Methods in Natural Language Processing (EMNLP), pp. 1532–1543 (2014)
6. Sultan, M., Salazar, C., Sumner, T.: Fast and easy short answer grading with high accuracy. In: Proceedings of the 2016 Conference of the North American Chapter of the Association for Computational Linguistics: Human Language Technologies, pp. 1070–1075 (2016)
7. Mathias, S., Bhattacharyya, P.: Thank "goodness"! a way to measure style in student essays. In: Proceedings of the 5th Workshop on Natural Language Processing Techniques for Educational Applications, pp. 35–41 (2018)
8. Salim, Y., Stevanus, V., Barlian, E., Sari, A., Suhartono, D.: Automated English digital essay grader using machine learning. In: 2019 IEEE International Conference on Engineering, Technology and Education (TALE), pp. 1–6 (2019)
9. Dong, F., Zhang, Y.: Automatic features for essay scoring-an empirical study. In: Proceedings of the 2016 Conference on Empirical Methods in Natural Language Processing, pp. 1072–1077 (2016)
10. Taghipour, K., Ng, H.: A neural approach to automated essay scoring. In: Proceedings of the 2016 Conference on Empirical Methods in Natural Language Processing, pp. 1882–1891 (2016)
11. Riordan, B., Horbach, A., Cahill, A., Zesch, T., Lee, C.: Investigating neural architectures for short answer scoring. In: Proceedings of the 12th Workshop on Innovative Use of NLP for Building Educational Applications, pp. 159–168 (2017)
12. Rodriguez, P., Jafari, A., Ormerod, C.: Language models and automated essay scoring. arXiv Preprint arXiv:1909.09482 (2019)
13. Lun, J., Zhu, J., Tang, Y., Yang, M.: Multiple data augmentation strategies for improving performance on automatic short answer scoring. In: Proceedings of the AAAI Conference on Artificial Intelligence, vol. 34, pp. 13389–13396 (2020)
14. Devlin, J., Chang, M., Lee, K., Toutanova, K.: BERT: pre-training of deep bidirectional transformers for language understanding. arXiv Preprint arXiv:1810.04805 (2018)
15. Yang, R., Cao, J., Wen, Z., Wu, Y., He, X.: Enhancing automated essay scoring performance via fine-tuning pre-trained language models with combination of regression and ranking. In: Findings of the Association for Computational Linguistics: EMNLP 2020, pp. 1560–1569 (2020)
16. Wang, Y., Wang, C., Li, R., Lin, H.: On the use of BERT for automated essay scoring: joint learning of multi-scale essay representation. arXiv Preprint arXiv:2205.03835 (2022)
17. Mizumoto, A., Eguchi, M.: Exploring the potential of using an AI language model for automated essay scoring. Res. Methods Appl. Linguist. **2**, 100050 (2023)
18. Naismith, B., Mulcaire, P., Burstein, J.: Automated evaluation of written discourse coherence using GPT-4. In: Proceedings of the 18th Workshop on Innovative Use of NLP for Building Educational Applications (BEA 2023), pp. 394–403 (2023)
19. Yancey, K., Laflair, G., Verardi, A., Burstein, J.: Rating short L2 essays on the CEFR scale with GPT-4. In: Proceedings of the 18th Workshop on Innovative Use of NLP for Building Educational Applications (BEA 2023), pp. 576–584 (2023)

20. Yan, L., et al.: Practical and ethical challenges of large language models in education: a systematic scoping review. Br. J. Edu. Technol. **55**, 90–112 (2024)
21. Kasneci, E., et al.: ChatGPT for good? On opportunities and challenges of large language models for education. Learn. Individ. Differ. **103**, 102274 (2023)
22. Peng, B., et al.: Check your facts and try again: improving large language models with external knowledge and automated feedback. arXiv Preprint arXiv:2302.12813 (2023)
23. Han, J., et al.: Fabric: automated scoring and feedback generation for essays. arXiv Preprint arXiv:2310.05191 (2023)
24. Wang, Y., et al.: Self-instruct: aligning language models with self-generated instructions. arXiv Preprint arXiv:2212.10560 (2022)
25. Jiang, A., et al.: Mistral 7B. arXiv Preprint arXiv:2310.06825 (2023)
26. Rasley, J., Rajbhandari, S., Ruwase, O., He, Y.: Deepspeed: system optimizations enable training deep learning models with over 100 billion parameters. In: Proceedings of the 26th ACM SIGKDD International Conference on Knowledge Discovery & Data Mining, pp. 3505–3506 (2020)
27. Dao, T.: Flashattention-2: faster attention with better parallelism and work partitioning. arXiv Preprint arXiv:2307.08691 (2023)
28. Hu, E., et al.: Lora: low-rank adaptation of large language models. arXiv Preprint arXiv:2106.09685 (2021)
29. Xiao, C., Ma, W., Xu, S., Zhang, K., Wang, Y., Fu, Q.: From automation to augmentation: large language models elevating essay scoring landscape. arXiv Preprint arXiv:2401.06431 (2024)
30. Touvron, H., et al.: Llama 2: open foundation and fine-tuned chat models. arXiv Preprint arXiv:2307.09288 (2023)

Phrase-Level Adversarial Data Generation for Bias Mitigation in Automatic Essay Scoring

Haddad Philip[1] and Tsegaye Misikir Tashu[2(✉)]

[1] Department of Data Science and Engineering, Eötvös Loránd University, Budapest, Hungary
[2] Artificial Intelligence Department, Bernoulli Institute, University of Groningen, Nijenborgh 4, 9747 AG Groningen, The Netherlands
t.m.tashu@rug.nl

Abstract. Automatic Essay Scoring (AES) is widely used to evaluate candidates for educational purposes. However, due to the lack of representative data, most existing AES systems are not robust, and their scoring predictions are biased towards the most represented data samples. In this study, we propose a model agnostic phrase-level method to generate an adversarial essay set to address the biases and robustness of AES models. Specifically, we construct an attack test set comprising samples from the original test set and adversarially generated samples using our proposed method. To evaluate the effectiveness of the attack strategy and data augmentation, we conducted a comprehensive analysis utilizing various neural network scoring models. Experimental results show that the proposed approach significantly improves AES model performance in the presence of adversarial examples and scenarios without such attacks.

Keywords: Automatic Essay Scoring · Adversarial Data Generation · Bias Mitigation

1 Introduction

Automatic essay scoring systems (AES) are used to reduce the workload of examiners, improve the feedback cycle in the teaching-learning process, and save time and costs in grading [1,17]. Training usable AES models depends on the availability of balanced and representative data across different class labels (essay scores). Due to the unavailability of such representative data, most existing AES systems are not robust, and the scoring predictions are biased towards the most represented data samples. Therefore, increasing AES models' usability requires more robustly trained models with respect to out-of-domain data and under-represented data samples [5,15,16]. Studies have shown that AES can be easily tricked by adding perturbations to the input, leading to incorrect predictions with high confidence [14]. These failures could hinder the safe deployment of these models in the real world and impact the trustworthiness of AES models.

F. Bellas and O. Fontenla-Romero (Eds.): AIEER 2024, CCIS 2519, pp. 67–78, 2025.
https://doi.org/10.1007/978-3-031-93409-4_6

Such perturbations can be added easily at different levels, with the most widely used being word-level perturbation. Several approaches have been proposed to address such challenges, improving resilience against these perturbations and reducing bias. Among these, data augmentation methods, which extend the training set to include adversarial examples, are widely used in the training process (fine-tuning) to improve the model's robustness. The problem of perturbations and the use of data augmentation have not been well addressed in the field of AES, especially at the phrase level. As the usage of AES systems is expanding from scoring essays for educational purposes to evaluating candidates [13] during interviews, minimizing biases and increasing the robustness of such models is relevant and creates trustworthiness towards the end users of the model. Therefore, in this study, we propose the use of a model-agnostic phrase-level method to generate an adversarial essay set to address the issue of biases and robustness of AES models. This study aims to train AES models on adversarially generated and augmented essays to build models that can score non-relevant generated essays properly.

2 Related Work

Automated Essay Scoring (AES) systems have become an important system in assessing student essays. With the adoption of advanced machine learning models including transformer-based architectures AES systems have become more effective. However, studies showed that neural network-based models are vulnerable to adversarial perturbations [12,13]. These adversarial examples or attacks are created by minor changes in the input data which mislead the algorithms into making wrong decisions [2]. Some research has been done to address these vulnerabilities. Gupta [3] explore the use of transformer models like BERT and RoBERTa for automated essay scoring (AES). It shows how data augmentation can help these models, especially with a wide range of essay topics. Their work showed that one model can be trained to grade essays across multiple subjects which is super helpful when there is limited data for certain topics and improves the model's accuracy and generalizability. The work by Park et al. introduces EssayGAN [11], an approach that uses generative adversarial networks (GANs) to generate synthetic essays. These essays are then scored and added to the existing datasets for AES systems. The results show that adding EssayGAN-generated essays to the training data improves the scoring of AES systems. Another work by [4] used data augmentation techniques like back-translation and score adjustment to improve AES models. The authors create a way to artificially add more essay-score pairs to the dataset and apply it to the Automated Student Assessment Prize dataset. The paper shows that data augmentation significantly improves the model's performance by training various AES models on this augmented data. This includes better handling of language variations and robustness to overfitting. The work by Tashu and Tomas [16] introduced a novel approach to enhancing the robustness of AES models against synonym-based adversarial attacks. Their focus is on synonym-based attacks, a specific type of adversarial attack that can be particularly challenging for AES models. This method involves generating new essays that are lexically similar to the original ones using keyword-based lexical substitution with BERT, and then using these adversarial samples to train the AES models.

Most of the existing works use semantic similarity to validate the perturbed examples. However, this method is unreliable in maintaining textual integrity as noted by Morris [10]. Lei et al. [6] have introduced methods to address the limitations of current approaches in preserving context-dependent content using label-preserving filters validated through human evaluation to enhance the fidelity of adversarially perturbed samples. This paper proposes a new model agnostic approach to generate phrase-level adversarial essays that extend and hybridise previous works [6,16]. By refining the training of AES models our approach aims to make the models robust to complex perturbations and to produce reliable scores across diverse and adversarially augmented datasets so that AES can be trusted and effective in educational and professional settings.

3 MA-PLAG: Model Agnostic Phrase-Level Adversarial Generation

One of the most widely used strategies to minimize bias and to train a robust model when there is small and unbalanced data is to generate adversarial samples and augment the training data. In this study, a phrase-level adversarial data generation strategy is used. The overview of the proposed adversarial essay generation architecture is presented in Fig. 1. The process is divided into several stages to generate label-preserved samples which have richer vocabulary required to train a more robust model. Given an essay E and to generate an adversarial essay E' from it, the proposed model agnostic phrase-level adversarial generation approached works as follows:

1. The sentence extractor using the text summarizer in step 3.1 will extract N important sentences.
2. The Phrase extracts in step 3.2 selects and extracts the relevant phrases from the sentences.
3. The blank-infilling model in step 3.3 will generate M perturbed phrases for each single sentence s, resulting in a set S' of perturbed sentences.
4. Label-preserving filter in step 3.4 will be applied on the set S', and only the relevant s' will be kept.
5. The final step is to replace each sentence s in E with the sentence s', resulting in the adversarial essay E'.

3.1 Sentence Extraction

Rather than randomly selecting sentences from a given essay, extracting the most important and content-bearing sentence from the given essay is beneficial. We used the extractive text summarization method to extract the most relevant sentence from the given essay. As the objective is to perturb the essay, it would be beneficial to reduce the text volume by condensing the information. We adopt the work by [9] which uses BERT and K-Means for extractive text summarization.

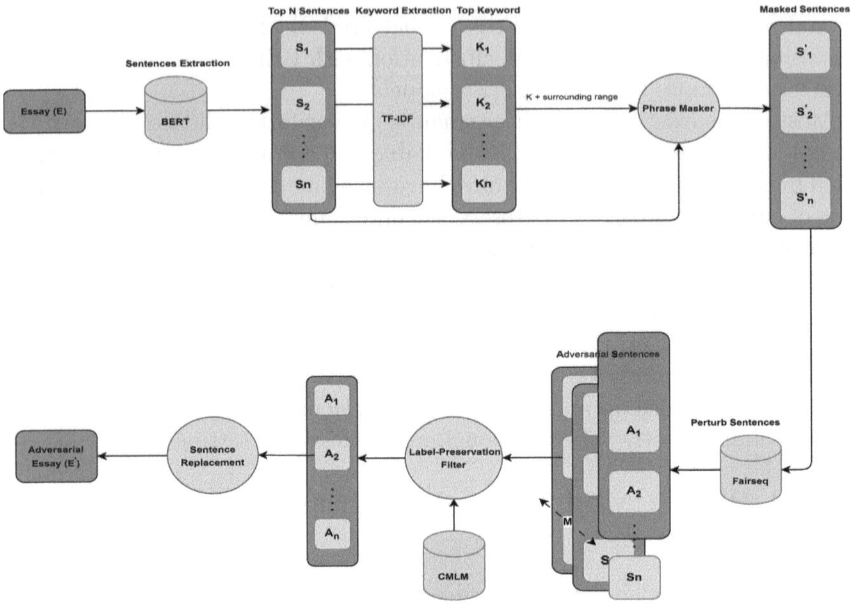

Fig. 1. The architecture of the proposed Model Agnostic Phrase-Level Adversarial Generation (MA-PLAG)

3.2 Phrase Extraction

For each sentence selected by the summarization algorithm, we extract the most significant keyword using the term frequency/inverse document frequency (TF-IDF) approach. These extracted keywords serve as the central element around which the phrase will be constructed. Considering the sentence length, typically ranging from 20 to 25 words, we adopt a phrase definition strategy that incorporates the TF-IDF keyword and the surrounding words within a specific range of length denoted by the parameter N. The determination of N is treated as a hyperparameter and can be adjusted according to specific requirements. Our phrase extraction approach gives MA-PLAG the flexibility to address a wide range of problem domains. Let s be a sentence in the essay E, and w be a word in s. The Keyword Extraction can be defined as follows:

$$w^* = \arg\max_{w \in s} \text{TF-IDF}(w, s, E) \tag{1}$$

where w^* is the most significant keyword in sentence s based on TF-IDF values. The Phrase Construction can be defined as follows:

$$P(w^*, s, N) = s[i^* - N : i^* + N + 1] \tag{2}$$

where i^* is the index of w^* in s, and N is the hyperparameter defining the number of words before and after w^* to include in the phrase P. The values of N and i^* are adjusted to ensure they fall within the valid indices of s.

3.3 Sentence Perturbation

To perturbate each sentence, a method called blank-infilling on each target phrase was adopted [6]. Firstly, we mask the phrase with a suitable token depending on the blank-infilling procedure, as shown in Fig. 2.

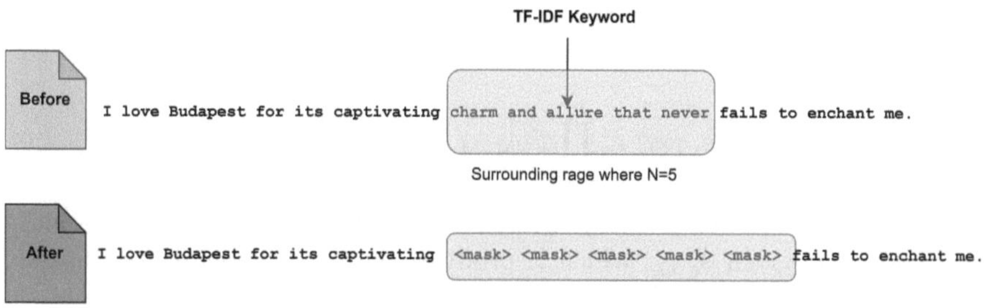

Fig. 2. Sentence; before and after masking the phrase

Subsequently, a pre-trained language model designed for blank-infilling tasks can be employed. Considering the surrounding context, this model takes the masked sentence as input and generates a phrase of M tokens to fill the masks. In our case, we used Fairseq[1] as an implementation of the blank infilling model BART [7]. The blank-infilling model will generate perturbed sentences by replacing the masked phrase with "different" new phrases, and the maximum length of the new phrases is not greater than the length of the original phrase plus a threshold. Let S be a sentence from a document, and S' be the version of S where a phrase P is masked. Let B represent a blank-infilling model. The sentence perturbation process can be defined as follows:

$$S'' = \begin{cases} \text{replace}(S', \text{mask}, B(S')) & \text{if } |B(S')| \leq |P| + \theta \\ S' & \text{otherwise} \end{cases} \tag{3}$$

where S'' is the final output sentence, $|P|$ is the length of the original masked phrase, $|Q|$ is the length of the generated phrase, and θ is a threshold for the maximum permissible length of Q relative to P.

3.4 Label-Preserving Filter

To ensure that the true label is preserved, we adopted the same strategy called class-conditioned masked language models (CMLMs) [6] to choose the most suitable perturbed sentence. In our case, we fine-tuned the RoBERTa Model [8], which is an extension of BERT. Since the AES task is being handled as a classification task, the true label, or the class-related characteristic, must be retained. To do this, a filter is applied directly to the perturbation

1 https://github.com/facebookresearch/fairseq.

using the likelihood supplied by the class-conditioned masked language models (CMLMs). Let's consider a sentence s of length n, a phrase p, and q as the perturbed phrase of length m filled by the model. The perturbed sentence will be $\tilde{s}_q(i,j) = s_1, \ldots, s_{i-1}, q_1, \ldots, q_m, s_{j+1}, \ldots, s_n$, where (i,j) represent the starting and ending indices of phrase p within the original sentence s, and $\tilde{s}_q(i,j)$ represents the version of sentence s where the phrase at indices (i,j) has been replaced with the perturbed phrase q. The equation for the class-conditioned likelihood of the adversarially perturbed phrase q in the sentence s can be calculated as:

$$L(s,q,y) = \prod_{k=1}^{m} P_{\text{CMLM}}\left(q_k \mid \tilde{s}_{q\backslash q_k}; \Theta_y\right). \tag{4}$$

where $\tilde{s}_{q\backslash q_k}$ is the sentence $\tilde{s}_q(i,j)$ with the token q_k masked, and P_{CMLM} is the likelihood of q_k given $\tilde{s}_{q\backslash q_k}$, which is produced by a class-conditioned masked language model Θ_y conditioned on class y. To avoid label changing from the true label, the phrase perturbations should get a higher likelihood on the true class's distribution and a lower likelihood on the others. This can be calculated as follows, where $\mathcal{Y}$ denotes the set of classes:

$$R(s,q,y) = L(s,q,y) / \max_{\tilde{y} \in \mathcal{Y}, \tilde{y} \neq y} L(s,q,\tilde{y}) \tag{5}$$

For better label preservation, the chosen phrase perturbations are required to have a likelihood ratio larger than a certain threshold δ.

4 Scoring Models

To thoroughly evaluate the efficiency of our proposed adversary generation methodology, both as an attack strategy and a data augmentation technique, we conducted a comprehensive analysis utilizing a variety of neural network scoring models. The models have an Embedding Layer, CNN layer, RNN layer and Dense layer. We used Glove and BERT, two popular pre-trained language models in the embedding layer to transform the input essay into dense numerical representations, capturing semantic and contextual information. CNN was used to extract local features from the embedded representations using convolutional filters. It efficiently captured patterns and relevant information within the text. Bidirectional Long Short-Term Memory (Bi-LSTM) and Bidirectional Gated Recurrent Unit (Bi-GRU) were also used to capture sequential dependencies and contextual information over longer text sequences. The bi-directional approach allowed the models to effectively incorporate information from both past and future contexts, enhancing their understanding of overall text semantics. To maintain consistency across all models, we used a uniform Dense layer architecture. This layer served as the final stage for score prediction, transforming the extracted features into a single scalar value. We utilized the mean squared error (MSE) as the loss function to measure the disparity between the predicted and target scores. MSE was chosen for its property of penalizing larger errors more severely, thereby emphasizing accurate score prediction. We used the RMSProp optimization algorithm, which adaptively adjusts the learning rate based on the gradient history. This approach facilitated efficient convergence and improved the overall training performance of the models. We constructed four distinct neural network models by employing these well-defined architectures and methodologies. Each model offered a unique combination of embedding techniques, convolutional and recurrent layers, and a shared dense layer, enabling a robust evaluation of our adversary generation methodology.

5 Experiments

5.1 Datasets and Evaluation Strategy

The experiments were performed on the dataset provided within the Automated Essay Scoring competition on the Kaggle[2] website. The datasets contain student essays for eight different prompts (essay discussion questions). Four datasets included essays of traditional writing genres such as persuasive, expository, or narrative. The other four datasets were source-based, i.e., the students had to discuss questions referring to a previously read source document. At least two human expert graders score each training set. The authors of the datasets already divided them into fixed training and test sets.

The dataset was split into three sets training, validation, and testing where 60% was used for training, 20% for evaluation, and 20% for testing. Subsequently, the models discussed in Sect. 4 were trained on the training set and individually fine-tuned by adjusting the layers, learning rate and the number of epochs. The best model with the highest Quadratic Weighted Kappa (QWK) value on the validation set was selected and finally evaluated using the test set. The variation in performance of the model across different prompts can be observed from the results presented.

5.2 Applying Attack Strategy

To assess the effectiveness of the proposed phrase-level attack strategy and augmentation, we formulated an attack test set comprising a combination of samples extracted from the original test set and those generated adversarially using our method. The primary objective of this test set was to evaluate the degree to which these samples were able to deceive the pre-trained models. To enhance the robustness of our experimental evaluation, we incorporated two key aspects in the construction of this attack set: Firstly, at the generation level, we applied varying ratios to mask individual sentences before inputting them into the blank-infilling model. For instance, given a sentence S with a length of 20 words and a generation ratio of 30%, this would mask six words from sentence S before supplying it to the blank-infilling model. The resulting sentence would contain 70% of the original, and the rest would be generated words. Secondly, we explored

[2] https://www.kaggle.com/c/asap-aes.

different attack sample sizes at the combination level while building the attack set. Suppose we have a data set with 100 samples, and the attack size ratio is set at 50%. In this scenario, we will generate 50 attack/adversarial samples to yield 150 samples within the attack set. In this phase, we considered the class imbalance issue so that more samples would be generated for underrepresented classes.

5.3 Data Augmentation

Given the objective of constructing robust models capable of withstanding sample perturbations and bias, we propose the adoption of phrase-level data augmentation as a strategy to address the problem. Specifically, we augment the adversarial examples generated with the original dataset in a manner consistent with the methodology employed during the creation of the attack set. Subsequently, we subject our AES models to retraining and evaluate their performance using the designated test set.

6 Experiment Results and Discussion

In this experiment, we mainly focused on the following masking and generation ratios: 30% and 40%, and with the adversarial attack generation and augmentation size of 50% and 75%. "No Attack" refers to the models being trained and tested on the original data, "With Augmentation" refers to the models being trained and tested on the augmented data, and "With Attack" means that the models were trained on the original data and tested on the adversarial attack data.

Table 1. Results for BERT model with a generation ratio of 30% and attack size of 50%.

Prompt	No Attack	With Attack	With Augmentation
2	0.611	0.346	0.610
3	0.757	0.707	0.827
4	0.695	0.683	0.808
5	0.837	0.783	0.907

The experimental results showed a notable decrease in model performance when adversarial attacks were used as a test set to evaluate models trained on the original trained data, indicating the vulnerability of the models to such attacks. All the models trained with original data and evaluated using the adversarial test set (referred to as the attack set) in all experiments showed a significant decrease in performance. This serves as evidence that our attacks can easily deceive these models. The adversaries' attacks had a considerable impact on the classification accuracy of the models. Specifically, for the Bi-LSTM-based model, the accuracy deteriorated by 0.105, 0.149, 0.101, and 0.112 for test sets 2, 3, 4, and 5, respectively. Similarly, the Bi-GRU-based model experienced accuracy deterioration of 0.109, 0.123, 0.152, and 0.104 for the corresponding test sets. The accuracy of the BERT model exhibited decreases of 0.267, 0.055, 0.011, and 0.073 for essay sets 2, 3, 4, and 5, respectively.

Table 2. Results with a generation ratio of 30% and attack size of 50%

Prompt	No Attack		With Attack		With Augmentation	
	Bi-LSTM	Bi-GRU	Bi-LSTM	Bi-GRU	Bi-LSTM	Bi-GRU
2	0.688	0.732	0.590	0.587	0.764	0.801
3	0.689	0.711	0.607	0.572	0.769	0.760
4	0.744	0.689	0.614	0.605	0.798	0.790
5	0.830	0.828	0.701	0.708	0.849	0.817

Table 3. Results with a generation ratio of 30% and attack size of 75%

Prompt	No Attack		With Attack		With Augmentation	
	Bi-LSTM	Bi-GRU	Bi-LSTM	Bi-GRU	Bi-LSTM	Bi-GRU
2	0.688	0.732	0.542	0.550	0.756	0.811
3	0.689	0.711	0.580	0.611	0.793	0.807
4	0.744	0.689	0.605	0.568	0.738	0.762
5	0.830	0.828	0.711	0.717	0.843	0.874

Table 4. Results for BERT with a generation ratio of 30% and attack size of 75%

Prompt	No Attack	With Attack	With Augmentation
2	0.611	0.354	0.609
3	0.757	0.700	0.797
4	0.695	0.692	0.803
5	0.837	0.783	0.897

Consequently, the classification accuracy declined across all four datasets utilized in the experiment. Notably, the most substantial deterioration occurred in the case of the BERT model, with a decrease of 0.267 in accuracy for essay

Table 5. Results for BERT with a generation ratio of 40% and attack size of 50%

Prompt	No Attack	With Attack	With Augmentation
2	0.611	0.302	0.617
3	0.759	0.628	0.828
4	0.695	0.616	0.756
5	0.837	0.722	0.882

Table 6. Results with a generation ratio of 40% and attack size of 50%

Prompt	No Attack		With Attack		With Augmentation	
	Bi-LSTM	Bi-GRU	Bi-LSTM	Bi-GRU	Bi-LSTM	Bi-GRU
2	0.688	0.732	0.595	0.593	0.742	0.744
3	0.689	0.711	0.622	0.654	0.760	0.737
4	0.744	0.689	0.617	0.709	0.714	0.767
5	0.830	0.828	0.727	0.609	0.807	0.638

set 2. This could be attributed to the fact that our BERT model[3] has a maximum sequence length of 512, and around 25% of samples in set 2 are longer than 512 words per sequence. The experiments indicate that the inclusion of adversarial examples into the original dataset, along with their utilization as a defence strategy, can enhance the performance of AES models. Specifically, when assessing the impact on classification accuracy, the Bi-LSTM-based model exhibited improvements of 0.174, 0.162, 0.083, and 0.066 for essays 2 through 5, respectively, after augmenting the dataset with adversarial examples. Similarly, the Bi-GRU-based model demonstrated enhanced classification accuracy of 0.194, 0.236, 0.173, and 0.159 for essays 2 through 5, respectively, compared to models that did not undergo adversarial attacks. By training the models with augmented examples generated using our proposed method, their overall performance on the combined test set showed average improvements of 0.163, 0.167, and 0.148 for Bi-LSTM, Bi-GRU, and BERT-based models, respectively.

6.1 Ablation Study

An ablation study was conducted to observe which component of the attack affects the performance of the model. Tables 1, 2, 3, 4, 5 and 6 depict the classification accuracy of the attack on Bi-LSTM, Bi-GRU and BERT models while varying the generation ratio and the attack size. In the first case, we varied the generation ratio from 30% to 40% while maintaining the attack size at 50% and compared the classification accuracy of the attacks. In the second case, we varied the attack size while maintaining the generation ratio at 30% and compared the classification accuracy of the attacks. The results of the ablation

[3] For technical resource concerns, we used DistilBERT.

study show that both generation ratio and attack size are important factors. When the generation ratio was increased from **30% to 40%**, the accuracy of both Bi-LSTM and Bi-GRU models slightly dropped. On the other hand, the performance of trained with augmentation remained almost unchanged implying that the augmentation process is insensitive to variation in generation ratio. For BERT, the performance of the model with a higher generation ratio of **40%** is more pronounced for the "With Attack" case, especially for Prompt 2, where the accuracy dropped from **0.346 to 0.302**. This implies that BERT is more sensitive to variation in generation ratio than Bi-LSTM and Bi-GRU. When the attack size was increased from **50% to 75%**, the Bi-LSTM and Bi-GRU models were noticeably affected. The accuracy of the models in the "With Attack" case dropped more for higher attack sizes thus showing that higher attack sizes yield more effective adversarial attacks. BERT also recorded decreased accuracy for higher attack sizes but the effect was less compared to the effect of changing the generation ratio. This shows that BERT is sensitive to generation ratio but relatively more stable to increase in attack size. Generally, this shows that both generation ratio and attack size should be carefully chosen when devising adversarial attacks and defence mechanisms. The generation ratio seems to have more effect on the BERT model than the attack size. On the other hand, the attack size has more effect on the Bi-LSTM and Bi-GRU models than the generation ratio. These observations can thus be employed to devise more effective AES models by balancing between the generation of adversarial examples and their attack strengths.

7 Conclusion

This study introduced a unified solution to counteract biases and improve the robustness of Automatic Essay Scoring (AES) models via a new phrase-level adversarial training method. By leveraging a model-agnostic approach to produce adversarial essay sets and using data augmentation, we showed how augmenting the training data can greatly improve the performance and robustness of different neural network-based AES models. Experiment results showed how AES models are sensitive to adversarial attacks and the accuracy significantly dropped when models trained on original datasets were tested on adversarially generated test sets. However, models retrained on the augmented datasets that included adversarial examples showed restored and even improved performance, as ranked scores produced by them achieved higher Quadratic Weighted Kappa (QWK).

The paper also discussed the need for a trade-off between generation ratio and attack size for adversarial training. It showed that higher generation ratios and attack sizes (in general) decreased the accuracy of models, but the effective data augmentation due to adversarial training mitigated the reduction, resulting in higher robustness. Finally, we can say that our proposed phrase-level adversarial training method using data augmentation is a viable solution to improve the robustness of AES systems against biases and adversarial attacks. It guarantees

AES models offer more accurate and unbiased essay scores and thus enhance their reliability and validity for real-world applications in educational institutions. As a by-product, this research can be extended to other natural language processing tasks to verify the effectiveness of this methodology in different domains.

References

1. Alikaniotis, D., Yannakoudakis, H., Rei, M.: Automatic text scoring using neural networks. In: Proceedings of the 54th Annual Meeting of the Association for Computational Linguistics (Volume 1: Long Papers). Association for Computational Linguistics (2016)
2. Ebrahimi, J., Rao, A., Lowd, D., Dou, D.: HotFlip: white-box adversarial examples for text classification. In: Proceedings of the 56th Annual Meeting of the Association for Computational Linguistics (Volume 2: Short Papers), pp. 31–36 (2018)
3. Gupta, K.: Data augmentation for automated essay scoring using transformer models. In: 2023 International Conference on Artificial Intelligence and Smart Communication (AISC) (2023)
4. Jong, Y.J., Kim, Y.J., Ri, O.C.: Improving performance of automated essay scoring by using back-translation essays and adjusted scores (2022)
5. Jurafsky, D., Chai, J., Schluter, N., Tetreault, J. (eds.): Proceedings of the 58th Annual Meeting of the Association for Computational Linguistics. Association for Computational Linguistics, Online (2020)
6. Lei, Y., Cao, Y., Li, D., Zhou, T., Fang, M., Pechenizkiy, M.: Phrase-level textual adversarial attack with label preservation (2022)
7. Lewis, M., et al.: Bart: denoising sequence-to-sequence pre-training for natural language generation, translation, and comprehension (2019)
8. Liu, Y., et al.: Roberta: a robustly optimized BERT pretraining approach. arXiv preprint arXiv:1907.11692 (2019)
9. Miller, D.: Leveraging BERT for extractive text summarization on lectures (2019)
10. Morris, J., Lifland, E., Lanchantin, J., Ji, Y., Qi, Y.: Reevaluating adversarial examples in natural language. In: Findings of the Association for Computational Linguistics: EMNLP 2020. Association for Computational Linguistics (2020)
11. Park, Y.H., Choi, Y.S., Park, C.Y., Lee, K.J.: Essaygan: essay data augmentation based on generative adversarial networks for automated essay scoring. Appl. Sci. (2022). https://api.semanticscholar.org/CorpusID:249455966
12. Pham, T., Bui, T., Mai, L., Nguyen, A.: Out of order: how important is the sequential order of words in a sentence in natural language understanding tasks? In: Findings of the Association for Computational Linguistics: ACL-IJCNLP 2021, pp. 1145–1160. Association for Computational Linguistics, Online (2021)
13. Singla, Y.K., Parekh, S., Singh, S., Li, J.J., Shah, R.R., Chen, C.: AES systems are both overstable and oversensitive: explaining why and proposing defenses. arXiv preprint arXiv:2109.11728 (2021)
14. Szegedy, C., et al.: Intriguing properties of neural networks (2014)
15. Tashu, T.M.: Off-topic essay detection using C-BGRU Siamese. In: 2020 IEEE 14th International Conference on Semantic Computing (ICSC), pp. 221–225 (2020). https://doi.org/10.1109/ICSC.2020.00046
16. Tashu, T.M., Horváth, T.: Synonym-based essay generation and augmentation for robust automatic essay scoring. In: Yin, H., Camacho, D., Tino, P. (eds.) Intelligent Data Engineering and Automated Learning - IDEAL 2022, pp. 12–21 (2022)
17. Tashu, T.M., Maurya, C.K., Horvath, T.: Deep learning architecture for automatic essay scoring. arXiv preprint arXiv:2206.08232 (2022)

Automated Essay Scoring with ChatGPT

Sebastian Maidl[1(✉)] and Annette Hautli-Janisz[2]

[1] University College Dublin, Belfield, Dublin 4, Ireland
sebastian.maidl@gmail.com
[2] Universität Passau, Innstraße 41, 94032 Passau, Germany

Abstract. In the past years, ChatGPT has proven that it is capable of handling tasks in many domains. This includes education. For education, the public discourse so far has been dominated by the possible adverse effects ChatGPT might have, as ChatGPT allows students to mask work done by AI as their own. This study tries to show a positive application for ChatGPT that can help students improve their work and save educators time. This paper is one of the first to compare ChatGPT and language professionals in grading essays. Although some research has been done, this study separates itself by placing a more significant emphasis on prompt engineering. Using the same criteria for the human raters and GPT while doing Zero-Shot prompt engineering has also not been done in this form. By doing that, this study aims to prove that ChatGPT can be used as an Automatic Essay Scoring system that can deliver grades comparable to those of human raters. With ChatGPT available to everyone, this study could show educators and students what potential AI systems have in grading Essays. The focus on prompt engineering can also help to understand how better prompts can be used to unlock ChatGPT's full potential.

Keywords: Automated Essay Scoring · AI · ChatGPT

1 Introduction

Generative AI (GenAI), and ChatGPT specifically, has been a hot-button topic for the last year [28]. ChatGPT has proven to be able to assist in many tasks and promises to change the working environment drastically by increasing efficiency and thereby revolutionizing what tasks need to be carried out by humans [10]. Artificial intelligence's ability to comprehend essay tasks and understand argument structure could also change the landscape of Automated Essay Scoring (AES). AES or Automated Essay Evaluation (AEE) is a research field within Natural Language Processing (NLP) that is concerned with grading essays based on different linguistic features [21]. These traditional AES systems are limited by the complicated process of adequately instructing and presenting them with all the required data to evaluate essays like argument annotations [24]. Additionally, the leading AEE systems also focus on catering to institutions and organizations

The original version of the chapter has been revised. The author name Sebastian Maidl has been corrected A correction to this chapter can be found at
https://doi.org/10.1007/978-3-031-93409-4_16

F. Bellas and O. Fontenla-Romero (Eds.): AIEER 2024, CCIS 2519, pp. 79–88, 2025.
https://doi.org/10.1007/978-3-031-93409-4_7

and cost money. If GenAI, with its understanding of arguments and language in general, could be used as a scoring system, it would create chances for students to educate themselves better and also allow educators to focus on teaching rather than grading essays manually [27]. In an attempt to answer these questions, this study will test the capabilities of ChatGPT as an automated scoring system for argumentative essays. In this process, the following research questions (RQ) are going to be answered:

1. Can ChatGPT be used as an AES system?
2. Are grades given by ChatGPT comparable to those provided by human raters?
3. Is GPT4 more capable of grading essays than GPT3.5?

While answering these questions, this study separates itself from other research papers done in the field of essay scoring with GenAI before. Previous papers have focused on GenAI's capabilities to give a holistic score, which means one overall grade for each essay instead of considering different aspects of argumentative essays [26,27,32]. Previous works also lacked a focus on prompt engineering, which is vital for receiving good responses from AI models. The paper by Herbold et al. in 2023 on "A large-scale comparison of human-written versus ChatGPT-generated essays" will serve as a basis for this research.

2 Related Work

2.1 AES

AEE or AES was first conceptualized in 1966 by E. B. Page and has now become one of the most critical fields in NLP [24]. Since then, more AES systems with different scoring methods have been developed. Compared to human graders, some advantages of AEE systems are higher consistency [29] and saving time and money [33] as less time for educators has to be used to grade essays. Additionally, AES allows students to train their skills [33] more frequently. Using AES systems has also been proven to help students write better essays. Although most improvements come in mechanics, such as punctuation and spelling, the advances were still significant [2]. Previous research [2] shows that students improved their essay scores from 2.28 to 3.93 out of six [7] for ten essays submitted to the "Criterion" system that evaluates essays [2] using one of the most popular AES systems, the "e-rater 2.0" [8]. Despite the proven success of systems such as e-rater, there is also criticism. Due to their statistical and pre-trained nature, it is possible to trick them by writing essays to satisfy the criteria for high scores but have low quality otherwise [33]. The lack of individual feedback is also a point of criticism for AES systems, especially concerning the relevance of content [29] and persuasiveness [22]. Better feedback in these areas could further students' improvements in more than just mechanics, like punctuation.

2.2 AES with AI

Due to the recent advances in Large Language Models (LLM) and GenAI, research started investigating the potential of using AI and GenAI systems such as ChatGPT to automate AES further [27]. Initial research comparing human raters and ChatGPT as a rater was done using essays from the TOEFL11 corpus. Grades given by ChatGPT were compared to the grades by the human raters and different linguistic features as well. This study showed that ChatGPT was able to grade papers with results similar to those of human raters [26]. In contrast to others, the research used GPT3.5 and did not provide example essays and ratings for those. Other studies done with GPT4 did provide example essays that proved to result in scores closer to those by human raters [27,32]. Other than the study on TOEFL11 essays, in this case, the essays were graded on the "Common European Framework of Reference" (CERF) and did not provide further details on the scale levels, as GPT4 showed built-in knowledge of the scale [32]. ChatGPT outperformed basic NLP models in these studies [27] and performed closely with traditional AES systems [32]. Overall, the research concluded that ChatGPT can grade essays [14], with results that can be compared to those of human raters and holistic AES systems [26,27,32]. The benefits of GPT compared to traditional AES are the higher potential for personalized feedback for the essay writer and the tone of the feedback, which can also be changed depending on how the prompt is set [16]. GPT can also be asked to provide an example of an essay that would have performed better based on the initial essay [3]. Additionally, ChatGPT can help educators save time by not having to assess each essay manually [27]. The downsides of GPT as a scoring system include the fact that scores are not reliably reproducible [26] and there is a fear of bias towards the writer of the essay [27]. However, one study tested for bias towards the authors by providing more information on the person who wrote the essay, like gender, but could not find evidence for biased assessment from GPT [32].

2.3 Prompt Engineering

Prompt engineering is one of the most crucial aspects of using GenAI in a more complex context [20] and optimizing the output for the given task [4]. Prompts can be improved in different ways. The first differentiation is between zero-shot, and few-shot prompts [9]. Some studies suggest that using few-shot prompting can already improve the quality of the response [5,9], but there are more ways to improve the output, even for zero-shot prompts. These methods include assigning a role to the model, giving context, diving the output length and/or format [12,20]. Chain-of-thought (CoT) prompts can also help to get a better response, especially in logical tasks, as they tell the model to build the answer step-by-step and show the logical structure of the response [9]. More advanced techniques in prompt engineering are, in most cases, only applicable when using an API or, for instance, the GPT playground, are to set the temperature and introduce a seed [4,9].

2.4 Advanced Prompt Engineering

"Are-You-Sure?" is a unique form of prompt engineering. The AI model is confronted with a previous response to let it critically assess whether the answer is correct [13]. This triggers the model to recalculate the response and compare it to the first, if the answers match, the response is confirmed. Otherwise, the new answer will be presented as correct, and the model might accept it as the new correct statement for future queries [13]. Simply asking the model, "Are-You-Sure?" or resending the prompt is only helpful for prompts whose task is to retrieve facts. In the case of argumentative tasks or summaries, the model will mostly reaffirm its initial answer [31]. Different techniques can be applied for more complex tasks with the same base idea as "Are-You-Sure?" prompts. One method is "Recursively Criticizes and Improves" (RCI) [23]. An algorithm called "SELF_REFINE" was developed to apply this, which improved the response quality by, on average, 20% and works when using zero-shot prompting [25]. RCI was compared to zero-shot prompting with CoT and performed better [23]. One concern with this type of prompting is that the response is getting better, not because the concept works but because giving the exact prompt multiple times can lead to better results. However, the "SELF_REFINE" algorithm delivered better results than reusing the same prompt numerous times [25]. This shows that AI models can find problems in their responses and use these findings to calculate a better response [23].

3 Method

3.1 Input Data

The essays written by humans stem from a corpus used in argument mining [30] and were also used in the study comparing quality of essays written by GPT and humans [19]. Since the Essays do not contain any biased related information [15] no evaluation of bias by GPT models was possible. The essays written by ChatGPT were generated using a zero-shot prompt asking GPT3.5 and GPT4 to write an essay on the given topic that consisted of 200 words. The criteria used to grade the essays were derived from a Ministry for Education of Lower Saxony guideline [19]. It consists of seven relevant categories for essay scoring, each graded on a seven-point Likert scale, with zero being the worst and six being the best score for each criterion [19]. The scores given by the human raters [19] also needed to be saved to compare the results from human raters and the results from the GPT models as raters. As seen before, it is essential to have a prompt that provides all necessary information to the model. Therefore, some of the concepts regarding well constructed prompt engineering were incorporated into the prompt for essay evaluation. The model was given the role of an English teacher. The context was to grade an essay written by a non-native English speaker. The criteria and the grades with the corresponding descriptions were also provided. The final prompt was: "'As an English teacher, please grade the following essay written by a non-native English speaker on the topic of topic. The Text: text Use the following list of criteria and description for the grades criteria"'. The "topic" and "text" were provided based on the instance of the iteration of the texts [1], "criteria" was the JSON file containing the criteria represented as a string. The temperature was set to 0.8 to get more consistent results. Lower temperatures caused runtime issues as the response did not change when the prompt was resent due to errors in the format. The OpenAI API was used, which has different parameters that assist in getting the best possible response. One that is very helpful is the "function" parameter [1]. Functions can improve the response by ensuring that a specific format, such as a JSON-like style, is being followed. This helps when 90 essays are graded one by one as the response format needs to be the same every time, and grading all essays at once exceeds the token limit. During this research the model sometimes did not assign values to all the required output properties, like essay topic or reasoning for the grade given, or did not grade single essays. As this can negatively impact the data quality, a check function was introduced that validated the response. If null, not a number (NaN) values were included, or the average grade for a topic was zero, the last prompt was resent to the model. As mentioned, this is a proven technique in prompt engineering and has provided good results.

3.2 Output

Since the function parameter has already predefined the output format, the resulting JSON could be extracted from the client's return statement and loaded into a DataFrame. Each author had one results table per grading model, coming to a total of six results DataFrames. Additionally, for each of the six results DataFrames, the average grade per topic and criteria and an overall average grade were calculated. For the prompt engineering techniques, a separate DataFrame was created for each method and each author rater combination. These DataFrames had different sizes as the size depended on the sample size and the amount of iteration provided in case of robustness.

4 Results

4.1 GPT as a System for Essay Scoring

The results showcase that GPT with both models can provide grades for the given criteria using zero-shot prompting. The output data indicates that GPT's grades follow a similar trend to those given by the human raters. Essays written by students have the lowest scores, and when graded by GPT4, the score is even lower. GPT4 has the highest scores, with the lowest difference in grades between GPT3.5 and 4. The difference between the grades given by GPT3.5 and 4 for the essays written by GPT3.5 is also small, but their grades are overall lower than those of the essays written by GPT4. Based on these grades and the overall fitting relation compared to the scores by the human rater the first RQ can be answered with yes: GenAI can be used as an essay evaluation system.

4.2 Grade Similarity Between Raters

First, the Student's t-test was calculated to evaluate the similarity between the grades of different raters [6]. For this, a two-sample t-test was required for the

H0 hypothesis that the grades given by human raters and both GPT models are different. The significance level of the p-value was set to 0.05, as it is the usual significance level. The results demonstrate that the differences in grades are not always statistically significant, which already showcases that the grades given are very similar. Second, an inter-rater agreement test was conducted to see the similarity between the grades. Here, Cronbach Alpha was used to test the inter-rater agreement. The Cronbach Alpha inter-rater agreement test was chosen over the Quadratic Cohen Kappa (QWK), as QWK has limited validity with ordinal scales like grades but performs much better with nominal scales [11]. For Cronbach Alpha, a value of over 0.7 suggests an acceptable inter-rater agreement, and a value higher than 0.9 indicates an excellent inter-rater agreement [17,18]. The Cronbach Alpha calculated for the grades given by either the GPT Model or human raters suggests a high agreement between GPT models and the language professionals. Except for the inter-rater agreement on some of the criteria, all Cronbach Alpha values for the overall grades suggest an acceptable to excellent inter-rater agreement, thereby performing as well or better than traditional AES systems. Based on those results, the second RQ can also be answered with yes. The inter-rater agreement between both GPT's models and human raters is at least acceptable, if not higher.

4.3 Comparison of GPT3 and GPT4

As the results show, both GPT models confirm what other studies have shown. Essays written by GPT4 receive higher grades than those written by GPT3, when graded by human raters. However, when graded by GPT models essays written by GPT3 surprisingly receive higher grades. The Cronbach Alpha values do not necessarily suggest that GPT4 is better at grading essays compared to GPT3.5. The values of GPT3/human raters and GPT4/human raters were almost identical. Since the inter-rater agreement for GPT4 is not higher than that of GPT3.5, it might not be the best solution for the given task. When using the OpenAI API, GPT4 takes considerably longer to respond. Also, using the GPT4 model is substantially more expensive, which must be considered, especially when requiring more extensive data. Additionally, the format in some cases suffers and, therefore, requires additional refinement before using the response. This is not an issue if only a single essay is sent, but when sending 90 essays the response format is essential to guarantee that the results can be used. The third RQ, therefore, has to be dismissed (Tables 1 and 2).

Table 1. Overall average grade for each 'author' per rater

Rater/Author	Student	GPT3.5	GPT4
Human	3.71	4.36	4.66
GPT3.5	4.20	4.61	4.26
GPT4	3.41	4.78	4.56

Table 2. Statistical evaluation between raters

	Human/GPT3.5		Human/GPT4		GPT3.5/GPT4	
Author	t-test	Cron.α	t-test	Cron.α	t-test	Cron.α
Student	<0.05	0.97	<0.05	0.94	<0.05	0.99
GPT3.5	<0.05	0.94	0.16	0.88	<0.05	0.99
GPT4	0.09	0.95	0.15	0.91	<0.05	0.95

5 Conclusion and Discussion

In this study, GPT has proven to be able to evaluate essays. GPT has also proven that it can compete with traditional AES systems regarding the inter-rater agreement. Therefore, this paper's first two RQs can be answered with yes. However, GPT4 proves to be more challenging to work with, raising the question of whether, in some areas, just marginally better scores justify these difficulties. Therefore, the last RQ has to be rejected as the results, besides the higher monetary and temporal demand, do not suggest higher capabilities. "Are-You-Sure?" prompts also showcased changes in grades and improved feedback provided by the AI model. Based on these findings, ChatGPT could be used by students and teachers alike to improve skills in argumentative writing. The option to have a grading system always at hand that is free to use (at least when using the web interface) can also help students become more comfortable writing essays as they have immediate access to personalized feedback. The capability of GenAI to give personalized feedback even sets it apart from regular AES systems. The use of "Are-You-Sure?" prompts can also improve this. When GPT is asked to provide further feedback, the resulting response includes ways to improve the essay further. However, one does not need access to OpenAI's API to receive individual feedback. Just asking ChatGPT's web interface to develop a grading scale is enough to get a personal AES system. AI as a rater can also remove bias from the grading process, as demonstrated in other studies [32]. One limitation of using ChatGPT as an AEE system is that the grades given can change when the essay is graded multiple times. Another limitation of using ChatGPT as an AES system could be that ChatGPT might not be suited for essay topics that require up-to-date information, especially ChatGPT-3. Also, grading large amounts of essays can be time-consuming, as the client can not be called with all essays at once. However, teaching students how to use ChatGPT as a personalized grading system can be a valuable lesson that educators can teach their students regarding the responsible usage of AI in education. Additional research can be done to improve the performance of this system by further improving the algorithm and even the prompts used in this study. Additionally, the new feature of "Batches" that is provided by OpenAI should be tested to grade essays in bulk more efficiently. Further research should be done to evaluate if ChatGPT can also be used for other tasks usually done by AES systems, like assessing linguistic and other features relevant to essay scoring, such as argument annotations. Additionally, future research could test ChatGPT's ability to grade tests in different subjects. Exciting questions include if ChatGPT can score history or social studies exams or if hallucinations hinder that process. Also, the question is how well-suited ChatGPT is to assess math tests on the one hand or, on the other hand, more creative tasks like poetry.

References

1. OpenAI Function Calling Tutorial: Generate Structured Output (2024). https://www.datacamp.com/tutorial/open-ai-function-calling-tutorial
2. Aluthman, E.S.: The effect of using automated essay evaluation on ESL undergraduate students' writing skill. Int. J. Engl. Linguist. **6**(5), 54 (2016). https://doi.org/10.5539/ijel.v6n5p54
3. Baidoo-Anu, D., Ansah, L.O.: Education in the era of generative Artificial Intelligence (AI): understanding the potential benefits of ChatGPT in promoting teaching and learning. J. AI **7**(1), 52–62 (2023). https://doi.org/10.61969/jai.1337500. https://dergipark.org.tr/en/pub/jai/issue/77844/1337500
4. Bozkurt, A., Sharma, R.C.: Generative AI and prompt engineering: the art of whispering to let the genie out of the algorithmic world. Asian J. Distance Educ. **18**(2), i–vii (2023). http://asianjde.com/ojs/index.php/AsianJDE/article/view/749
5. Brown, T.B., et al.: Language models are few-shot learners (2020). http://arxiv.org/abs/2005.14165 [cs]
6. Bruce, P., Bruce, A., Gedeck, P.: Practical Statistics for Data Scientists: 50+ Essential Concepts Using R and Python. O'Reilly Media, Inc. (2020)
7. Burstein, J., Chodorow, M.: Automated essay scoring for nonnative English speakers. In: Proceedings of a Symposium on Computer Mediated Language Assessment and Evaluation in Natural Language Processing - ASSESSEVALNLP 1999, p. 68. Association for Computational Linguistics, College Park, Maryland (1999). https://doi.org/10.3115/1598834.1598847. http://portal.acm.org/citation.cfm?doid=1598834.1598847
8. Burstein, J., Chodorow, M., Leacock, C.: Automated essay evaluation: the criterion online writing service. AI Mag. **25**(3), 27–27 (2004). https://doi.org/10.1609/aimag.v25i3.1774. https://ojs.aaai.org/aimagazine/index.php/aimagazine/article/view/1774
9. Chen, B., Zhang, Z., Langrené, N., Zhu, S.: Unleashing the potential of prompt engineering in Large Language Models: a comprehensive review (2023). http://arxiv.org/abs/2310.14735, [cs]
10. Chui, M., et al.: The economic potential of generative AI: The next productivity frontier - Frankfurt Main Finance e.V. Technical report (2023). https://www.mckinsey.com/capabilities/mckinsey-digital/our-insights/the-economic-potential-of-generative-ai-the-next-productivity-frontier#introduction
11. Cohen, J.: A coefficient of agreement for nominal scales. Educ. Psychol. Measur. **20**(1), 37–46 (1960). https://doi.org/10.1177/001316446002000104
12. Ekin, S.: Prompt engineering for ChatGPT: a quick guide to techniques, tips, and best practices (2023). https://doi.org/10.36227/techrxiv.22683919.v2
13. Eliot, L.: Prompt engineering boosted via are-you-sure AI self-reflective self-improvement techniques that greatly improve generative AI answers (2023). https://www.forbes.com/sites/lanceeliot/2023/08/30/prompt-engineering-

boosted-via-are-you-sure-ai-self-reflective-self-improvement-techniques-that-greatly-improve-generative-ai-answers/
14. Ercikan, K., McCaffrey, D.F.: Optimizing implementation of artificial-intelligence-based automated scoring: an evidence centered design approach for designing assessments for AI-based scoring. J. Educ. Measur. **59**(3), 272–287 (2022). https://doi.org/10.1111/jedm.12332
15. EssayForum: About Us. https://essayforum.com/about/
16. Farrokhnia, M., Banihashem, S.K., Noroozi, O., Wals, A.: A SWOT analysis of ChatGPT: implications for educational practice and research. Innov. Educ. Teach. Int. 1–15 (2023). https://doi.org/10.1080/14703297.2023.2195846
17. George, D., Mallery, P.: SPSS for Windows Step by Step: A Simple Guide and Reference, 11.0 Update. Allyn and Bacon (2003)
18. Guide, V.D.R., Jr., Ketokivi, M.: Notes from the Editors: redefining some methodological criteria for the journal. J. Oper. Manag. **37**(1), v–viii (2015). https://doi.org/10.1016/S0272-6963(15)00056-X
19. Herbold, S., Hautli-Janisz, A., Heuer, U., Kikteva, Z., Trautsch, A.: A large-scale comparison of human-written versus ChatGPT-generated essays. Sci. Rep. **13**(1), 18617 (2023). https://doi.org/10.1038/s41598-023-45644-9. https://www.nature.com/articles/s41598-023-45644-9
20. Heston, T., Khun, C.: Prompt engineering in medical education. Int. Med. Educ. **2**(3), 198–205 (2023). https://doi.org/10.3390/ime2030019. https://www.mdpi.com/2813-141X/2/3/19
21. Hussein, M.A., Hassan, H., Nassef, M.: Automated language essay scoring systems: a literature review. PeerJ Comput. Sci. **5**, e208 (2019). https://doi.org/10.7717/peerj-cs.208. https://peerj.com/articles/cs-208
22. Ke, Z., Ng, V.: Automated essay scoring: a survey of the state of the art, pp. 6300–6308 (2019). https://doi.org/10.24963/ijcai.2019/879
23. Kim, J.H., Kim, S.K., Choi, J., Lee, Y.: Reliability of ChatGPT for performing triage task in the emergency department using the Korean Triage and Acuity Scale. Digit. Health **10**, 20552076241227132 (2024). https://doi.org/10.1177/20552076241227132
24. Lagakis, P., Demetriadis, S.: Automated essay scoring: a review of the field. In: 2021 International Conference on Computer, Information and Telecommunication Systems (CITS), pp. 1–6. IEEE, Istanbul, Turkey (2021). https://doi.org/10.1109/CITS52676.2021.9618476. https://ieeexplore.ieee.org/document/9618476/
25. Madaan, A., et al.: Self-refine: iterative refinement with self-feedback. In: Advances in Neural Information Processing Systems, vol. 36, pp. 46534–46594 (2023). https://proceedings.neurips.cc/paper_files/paper/2023/hash/91edff07232fb1b55a505a9e9f6c0ff3-Abstract-Conference.html
26. Mizumoto, A., Eguchi, M.: Exploring the potential of using an AI language model for automated essay scoring. Res. Methods Appl. Linguist. **2**(2), 100050 (2023). https://doi.org/10.1016/j.rmal.2023.100050
27. Naismith, B., Mulcaire, P., Burstein, J.: Automated evaluation of written discourse coherence using GPT-4. In: Proceedings of the 18th Workshop on Innovative Use of NLP for Building Educational Applications (BEA 2023), pp. 394–403. Association for Computational Linguistics, Toronto, Canada (2023). https://doi.org/10.18653/v1/2023.bea-1.32. https://aclanthology.org/2023.bea-1.32
28. Patnaik, D.: The 10 biggest stories of 2023 that say the future is here. https://www.forbes.com/sites/devpatnaik/2023/12/10/the-10-biggest-stories-of-2023-that-say-the-future-is-here/

29. Ramesh, D., Sanampudi, S.K.: An automated essay scoring systems: a systematic literature review. Artif. Intell. Rev. **55**(3), 2495–2527 (2022). https://doi.org/10.1007/s10462-021-10068-2
30. Stab, C., Gurevych, I.: Annotating argument components and relations in persuasive essays. In: Tsujii, J., Hajic, J. (eds.) Proceedings of COLING 2014, the 25th International Conference on Computational Linguistics: Technical Papers, pp. 1501–1510. Dublin City University and Association for Computational Linguistics, Dublin, Ireland (2014). https://aclanthology.org/C14-1142
31. Teubner, T., Flath, C.M., Weinhardt, C., Van Der Aalst, W., Hinz, O.: Welcome to the Era of ChatGPT et al.: The prospects of large language models. Bus. Inf. Syst. Eng. **65**(2), 95–101 (2023). https://doi.org/10.1007/s12599-023-00795-x
32. Yancey, K.P., Laflair, G., Verardi, A., Burstein, J.: Rating short L2 essays on the CEFR scale with GPT-4. In: Proceedings of the 18th Workshop on Innovative Use of NLP for Building Educational Applications (BEA 2023), pp. 576–584. Association for Computational Linguistics, Toronto, Canada (2023). https://doi.org/10.18653/v1/2023.bea-1.49. https://aclanthology.org/2023.bea-1.49
33. Zupanc, K., Bosnic, Z.: Advances in the field of automated essay evaluation. Informatica **39**(4) (2016). https://www.informatica.si/index.php/informatica/article/view/815

More Than a Technical Fix: An Interdisciplinary Approach to AI in Education

Franco Rau(✉), Lina Franken, and Annekatrin Bock

FAU University of Erlangen–Nuremberg, Regensburger Straße 160, D-90478 Nuremberg, Germany

franco.rau@fau.de

Abstract. Implementing artificial intelligence (AI) in education is envisioned as a revolutionary change addressing fundamental pedagogical issues. However, this perspective tends to overlook educational systems' complexity, and the profound social and cultural dimensions associated with these technologies. This paper proposes an interdisciplinary framework integrating educational, media, and cultural studies to describe and analyze AI's diverse educational phenomena and impacts, presenting a visionary outlook for future research projects. Our ongoing research critiques the recurring repetitive discourse surrounding educational technologies—characterized by hype, hope, and disappointment cycles. Rather than viewing technology merely as a tool to solve fundamental pedagogical challenges, we emphasize the necessity of a nuanced, interdisciplinary perspective that accounts for the intricate interplay between AI and the sociocultural context of education.

Keywords: AI in Education · Interdisciplinary Approach · Educational technology

1 Introduction: More Than a Technical Fix

There is significant interest in how AI will transform education in public and academic discourse [1, 12, 15]. Terms like "educational revolution," "key technology," and "disruption" are commonly circulated, especially in public spheres. The discourse around the hope for fundamental change ties into well-known discussions about earlier educational technologies. Historically, educational technologies have sparked initial enthusiasm and hope for transformation, often followed by disappointment when anticipated changes fail to materialize. While one technology is still under scrutiny, another emerges, generating a new hype before the previous one has been thoroughly evaluated [4, 7, 13]. This cyclical nature has been observed with various technologies, from radio and television to digital tools, each promising to revolutionize teaching and learning but ultimately delivering limited substantive changes in pedagogical practice [2, 7, 9].

One prevalent issue in these discussions is the tendency to view new technologies as a "technical fix" for complex educational problems. This perspective simplifies the multifaceted nature of educational processes and overlooks the broader social, cultural,

F. Bellas and O. Fontenla-Romero (Eds.): AIEER 2024, CCIS 2519, pp. 89–95, 2025.
https://doi.org/10.1007/978-3-031-93409-4_8

and ethical implications of technology integration [17]. The notion that a single technological tool can resolve fundamental pedagogical tensions has repeatedly proven overly simplistic [9, 14], as is the case for societal debates more generally [8, 16]. Imaginations of problem solutions via technology tend to focus on the near future instead of being realized in the present time, this future constantly moving further away. Moreover, current research practices in educational technology often emphasize the potential of new technologies without adequately examining their practical outcomes or pedagogical value. As Bigum and Rowan [2] noted, much of the existing research on educational technologies is "long on hope and hype and short on reports of outcomes that might be judged worthwhile." This lack of rigorous evaluation contributes to the perpetuation of hype cycles and prevents a deeper understanding of how these technologies can be integrated and discussed in educational contexts.

Against this background, we propose an interdisciplinary framework that aims to move beyond the simplistic view of AI as a mere technical fix. By integrating educational science, media studies, and cultural studies perspectives, we seek to provide a nuanced understanding of AI's phenomena and its ambivalences instead of focusing on its impacts on education and its limits. This framework emphasizes the need for interdisciplinary research considering the complex interplay between technology and education's social, cultural, and ethical dimensions.

2 Proposed Framework

As an adaptation of the "Frankfurt Triangle" [5], the framework aims to provide comprehensive orientation and reflection for educational processes in digital transformation.

Our specified framework focuses on the impacts of AI in education, drawing heavily from educational sciences, media studies, and cultural studies. The framework systematically and iteratively addresses AI's technological, social, and ethical dimensions, offering a holistic approach to their understanding and evaluation. This framework enables a nuanced understanding of AI's role in education, moving beyond one-dimensional views and fostering informed, inclusive, and responsible use of AI technologies in educational settings.

2.1 Educational Science Perspective

The educational science perspective focuses on integrating AI technologies into teaching and learning processes to promote critical, competency-based, and inclusive education. This approach emphasizes a didactic-interactional approach, competency development, as well as a critical perspective:

- Didactic-Interactional Approach: This approach analyzes how individuals and groups use AI technologies in educational settings. It involves studying how AI tools are adopted, adapted, and integrated into social practices and educational routines. It also examines how these tools can facilitate interactive and collaborative learning experiences, exploring the potential of AI to support diverse learners.

- Competency Development: Evaluating AI's potential to support the development of essential skills and competencies. This aspect includes assessing the effectiveness of AI-driven personalized learning systems and adaptive learning technologies in enhancing students' critical thinking, problem-solving, and digital literacy skills.
- Critical Pedagogy: This focus involves applying the principles of critical pedagogy to the study of AI in education. It involves fostering a critical awareness of the ways in which AI technologies influence educational practices and outcomes and empowering educators and learners to engage critically with these technologies in ways that promote social change and educational equity (Fig. 1).

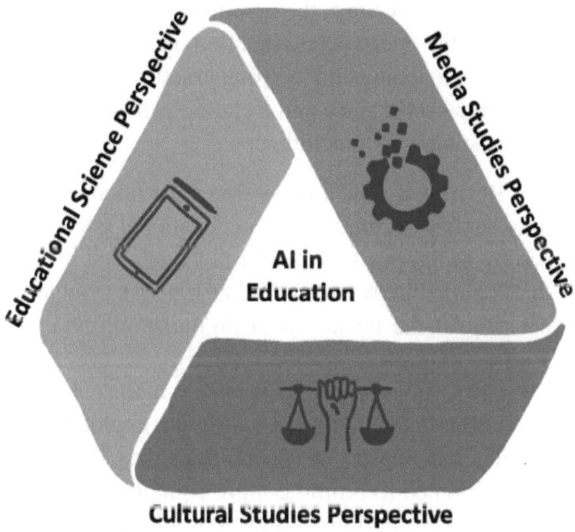

Fig. 1. A modified framework guiding educational processes in digital transformation, inspired by the "Frankfurt Triangle" [5]

2.2 Media Studies Perspective

The media studies perspective explores how AI technologies shape educational content, formats, and processes. This perspective draws on critical app studies and EdTech studies and includes:

- Technological Mediation: Examining how AI technologies mediate educational experiences and interactions. With this focus in mind, we analyze the affordances and constraints of AI tools and how they are entangled with teaching practices, learning activities, and communication in educational settings.
- Reflective Dimension: Identifying structures and functions of digital phenomena and artefacts created by the ongoing digitalization of the world. A reflective approach to digital systems, the consideration of cultural inscriptions, and the active (co-)design and reflection of technological and media phenomena form the basis for reflective

participation in a digitally shaped world. This aspect involves reflecting on technology affordances, data practices, and automation, taking into account their impact on social desires and expectations with regard to education and learning in a culture of digitality.
- Ethical Implications: This idea addresses the ethical considerations related to the use of AI in education. It involves critically examining issues such as data privacy, algorithmic bias [11], and the impact of AI on teacher autonomy and student agency. It also includes analyzing guidelines and frameworks for AI's responsible and ethical use in educational contexts.

2.3 Cultural Studies Perspective

The cultural studies perspective considers the broader social, cultural, and ethical dimensions of AI in education and the interwoven reflection on AI shaping teaching and learning practices and, vice versa, teaching and learning practices shaping future AI developments. This perspective draws on science and technology studies, cultural anthropology and critical code and data studies and includes:

- Human-Technology Relations: This area explores the interactions between individuals, groups, society, and AI technologies in educational contexts. It examines how AI tools are shaped by social practices, cultural values, and institutional structures, focusing on the interactions between individuals, groups, society, digital systems, soft- and hardware against the backdrop of digitalization and the cultural change involved in that.
- Cultural Inscriptions: This focus involves investigating the cultural narratives, values and practices embedded in AI technologies. It includes exploring how these technologies reinforce societal norms, biases, and power dynamics, how these can be reflected and how they can be designed to promote more equitable and inclusive educational practices. This perspectice also addresses questions related to personal rights, privacy, data property and other ethical aspects of social participation.
- Social Justice and Equity: Investigating the impact of AI on social justice and equity in educational processes. This idea includes examining how AI technologies can both mitigate and reinforce existing educational inequalities and how the technology can be designed and implemented to promote more equitable learning opportunities for all teaching and learning situations.

3 An Exemplary Case Study: Analyzing Gender Bias in AI-Generated Images

In our current project, "Beyond Prompting," we utilize our adapted "Frankfurt Triangle" framework, emphasizing analysis, reflection, and design—key processes for understanding and effectively integrating AI into educational contexts. To illustrate the practical application of this interdisciplinary framework, we outline a case study focusing on the issue of sexualization in AI-generated images. This example demonstrates how perspectives from educational science, media studies, and cultural studies contribute to understanding and addressing this complex issue.

3.1 Phenomenon: Sexualization in AI-Generated Images

A notable phenomenon explored with our framework is the depiction of sexualized AI-generated images of female athletes, specifically in the context of beach volleyball. For instance, when using the English prompt "female beach volleyball player in long pants" with Leonardo AI, only about half of the generated images depict athletes in long pants. In contrast, using the corresponding German prompt results in none of the beach volleyball players being shown wearing long pants after more than 30 iterations This discrepancy highlights the limitations and biases embedded in AI technologies regarding gender representation and appropriateness in educational contexts. Additionally, "SchulKI," an educational AI, sometimes blocks the German prompt for violating guidelines on sexualized content while allowing requests for male beach volleyball players. This example underscores the need to address the biases in AI technologies concerning gender representation and appropriateness (Fig. 2).

Fig. 2. Sample of AI-generated images by Leonardo AI based on the German translation of the prompt, "female beach volleyball player with long pants."

3.2 Applying the Framework

From the educational sciences perspective, this case study examines how AI technologies can influence teaching and learning processes regarding gender representation and inclusivity. Researchers and educational practitioners can use this scenario to discuss the implications of biased AI outputs on perceptions and learning outcomes. Analyzing how AI tools either fail to produce non-sexualized images or block specific prompts reveals how crucial it is to develop critical digital literacy skills. This involves recognizing and challenging biases in AI-generated content and understanding the ethical implications of AI in educational settings.

The media studies perspective explores the narratives and technological mediation involved in this phenomenon. This perspective investigates how AI technologies perpetuate societal norms and biases [9, 10], particularly regarding gender representation. By analyzing AI's failure to generate appropriate images of female athletes, media studies scholars can highlight how these technologies reinforce existing stereotypes and power dynamics. This perspective also emphasizes the need for ethical guidelines and frameworks to ensure that AI tools promote equitable and inclusive practices in media production and education.

The cultural studies perspective considers the interactions between individuals, society, and digital systems that become visible within the outputs of the case study. They show that the sexualization of female athletes is deeply embedded into social norms, forming bias within the training sets for AI-generated images. In its outcome, this impacts societal perceptions and the experiences of individuals within educational contexts, as well as cultural norms connected to body and sport. Intersections of technology, culture, and power are related by connecting the picture to a broader discourse on female body norms in both the present and past. This perspective allows for a critical analysis of the ways in which AI technologies are being shaped by and at the same time shaping social norms and advocates for more equitable and inclusive uses of AI.

4 Conclusion und Research Directions

The updated "Frankfurt Triangle" model [5] offers a comprehensive framework for analyzing and addressing complex phenomena in AI and education by integrating educational sciences, media studies, and cultural studies. Bringing together different disciplinary perspectives on AI allows to overcome monocausal technology hype circles and provides nuanced insights into the interconnectedness of technology and its uptake in educational contexts. This model actively fosters the informed, inclusive, and responsible use of AI technologies, systematically addressing social, cultural, and ethical dimensions. To further advance this interdisciplinary framework, we propose developing case studies through workshops, conducting empirical studies with mixed-methods approaches, or applying future methods for researching possible futures of AI in education [3, 6]. We would encourage research approaches that engage educators, students, and stakeholders in participatory research to co-design and evaluate AI technologies. Such approaches would ensure that diverse perspectives, needs, and values are at the core of AI-driven educational innovations.

Our specified framework focuses on the impacts of AI in education, drawing heavily from educational sciences, media studies, and cultural studies. The framework systematically and iteratively addresses AI's technological, social, and ethical dimensions, offering a holistic approach to their understanding and evaluation. This framework enables a nuanced understanding of AI's role in education, moving beyond one-dimensional views and fostering informed, inclusive, and responsible use of AI technologies in educational settings.

Acknowledgments. This study was funded by the Ministry for Science and Culture of Lower Saxony, Germany (2024 ZN 4331).

Disclosure of Interests. The authors have no competing interests to declare that are relevant to the content of this article.

References

1. Adeshola, I., Adepoju, A.P.: The opportunities and challenges of ChatGPT in education. Interact. Learn. Environ. 1–14 (2023). https://doi.org/10.1080/10494820.2023.2253858
2. Bigum, C., Rowan, L.: Landscaping on shifting ground: teacher education in a digitally transforming world. Asia-Pacific J. Teach. Educ. **36**, 245–255 (2008)

3. Bock, A., Macgilchrist, F., Rabenstein, K., Wagener-Böck, N.: Hoping for community in a technologically decelerated world—a critical utopian approach. Futures **163**(103434), 1–9 (2024). https://doi.org/10.1016/j.futures.2024.103434
4. Bock, A., Dander, V., Rau, F.: Raus aus dem ‹Loop›! Mögliche Zukünfte für Medienbildung with(out) KI. MedienPädagogik (Jahrbuch Medienpädagogik 21) 231–249 (2024). https://doi.org/10.21240/mpaed/jb21/2024.09.11.X
5. Brinda, T., et al.: Frankfurt-Dreieck zur Bildung in der digital vernetzten Welt. Ein interdisziplinäres Modell. In: Knaus, T., Merz, O. (eds.) Schnittstellen und Interfaces. Digitaler Wandel in Bildungseinrichtungen, pp. 157–167, Kopaed, München (2020). https://doi.org/10.25656/01:22117
6. Franken, L.: Digitale Methoden für qualitative Forschung. UTB Verlag, Münster, Computationelle Daten und Verfahren (2023)
7. Gouseti, A.: Web 2.0 and education: not just another case of hype, hope and disappointment? Learn. Med. Technol. **35**(3): 351–356 (2010). https://doi.org/10.1080/17439884.2010.509353
8. Jasanoff, S.: Future imperfect. science, technology, and the imaginations of modernity. In: Jasanoff, S., Kim, S.-H. (eds.) Dreamscapes of Modernity. Sociotechnical Imaginaries and the Fabrication of Power, pp. 1–33. University of Chicago Press, Chicago/London (2015)
9. Mayes, J.: Learning technology and groundhog day. In: Proceedings of Hypermedia at Work: Practice and Theory in Higher Education, University of Kent, pp. 10–12 (1995)
10. Nemorin, S., Vlachidis, A., Ayerakwa, H.M., Andriotis, P.: AI hyped? A horizon scan of discourse on artificial intelligence in education (AIED) and development. Learn. Media Technol. **48**(1), 38–51 (2023). https://doi.org/10.1080/17439884.2022.2095568
11. Noble, S.U.: Algorithms of Oppression: How Search Engines Reinforce Racism. NYU Press (2018). https://doi.org/10.2307/j.ctt1pwt9w5
12. Potter, J.: Micro studies in macro digital ecosystems: AI dystopias, assemblages, and qualitative research in challenging times. Learn. Media Technol. **48**(3), 369–371 (2023). https://doi.org/10.1080/17439884.2023.2235988
13. Rau, F.: Hochschullehre mit dem Social Web? Zur Einschätzung von Trendthemen in Bildungskontexten. In: Bücker, D., et al. (eds.) Trendy, hip und cool. Auf dem Weg zu einer innovativen Hochschule?, pp. 95–105. W. Bertelsmann Verlag, Bielefeld (2017)
14. Sims, C.: Disruptive Fixation: School Reform and the Pitfalls of Techno-Idealism. Princeton University Press (2018). https://doi.org/10.23943/princeton/9780691163987.001.0001
15. Schmohl, T., Watanabe, A., Schelling, K.: Künstliche Intelligenz in der Hochschulbildung. Chancen und Grenzen des KI-gestützten Lernens und Lehrens. 283 pp. (2023). https://doi.org/10.25656/01:26427
16. Strathern, M.: Robust knowledge and fragile futures. In: Ong, A., Collier, S.J. (eds.) Global Assemblages. Technology, Politics, and Ethics as Anthropological Problems, pp. 464–481. Blackwell Publishing, Malden/Oxford/Victoria (2005)
17. Wagener-Böck, N., Macgilchrist, F., Rabenstein, K., Bock, A.: From automation to symmation: ethnographic perspectives on what happens in front of the screen. Postdigit. Sci. Educ. (2022). https://doi.org/10.1007/s42438-022-00350-z

To Accept or Not to Accept? An IRT-TOE Framework to Understand Educators' Resistance to Generative AI in Higher Education

Jan-Erik Kalmus and Anastasija Nikiforova(✉)

University of Tartu, Narva mnt 18, 51009 Tartu, Estonia
anastasija.nikiforova@ut.ee

Abstract. Since the public release of Chat Generative Pre-Trained Transformer (ChatGPT), extensive discourse has emerged concerning the potential advantages and challenges of integrating Generative Artificial Intelligence (GenAI) into education. In the realm of information systems, research on technology adoption is crucial for understanding the diverse factors influencing the uptake of specific technologies. Theoretical frameworks, refined and validated over decades, serve as guiding tools to elucidate the individual and organizational dynamics, obstacles, and perceptions surrounding technology adoption. However, while several models have been proposed, they often prioritize elucidating the factors that facilitate acceptance over those that impede it, typically focusing on the student perspective and leaving a gap in empirical evidence regarding educators' viewpoints. Given the pivotal role academics staff play in higher education, this study aims to develop a theoretical model to empirically predict the barriers preventing educators from adopting GenAI in their classrooms. Acknowledging the lack of theoretical models tailored to identifying such barriers, our approach is grounded in the Innovation Resistance Theory (IRT) framework and augmented with constructs from the Technology-Organization-Environment (TOE) framework. This model is transformed into a measurement instrument employing a quantitative approach, complemented by a qualitative approach to enrich the analysis and uncover concerns related to GenAI adoption in the higher education domain.

Keywords: ChatGPT · Generative AI · GenAI · Higher Education · Innovation Resistance Theory · technology adoption

1 Introduction

Generative Artificial Intelligence (GenAI) - a type of artificial intelligence (AI) systems - excels at generating diverse content, thereby offering unprecedented capabilities, however, raising ethical concerns regarding disinformation, accuracy, bias, privacy, and ownership [6, 7, 9, 12]. Academic institutions responded swiftly due to concerns about misuse, particularly academic fraud. Some governments restricted or even banned ChatGPT [18, 35], while others provided guidelines for its ethical use [1].

F. Bellas and O. Fontenla-Romero (Eds.): AIEER 2024, CCIS 2519, pp. 96–107, 2025.
https://doi.org/10.1007/978-3-031-93409-4_9

Digital technology in education, including AI systems, addresses challenges such as those posed by the COVID-19 pandemic and aims to enhance learning experiences [14]. By personalizing learning, enriching educational resources, boosting student engagement, and fostering lifelong learning, these technologies can potentially contribute to the Education 5.0 movement, creating a more flexible and inclusive educational environment. However, integrating such technology requires understanding both its benefits and challenges. Research typically emphasizes identifying factors facilitating acceptance rather than barriers hindering it [11, 15, 28–30], crucial for promoting responsible adoption. This focus often centers on the student perspective, neglecting empirical evidence on educators' views (or academic staff), who are key actors in the educational ecosystem. Furthermore, research tends to concentrate solely on ChatGPT, disregarding other GenAI tools (see Sect. 2).

This study aims to develop a theoretical model to empirically predict barriers hindering educators[1] from adopting GenAI in their classrooms. Considering a lack of models focusing on these barriers, the developed model integrates Innovation Resistance Theory (IRT) with elements of the Technology-Organization-Environment (TOE) framework.

The remainder of the paper is structured as follows: Sect. 2 provides background, Sect. 3 presents the model and methodology, while Sect. 4 concludes the paper.

2 Background

To study technology adoption, researchers widely use various models and theories to understand factors influencing an individual's decision to adopt technology. In this context, *technology acceptance* refers to perceived usefulness and attitudes towards a technology, considered a preliminary step to *technology adoption*, defined as actual technology use [13].

Research in this field has produced many empirically validated models over decades. Some theories focus on the perception-based pre-adoption phase, primarily using the Theory of Planned Behavior (TPB), which argues that perceptions drive actions [26]. However, Schwartz et al. [26] criticize the field for overlooking post-adoption perspectives lack of examination on why technology adoption is resisted. These gaps hinder a holistic understanding of motives towards certain technologies, particularly reluctance towards their adoption.

Prominent theories used in technology acceptance research include Technology Acceptance Model (TAM), Unified Theory of Acceptance and Use of Technology (UTAUT), Theory of Planned Behavior (TPB), and Technology-Organization-Environment (TOE).

TAM posits that user attitude towards a system is the most accurate predictor of actual use, which is based on perceived usefulness and perceived ease of use, emphasizing user perception [10].

[1] Educators or academic staff of universities are faculty members in teaching positions such as academics, teaching assistants, professors, and researchers, irrespective of institutions and fields of these universities.

UTAUT [32] claims the likelihood of adopting a technology depends on performance expectancy, effort expectancy, social influence, and facilitating conditions. UTAUT2 added hedonic motivation, price value, and habit to the model [33].

TPB predicts and explains human behavior through perception, attitude, and control over behavior [2]. It improves upon the Theory of Reasoned Action (TRA), focusing on intention driven by attitude, subjective norm, and perceived behavioral control.

TOE framework posits that technology adoption in organizations is influenced by the characteristics of the technology, the organizational context, and the external environment [21].

While these models are valuable for understanding factors that facilitate technology acceptance, they do not primarily focus on identifying barriers to adoption. Understanding both acceptance and resistance aspects is essential for a comprehensive view of technology integration. Innovation Resistance Theory (IRT) plays a crucial role in understanding barriers and resistance factors overlooked by TAM, UTAUT, TOE, and TPB.

IRT aims to explain consumer response to innovation and why some innovations are met with resistance [22]. According to Ram, resistance is a natural response to change and products that respond to the sources of resistance are more likely to overcome the resistance barriers [22]. IRT accounts for *functional* and *psychological barriers*, where functional barriers are associated with value, patterns and risks associated with product use, while psychological barriers are related to the traditions, norms and perceptions of the customer [23]. According to IRT, three major groups of factors affect innovation resistance: (1) *perceived innovation characteristics*, (2) *consumer characteristics*, and (3) *characteristics of propagation mechanisms*. The theory has its roots in business and marketing research and contrary to the previous models and frameworks introduced in this section, IRT attempts to understand *why consumers or organisations reject technology instead of embracing it?*

Transitioning to the current state of research on GenAI adoption, our investigation delved into existing studies through a systematic literature review (SLR). While we do not present the SLR findings in this paper due to their peripheral role, it is accessible on Zenodo[2]. The analysis revealed that the majority of existing research predominantly focuses on ChatGPT as the GenAI tool of choice [3, 11, 15, 28–30] (as of December 2023), which is unsurprising. However, it also underscores a research gap, indicating the necessity to encompass a broader range of GenAI tools.

Most studies focus on students as their primary group [11, 15, 28–30], with only one study focusing on academics [3]. The most popular technology adoption model in these studies was UTAUT, with two studies using the updated UTAUT2 [28, 29], and one using the original version [15]. Additionally, two studies employed TAM [11, 30], and one used Social Cognitive Theory (SCT) as its theoretical foundation [3]. Existing studies have primarily examined factors affecting the acceptance of GenAI technology, neglecting research on resistance, barriers, and limitations to adoption. This aligns with [25], emphasizing the need to understand why technology adoption is resisted—a perspective largely overlooked.

[2] https://doi.org/10.5281/zenodo.13122996.

Research on the adoption of GenAI tools by academics and educators is notably limited. Doung et al. [11] have called for such research, which is particularly relevant in settings where educators have the final say on the use of these technologies (e.g., Estonian higher education). Given the identified research gaps, this study has a long-term aim to explore GenAI adoption through the lens of resistance and educator perception, thereby being unique in all three components.

3 Model Development

This ongoing research aims to uncover barriers hindering academics and higher education staff from adopting GenAI tools in classrooms. To this end, we develop a model integrating Innovation Resistance Theory (IRT) with Technology-Organization-Environment (TOE) constructs, considering both individual sentiment and organizational context. The model, rooted in IRT, is expanded with *Organization* and *Environment* constructs from TOE to incorporate institutional and external factors. The Technology construct is omitted to prevent redundancy as IRT captures the potential limitations of the technology from the perspective of the user.

Let us introduce the model's constructs (Fig. 1), where hypotheses and measurement items (Table 1) are formulated based on the underlying constructs and theory, existing research, and assumptions drawn from the current state of the art, providing a structured approach to hypothesis development.

3.1 Hypotheses Development

The initial reception of GenAI by the education community can be perceived negative as implies from several bans and concerns of cheating conveyed through mainstream media [5, 7, 9, 35]. This leads us to **H1**: *More than half of educators prohibit the use of GenAI tools in their courses.*

The first of the psychological barriers in IRT – the tradition barrier (TB) – refers to the psychological impact of an innovation's deviation from the established traditions or societal norms of its user [23]. The intent to maintain existing processes and norms affects openness to change as change presents a threat to the *status quo*. The tradition barrier signifies resistance to change stemming from entrenched norms and practices, which Shills defines as "*anything which is handed down from past to present*" [27, p. 112]. Academic institutions, proud of their traditions and heritage, are often resistant to change, driven by concerns over disrupting established processes, workload implications, and distrust towards administration [4]. This reluctance is compounded by the autonomy of teaching staff. Organisation for Economic Cooperation and Development (OECD) echoes these concerns, suggesting that they may challenge traditional teaching methods and alter perceptions of education, impacting student engagement [20]. Consequently, we define **H2**: *Tradition barrier has a positive effect on academics' resistance towards the adoption of GenAI within the academic environment.*

The image barrier (IB) addresses how users perceive an innovation's impact on their social image or identity [23]. Bin-Nashwan et al. [3] exemplify this through academics' negative sentiment towards ChatGPT, driven by their dedication to academic integrity, which is integral to their personal reputation and self-identity. Consequently, we define **H3**: *Image barrier has a positive effect on academics' resistance towards the adoption of GenAI within the academic environment.*

The risk barrier (RB) encompasses the emotions stemming from uncertainty, unintended outcomes, or side-effects of innovation, categorized into physical, economic, functional, and social risks [23]. In the context of GenAI in higher education, concerns about academic fraud and cheating are prominent. Kasneci et al. highlight various issues, including overreliance, adaptability, and output verification, associated with GenAI use in education [16]. Additionally, GenAI tools are perceived as susceptible to producing inaccurate information and bias [16, 24]. Considering these risks, academics may resist GenAI adoption within the academic environment. For instance, the potential inaccuracy of credit point representations due to significant assistance from GenAI tools could impact the perceived value of students' efforts, rendering current estimations inaccurate. This leads us to **H4**: *Risk barrier has a positive effect on academics' resistance towards the adoption of GenAI within the academic environment.*

The usage barrier (UB) represents resistance to innovation when it clashes with existing workflows, practices, and habits [23]. In the context of GenAI in education, one significant issue is the challenge of discerning GenAI-generated outputs from student-produced work [16]. This poses difficulties in evaluating students' knowledge against course learning outcomes, as exemplified by the deprecation of essays as an evaluation method due to students' ability to generate them easily with GenAI tools. Addressing this challenge requires educators to adapt and improve evaluation methods [19] as done by a number of top-ranked universities worldwide, which may demand significant effort depending on course content and structure. Moreover, the usage barrier encompasses the incompatibility of GenAI within specific courses, such as language courses focused on reading and writing, where GenAI capabilities may exceed course requirements. Thus, **H5:** *Usage barrier has a positive effect on academics' resistance towards the adoption of GENAI within the academic environment.*

The value barrier (VB) asserts that customers are unlikely to embrace a product if its performance does not justify its cost [23]. In the educational context, educators lack control over financial decisions affecting students' access to GenAI tools. Therefore, this study considers the value barrier from the perspective of the intrinsic value of the technology in education—whether its use in courses provides any value to students at all.

Effective technology integration in education necessitates equal access for all students, ensuring digital equity in classrooms [8, 12]. Historically, concerns about access and equity have been raised regarding the widespread availability of the internet in education [17], similar to the adoption of GenAI. Educators recognize the benefits of technology but emphasize the importance of equal availability and access. Within this barrier, it's crucial to weigh the required effort against the technology's potential benefits in a given course. Considering these factors allows for a more holistic understanding of the value barrier within this study's context. This leads us to **H6**: *Value barrier has a positive effect on academics' resistance towards the adoption of GenAI within the academic environment.*

The organizational context (OB) within the TOE framework considers how an organization's staff, internal structure, and processes influence the adoption of technology [31]. In this study, organization refers to the educational institutions where educators are employed. Webb and Cox identified that for effective technology integration in classrooms, teachers require knowledge on how to effectively incorporate these technologies into teaching practices [34]. Institutions may need to provide additional support to educators in the form of knowledge sharing, training, and guidelines to facilitate these changes. Additionally, educators may feel pressured to adopt these tools due to their increasing popularity and promotion as the future of education, which could lead to resistance. This leads us to **H7**: *Organisational context has a positive effect on academics' resistance towards the adoption of GenAI within the academic environment.*

The environment context (EB) within the TOE framework considers the impact of external variables such as regulation, market conditions, and societal and cultural factors [31]. Various governmental restrictions have been observed on the use of ChatGPT since their public availability. For example, Italy initially prohibited the use of ChatGPT over privacy concerns [18], and local governments in Australia, and the United States also imposed restrictions on its use in education [5, 35]. These examples highlight the susceptibility of GenAI technology to government regulation. Additionally, educators may feel pressured to integrate GenAI tools into their courses due to the technology's popularity and its increasing use in other fields, which could lead to resistance. This leads us to **H8**: *Environment context has a positive effect on academics' resistance towards the adoption of GenAI within the academic environment.*

3.2 Model

The developed model (see Fig. 1) uses the constructs of the IRT and the Environment and Organisation constructs of the TOE models to capture the potential resistance sentiment of educators towards GenAI tools use in the classroom. The model uses demographic variables – gender, age, university, academic field – as control variables.

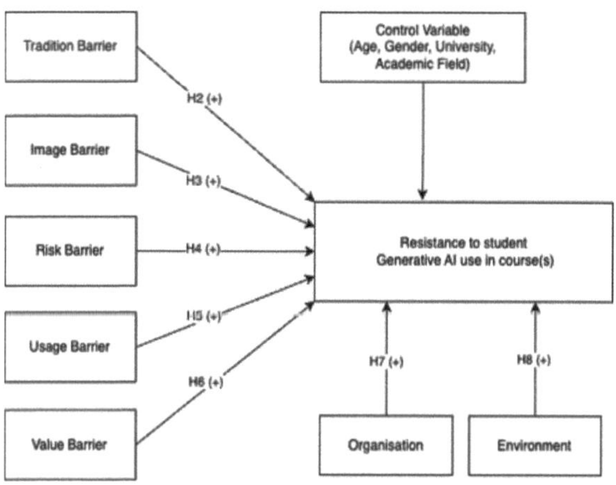

Fig. 1. Consolidate theoretical model.

We propose a mixed-method approach to test the hypotheses and refine the developed theoretical model. Utilizing Structural Equation Modelling (SEM) and statistical analysis, the quantitative method will test the accuracy of the model and identify potential areas for improvement. To gain deeper insights, we recommend complementing this with qualitative data collection, which is expected to be analyzed using response coding technique.

To this end, we develop a questionnaire for data collection (available on Zenodo[3]), which also gathers qualitative insights from educators on their perspectives regarding GenAI use. The survey is divided into three sections: (1) demographic profile, (2) core measurement instrument, and (3) additional questions. This mixed-method approach ensures a robust analysis and a comprehensive understanding of the factors influencing GenAI adoption in education.

The demographic profile section focuses on collecting demographic data related to gender, age range, university, and general academic field. In addition to the initial closed-ended questions aimed at recording the respondents' demographic profile, two additional closed-ended questions are included in the general information section: *Do you allow students to use GenAI in your courses? Do you use GenAI in your academic work?*

The first question is used to capture data for the H1. To more accurately reflect the sentiment towards using GenAI tools in courses, the possible answers are: *No, Allow*, and *Recommend*. The second question gathers information on the number of educators using GenAI in their academic work, helping to distinguish between respondents with prior experience using the tools and those whose perceptions may be influenced by a lack of familiarity with GenAI.

The second part of the questionnaire contains the measurement instrument consisting of 31 measurement items (see Table 1) derived from the constructs they are associated with based on existing research and underlying theory, wherein measurement items are measured using a five-point Likert scale.

The questionnaire is complemented with open-ended questions to gain a descriptive insight into the general sentiment of educators towards GenAI, covering multiple aspects of educators' personal experience with GenAI from personal use to necessary adjustments in courses.

The third section includes optional open-ended questions to provide respondents with a platform for a more nuanced interpretation of results. These questions inquire:

- *Are there any additional challenges associated with letting students use GenAI in your course(s) that were not covered by this study?*
- *What kind of tasks in your courses are most affected by the use of GenAI?*
- *How would you describe your own experience of using GenAI tools?*
- *Have you already integrated the use of GenAI in your course(s)?*
- *What were the adaptations you already did to integrate GenAI use in your course(s)?*

[3] https://doi.org/10.5281/zenodo.13122996.

Table 1. Developed measurement instrument.

Barrier	Item
Tradition barrier	**TB1**: Student use of GenAI reduces student participation in traditional course delivery methods
	TB2: Student use of GenAI makes traditional teaching methods ineffective
	TB3: Student use of GenAI creates a need for new teaching methods
	TB4: Student use of GenAI conflicts with general academic norms or traditions of my institution
Image barrier	**IB1**: Allowing students use GenAI in my courses causes criticism from my colleagues
	IB2: Allowing students use GenAI in my courses has a negative effect on my academic reputation
	IB3: Not allowing students use GenAI in my courses has a negative effect on my reputation among students
Risk barrier	**RB1**: Students using GenAI can become overly reliant on the tools
	RB2: Student use of GenAI has a negative effect on the development of problem solving and critical thinking skills
	RB3: Students using GenAI in my courses can complete the course with reduced effort
	RB4: Students using GenAI risk their academic integrity
	RB5: Students using GenAI can receive misleading information from the tools
	RB6: Students may have difficulties verifying the accuracy of GenAI outputs
Usage barrier	**UB1**: The contents of my courses are not suitable for GenAI use by students
	UB2: Student produced work is difficult to distinguish from GenAI outputs
	UB3: Students use of GenAI makes measuring learning outcomes in my courses more difficult
	UB4: Current evaluation methods in my courses are less effective when GENAI is used by students
	UB5: Improved evaluation methods in my courses are necessary when GENAI is used by students
Value barrier	**VB1**: Students do not have equal access to GenAI tools that are useful in my courses
	VB2: Students do not receive significant value from the use of GenAI tools in my courses

(continued)

Table 1. (*continued*)

Barrier	Item
	VB3: The risk of misuse of GenAI tools outweighs its potential benefits
	VB4: The resources required to allow the use of GenAI tools outweigh its potential benefits
Organizational barrier	**O1**: Institutional policy is required to allow student GenAI use
	O2: Current institutional policy does not support student GenAI use in courses
	O3: My institution does not promote student GenAI use
	O4: My institution does not provide me support (e.g., guidance, training) to allow students GenAI use in my courses
	O5: My institution does not provide students support (e.g., guidance, training) to allow them use GenAI in my courses
Environmental barrier	**E1**: Government policy is required to allow the use of GenAI tools by students
	E2: Current government policy does not support student GenAI use
	E3: My institution expects me to allow students use GenAI tools in my courses
	E4: Students expect me to allow them use GenAI tools in my courses

The instrument was subject to iterative expert review throughout its development process to improve the quality of the measurement items. Reviews were performed by two experts from the domains of technology acceptance research and modern educational theory. The instrument is made available on Zenodo[4].

4 Conclusion

This study proposes a novel theoretical model aimed to uncover barriers preventing academic staff from adopting GenAI tools in their courses. Drawing on constructs from Innovation Resistance Theory (IRT) and Technology-Organization-Environment (TOE), it is aimed at examining individual, organizational, and environmental aspects to empirically assess potential resistance to GenAI use by students. Utilizing these constructs and the state of the art, we define eight hypotheses regarding resistance to GenAI use in higher education. The model is transformed into a measurement instrument that employs quantitative and qualitative approaches to enrich the analysis and discover concerns related to GenAI adoption in higher education.

Future research is recommended to validate the developed model in real-world settings with its further refinement. As such, we are currently applying the model in Estonian

[4] https://doi.org/10.5281/ zenodo.13122996.

higher education settings [36] to examine whether academic staff of public universities in Estonia, known as a "digital nation" and early adopters of emerging technologies like GenAI, are reluctant to allow students to use GenAI tools, identifying concerns related to GenAI adoption in higher education.

The study contributes to the research by proposing a novel theoretical model that addresses the often-neglected perspective of technology resistance. It is one of the first to encompass educators' viewpoints as integral to the educational ecosystem. However, while we cover a neglected perspective, further research would benefit from unifying student and educator perspectives to comprehensively understand factors affecting GenAI adoption in higher education.

Declaration of Generative AI and AI-Assisted Technologies in the Writing Process. During the preparation of this work the authors used Google Gemini and ChatGPT-3.5 in order to improve readability and language. After using this tool/service, the authors reviewed and edited the content as needed and takes full responsibility for the content of the publication.

References

1. TLU Recommendations for the Use of Artificial Intelligence. Tallinn Univeristy. https://www.tlu.ee/en/ai#sources. Accessed 20 Feb 2024
2. Ajzen, I.: The theory of planned behavior. Org. Behav. Hum. Decis. Processes **50**, 179–211 (1991). https://doi.org/10.1016/0749-5978(91)90020-T
3. Bin-Nashwan, S.A., Sadallah, M., Bouteraa, M.: Use of ChatGPT in academia: academic integrity hangs in the balance. Technol. Soc. **75**, 102370 (2023). https://doi.org/10.1016/j.techsoc.2023.102370, ISSN 0160–791X
4. Caruth, G., Caruth, D.: Understanding resistance to change: a challenge for universities. Turk. On. J. Dist. Educ. **14**, 12–21 (2013)
5. Cassidy, C.: Queensland public schools to join NSW in banning students from ChatGPT. https://www.theguardian.com/australia-news/2023/jan/23/queensland-public-schools-to-join-nsw-in-banning-students-from-chatgpt. Accessed 30 Oct 2024
6. Cassidy, D., et al.: Use scenarios & practical examples of AI use in education. arXiv preprint, arXiv:2309.12320 (2023)
7. Chow, A., Perrigo, B.: The AI Arms Race Is Changing Everything. https://time.com/6255952/ai-impact-chatgpt-microsoft-google/. Accessed: 30 Oct 2024
8. E. Commission, S. Directorate-General for Education, Youth, Culture. Enhancing learning through digital tools and practices – How digital technology in compulsory education can help promote inclusion – Final report – October 2021. Publications Office (2021). https://doi.org/10.2766/365846
9. Currie, G.M.: Academic integrity and artificial intelligence: is ChatGPT hype, hero or heresy? Sem. Nuclear Med. **53**(5), 719–730 (2023). https://doi.org/10.1053/j.semnuclmed.2023.04.008, ISSN 0001-2998
10. Davis, F.D.: A technology acceptance model for empirically testing new end-user information systems: theory and results. Ph.D. thesis, Massachusetts Institute of Technology (1985). https://dspace.mit.edu/handle/1721.1/15192
11. Duong, C.D., Vu, T.N., Ngo, T.V.N.: Applying a modified technology acceptance model to explain higher education students' usage of ChatGPT: a serial multiple mediation model with knowledge sharing as a moderator. Int. J. Manage. Educ. **21**(3), 100883 (2023). https://doi.org/10.1016/j.ijme.2023.100883, ISSN 1472–8117

12. Dwivedi, Y.K., et al.: "So what if ChatGPT wrote it?" Multidisciplinary perspectives on opportunities, challenges and implications of generative conversational AI for research, practice and policy. Int. J. Inf. Manage. **71**, 102642 (2023)
13. Granić, A.: Technology Acceptance and Adoption in Education, pp. 183–197 (2023). https://doi.org/10.1007/978-981-19-2080-6_11,ISBN 978-981-19-2079-0
14. Haleem, A., Javaid, M., Qadri, M.A., Suman, R.: Understanding the role of digital technologies in education: a review. Sustain. Oper. Comput. **3**, 275–285 (2022). https://doi.org/10.1016/j.susoc.2022.05.004, ISSN 2666- 4127
15. Hernandez, A.A., Padilla, J.R.C., Montefalcon, M.D.L.: Information seeking behavior in ChatGPT: the case of programming students from a developing economy. In: 2023 IEEE 13th International Conference on System Engineering and Technology (ICSET), pp. 72–77 (2023). https://doi.org/10.1109/ICSET59111.2023.10295122
16. Kasneci, E., et al.: ChatGPT for good? On opportunities and challenges of large language models for education. Learn. Individ. Diff. **103**, 102274 (2023). https://doi.org/10.1016/j.lindif.2023.102274, ISSN 1041–6080
17. Maddux, C.D.: The Internet: educational prospects—and problems. Educ. Technol. **34**(7), 37–42 (1994). ISSN 00131962
18. McCallum. S.: ChatGPT banned in Italy over privacy concerns. https://www.bbc.com/news/technology-65139406. Accessed 30 Oct 2024
19. Moorhouse, B.L., Yeo, M.A., Wan, Y.: Generative AI tools and assessment: guidelines of the world's top-ranking universities. Comput. Educ. Open **5**, 100151 (2023). https://doi.org/10.1016/j.caeo.2023.100151, ISSN 2666-5573
20. OECD. Generative AI in the classroom: From hype to reality? (2023). https://one.oecd.org/document/EDU/EDPC(2023)11/en/pdf
21. Oliveira, T., Martins, M.R.: Literature review of information technology adoption models at firm level **14**(01), 1566–6379 (2011)
22. Ram, S.: A model of innovation resistance. Adv. Consum. Res. **14**, 208–212 (1987)
23. Ram, S., Sheth, J.: Consumer resistance to innovations: the marketing problem and its solutions. J. Consum. Mark. 6:5+ (1989). https://doi.org/10.1108/EUM0000000002542
24. Ray, P.P.: ChatGPT: a comprehensive review on background, applications, key challenges, bias, ethics, limitations and future scope. Internet Things Cyber-Phys. Syst. **3**, 121–154 (2023). https://doi.org/10.1016/j.iotcps.2023.04.003, ISSN 2667-3452
25. Samhan, B.: Revisiting technology resistance: Current insights and future directions. Australas. J. Inf. Syst. **22**, 01 (2018). https://doi.org/10.3127/ajis.v22i0.1655
26. Schwarz, A., Chin, W.W., Hirschheim, R., Schwarz, C.: Toward a process-based view of information technology acceptance. J. Inf. Technol. **29**(1), 73–96 (2014). https://doi.org/10.1057/jit.2013.31
27. Shils, E.: Tradition. University of Chicago Press (1981). ISBN 9780226753263
28. Strzelecki, A.: Students' acceptance of ChatGPT in higher education: an extended unified theory of acceptance and use of technology **49**(2), 223–245. https://doi.org/10.1007/s10755-023-09686-1, ISSN 1573-1758
29. Strzelecki, A.: To use or not to use ChatGPT in higher education? A study of students' acceptance and use of technology. Interact. Learn. Environ. 1–14 (2023). https://doi.org/10.1080/10494820.2023.2209881
30. Tiwari, C., Bhat, M., Subramaniam, R., Khan, M., Khan, S.: What drives students toward ChatGPT? An investigation of the factors influencing adoption and usage of ChatGPT. Interact. Technol. Smart Educ. (2023). https://doi.org/10.1108/ITSE-04-2023-0061, ISSN 17588510
31. Tornatzky, L.G., Fleischer, M.: The Processes of Technological Innovation. Lexington Books (1990)
32. Venkatesh, V., Morris, M.G., Davis, G.B., Davis, F.D.: User acceptance of information technology: toward a unified view. MIS Q. **27**(3):425–478 (2003). ISSN 02767783

33. Venkatesh, V., Thong, J.Y.L., Xu, X.: Consumer acceptance and use of information technology: extending the unified theory of acceptance and use of technology. MIS Q. **36**(1), 157–178 (2012). ISSN 02767783
34. Webb, M., Cox, M.: A review of pedagogy related to information and communications technology. Technol. Pedagogy Educ. **13**(3), 235–286 (2004). https://doi.org/10.1080/14759390400200183
35. Yang, M.: New York City schools ban AI chatbot that writes essays and answers prompts, 01 2023. https://www.theguardian.com/us-news/2023/jan/06/new-york-city-schools-ban-ai-chatbot-chatgpt. Accessed 30 Oct 2024
36. Kalmus, J.E., Nikiforova, A.: Generative AI adoption in higher education: exploring educator resistance in Estonian Universities. In: Proceedings of the 2024 Pre-ICIS SIGDSA Symposium, 13 (2024) https://aisel.aisnet.org/sigdsa2024/13

Potential of GPT-4o in Learning Analytics: A Comparative Study with Moodle Logs Analytics

Raidell Avello-Martínez[1,2,4](✉), Víctor G. Gómez-Rodríguez[2,4], and Carlos E. George-Reyes[3,4]

[1] Universidad Bolivariana del Ecuador, 092405 Guayas, Ecuador
raidell.avello@udc.es
[2] CITIC Research Center, University of A Coruña, A Coruña, Spain
[3] Instituto Tecnológico Superior Urdesa, Guayaquil, Ecuador
[4] Monterrey Institute of Technology and Higher Education (ITESM), Monterrey, Mexico

Abstract. This study explores the use of the generative AI model GPT-4o for analyzing Moodle logs, comparing it with Moodle Logs Analytics (MLA), a specialized educational analytics tool. Focusing on a Digital Narratives course at the Universidad Bolivariana del Ecuador, logs were analyzed using both methods to evaluate the accuracy, ease of use, and utility of GPT-4o against MLA. Results indicate that GPT-4o can generate detailed reports and comparable graphs to MLA in various aspects of educational data analysis. However, technical limitations were encountered in creating complex geographical visualizations, such as world maps of accesses by country. Despite these challenges, GPT-4o proved to be a powerful tool for transforming raw data into valuable insights, enabling educators to make informed decisions to enhance teaching and learning.

Keywords: Learning Analytics · Generative AI · ChatGPT · Moodle Logs · Educational Data Analysis

1 Introduction

Learning Management Systems (LMS) like Moodle are fundamental tools in modern education, offering a robust platform for e-learning and hybrid learning [1]. Moodle is especially prominent for its open source nature, which facilitates continuous innovation and the development of plugins that enrich its functionality [2]. However, truly exploiting the data generated by Moodle remains a complex process, highlighting the importance of effective analytical tools that can transform raw records into valuable insights to improve teaching and learning.

In the literature, Moodle log analysis has been explored using various tools, which offers visual analysis of student activity in Moodle [3]. These tools make data visualization easier, but often require specific technical skills and may not integrate easily with all Moodle features.

F. Bellas and O. Fontenla-Romero (Eds.): AIEER 2024, CCIS 2519, pp. 108–117, 2025.
https://doi.org/10.1007/978-3-031-93409-4_10

The advent of Generative Artificial Intelligence (GenAI), and in particular advanced models such as GPT-4o, offers new possibilities for LMS log analysis [4]. GPT-4o can process large volumes of text and generate complex understandings that can be used to analyze students' interaction with digital resources, their participation in forums, and their progression through course materials. This study aims to explore how GPT-4o can be used to enrich learning analytics in Moodle, providing an additional layer of analysis that goes beyond the capabilities of existing tools.

This work addresses the use of GPT-4o in Moodle log analysis, highlighting how generative artificial intelligence can complement and extend traditional educational analytics methodologies. By integrating GPT-4o, we seek to offer a more detailed and contextualized view of learning activities, helping educators make more informed decisions based on rich and multifaceted data. To achieve this objective, the results of log analysis from a course of the Master's Degree in Digital Environments at the Bolivarian University of Ecuador will be compared using GPT-4o and the Moodle Logs Analytics tool, a widely accepted open source solution. This comparison will allow us to evaluate the accuracy, ease of use, and usefulness of GPT-4o, providing a comprehensive evaluation of its effectiveness in the educational context.

1.1 Literature Review

Log analysis in learning management systems has been an active and crucial field of research to improve the understanding of student behavior and the effectiveness of pedagogical practices. Moodle, as one of the most used LMS worldwide, has generated a considerable amount of research focused on the exploitation of its data for educational improvement.

Tools and Techniques for Log Analysis in Moodle

Various tools have been developed to analyze Moodle logs, facilitating the work of educators and researchers. UBUMonitor, for example, is a tool that facilitates visual analysis of student activity, allowing educators to obtain an overview of interactions with course resources [5]. UBUMonitor stands out for its customization capacity, allowing users to adjust the analysis parameters according to the specific needs of the course and the researcher.

Another significant tool is GISMO, which provides visual reports on student activity in Moodle. GISMO has been widely used, but has faced maintenance and update issues, limiting its functionality with newer versions of Moodle [6]. MOCLog is another tool that offers detailed analyzes of student behavior, although it has also struggled to keep up with Moodle updates, affecting its ability to provide accurate and up-to-date analysis [7].

In the context of digital education, Moodle Logs Analytics has emerged as an open source solution for analyzing activity logs in Moodle [8]. This tool, developed to provide interactive and detailed graphics, has been used to analyze five editions of a Digital Storytelling course in a master's program, revealing significant patterns in access to resources, participation in forums and submission of assignments. The results have allowed us to suggest adaptive pedagogical strategies based on these findings (Avello-Martínez, Delgado Álvarez, & Gómez Rodríguez, 2024).

Generative Artificial Intelligence in Learning Analytics
The introduction of generative artificial intelligence has opened new possibilities in learning analytics [4]. Advanced models like GPT-4o can process large volumes of text and generate detailed and contextual analyses of log data. These models allow educators to gain deeper insights into students' interactions with the course, their participation in forums, and their progression through learning materials.

Studies have explored how ChatGPT can become a student-centered educational technology and how it can be applied in learning analytics. For example, using ChatGPT to interpret and analyze text-based data can be a valuable technique when dealing with qualitative educational records. However, these studies only proposed the concept of using ChatGPT to address deficiencies in qualitative analysis in existing LA techniques without conducting further related experiments [9].

In the past, LA predictions and identifying at-risk students were primarily done using machine learning models or statistical analysis, which have limitations in handling text data [10]. Students' thoughts can also be an important feature in predicting risk, and integrating ChatGPT with current LA techniques can broaden the data sources for analysis. Additionally, if ChatGPT performs comparably to current methods in analyzing numerical data, it could offer educators and researchers a powerful and convenient LA tool.

The work of Susnjak [10] is notable in this context, as it proposes a framework that combines both explainable AI (XAI) and prescriptive analytics, integrating generative language models to communicate insights in a comprehensible manner to students. This approach not only identifies at-risk students but also provides prescriptive feedback based on data, translated into natural language using GPT, offering actionable and personalized recommendations.

2 Methodology

2.1 Study Objective and Context

The objective of this study is to exemplify the effectiveness of the GPT-4o model to perform some cases of analysis of Moodle logs, specifically for the Digital Narratives course, within the Master's Degree in Digital Environments at the Universidad Bolivariana del Ecuador. The Digital Narratives course was selected for its rich structure and diversity of activities used, which allows the evaluation of students' interactions with the resources. In addition, the principal investigator of this work is the course professor.

The choice of GPT-4o is justified by its advanced natural language processing capabilities and its accuracy in analyzing educational data [11]. Moodle Logs Analytics (MLA) was used to verify the accuracy and validity of the results generated by GPT-4o, a tool with which the researchers already have previous experience. This verification is crucial due to the possible hallucinations of ChatGPT, where the model can generate inaccurate or fictitious information. Comparing results with MLA helps ensure consistency and accuracy in analyses, mitigating the risks associated with these hallucinations and strengthening the reliability of the results obtained with GPT-4o.

2.2 Data Collection

Activity logs of students from the Digital Narratives course were collected using the CSV report download option within the Moodle platform. The data were preprocessed to remove irrelevant or duplicate information and ensured to be in a suitable format for analysis. Additionally, the data were anonymized using a Python procedure before uploading to GPT-4o to protect the privacy of students and instructors.

2.3 Analysis with GPT-4o

The Moodle logs were uploaded into ChatGPT, which was the selected interface. Report Generation: GPT-4o was tasked with generating detailed reports on student activity, following the same reports generated by Moodle Logs Analytics, identifying behavior patterns, participation analysis, and performance. Additionally, recommendations for instructors were requested, which are not provided by Moodle Logs Analytics.

2.4 Verification with Moodle Logs Analytics (MLA)

The same Moodle logs were uploaded into the Moodle Logs Analytics tool. MLA functionalities were used to generate interactive and detailed graphs on student activity. The patterns identified by GPT-4o were compared with those visualized in MLA to verify consistency. The results from GPT-4o were validated by checking their consistency with the analyses provided by MLA.

2.5 Evaluation of Results

The accuracy of the results obtained with GPT-4o was evaluated by comparing them with those generated by MLA. The ease of use of GPT-4o was documented, considering the setup time, ease of interpreting the results, and overall interface usability. The utility of the reports generated by GPT-4o for instructors and administrators was analyzed, evaluating how understandable and actionable the provided recommendations were.

3 Results and Analysis

3.1 Data Filtering and Anonymization

Before performing the analysis, the dataset was filtered to include only records between March 20, 2024, and April 22, 2024, which corresponds to the duration of the course. User names were anonymized by replacing student names with "Student X" and instructor names with "Professor X" based on a provided list of instructor names. This was done locally using a Python script to ensure data privacy and integrity.

The prompt used to obtain the code to prepare the data in Python with GPT-4o was as follows: "Give me the python code to filter the dataset to include only records between March 20, 2024, and April 22, 2024. Anonymize the user names by replacing student names with 'Student X' and instructor names with 'Professor X' based on the provided list of instructor names.". The structure of the dataset was previously provided.

To visualize the daily accesses to the Digital Narratives course (Fig. 1), a line graph was generated using the anonymized and filtered data. The graph displays the number of accesses each day between March 20, 2024, and April 22, 2024. Additionally, a red dashed line representing the overall average daily accesses was included to provide a clearer understanding of access patterns.

The prompt used to generate this analysis with GPT-4o was as follows: "Here is a dataset of activity logs from Moodle. Please analyze the daily access patterns and generate a line graph showing the number of accesses each day. Include a red dashed line indicating the overall average daily accesses.". This visualization helps in identifying peak access days and understanding student engagement throughout the course duration. Comparing this with the output from Moodle Logs Analytics, we observed similar patterns, validating the consistency and accuracy of GPT-4o's analysis capabilities.

The line graph showing daily accesses can not only highlight periods of heightened engagement, but also reveal underlying trends in student behavior over time. For example, consistent increases in accesses toward the end of the week could indicate students' tendency to engage more intensely as deadlines approach, suggesting a need for additional support or resources during these times. Additionally, decreases in activity could highlight periods where students might benefit from motivational interventions or additional content reviews. These insights can help educators not only schedule activities more effectively, but also develop specific strategies aimed at maintaining consistent student engagement throughout the course.

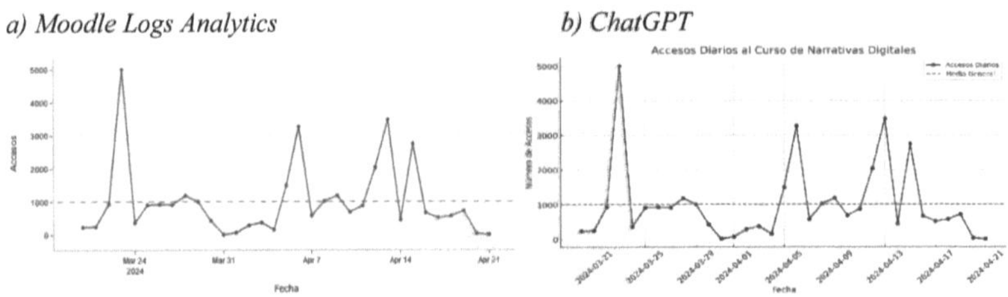

Fig. 1. Daily accesses

To further analyze participant engagement (Fig. 2), a heatmap was created to show accesses by day of the week and hour of the day. This visual representation helps in identifying peak access times and days. The prompt used to generate this analysis with GPT-4o was as follows: "Please analyze the access patterns by day of the week and hour of the day and generate a heatmap showing these patterns.". The heatmap provides a clear view of the times when students are most active, which can inform decisions about the best times for scheduling interactive activities or assignments. It is important to note that the instructor teaches from Poland, which explains the early morning access logs due to the time difference.

The heatmap, not only highlights peak access times, but also reveals patterns that can inform more effective scheduling of interactive activities and assignments [8]. This data-driven approach allows instructors to tailor their teaching strategies to better meet the needs of their students, potentially increasing engagement and improving learning outcomes [12]. Furthermore, the ability to monitor student activity in such detail allows for early identification of at-risk students, enabling timely interventions.

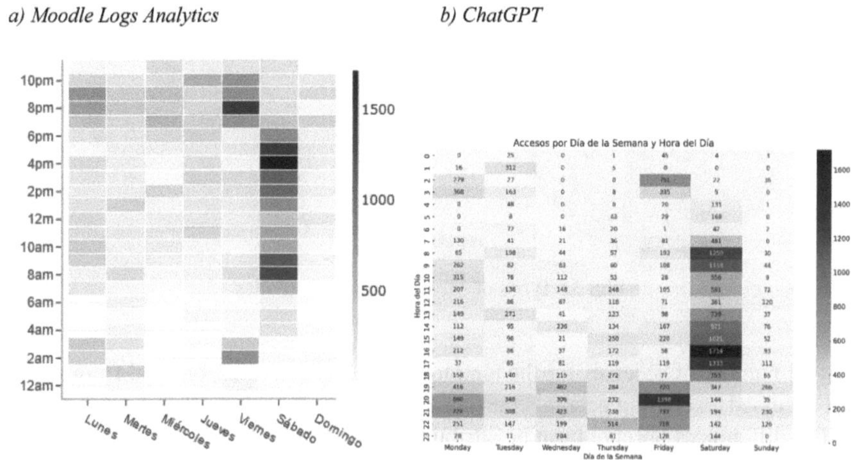

Fig. 2. Participant engagement

The pic chart illustrates the distribution of the types of activities most accessed by participants in the Digital Narratives course (Fig. 3). Each segment represents a different type of activity, showing the proportion of total accesses attributed to each type. The prompt used to generate this analysis with GPT-4o was as follows: "*Please analyze the types of activities accessed and generate a pie chart showing the distribution of the most accessed activities.* ". This visualization helps in understanding which types of activities are most engaging for the participants, allowing educators to identify key resources and potentially adjust their focus to enhance student interaction with the course content.

The detailed breakdown provided by the pie chart offers educators valuable insights into student preferences and behaviors. By identifying which types of activities receive the most engagement, instructors can refine their course design to prioritize these elements, potentially increasing overall student engagement and satisfaction [13]. For example, if interactive forums and quizzes prove to be particularly popular, educators could expand these components, integrating them more deeply into the curriculum. Additionally, understanding less-accessed activities can lead to a re-evaluation of their design or relevance, potentially resulting in modifications that make them more engaging or useful. This targeted approach not only improves the learning experience, but also ensures that educational content closely aligns with students' interests and learning styles, thereby fostering a more effective and engaging educational environment.

The horizontal bar chart illustrates the ten most accessed specific activities in the course based on the total number of accesses (Fig. 4). Each bar represents a different activity, showing the total number of accesses for each. The prompt used to generate this analysis with GPT-4o was as follows: "Please analyze the specific activities accessed based on the 'Contexto del evento' column and generate a horizontal bar chart showing

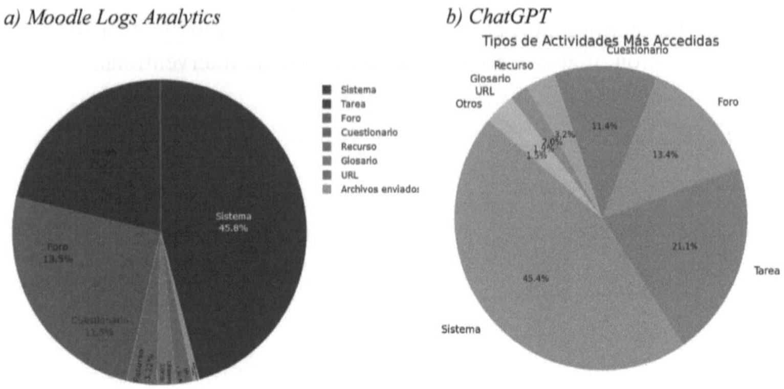

Fig. 3. Types of Most Accessed Activities

the total number of accesses for the ten most accessed activities, ordered from most to least accessed, excluding general course access."

The differences observed can be attributed to the following factors:

- Counting Method: The initial analysis counted unique accesses per user per activity, whereas this analysis counts all accesses, regardless of how many times the same user accessed an activity.
- Activity Type: Some activities, like URLs, might have been accessed multiple times by fewer users, which explains their higher presence in a total access count compared to unique access count.

In this sense, an analysis of the precision of the results provided by MLA is required, first of all, to adjust the prompt and achieve a graph that is truly useful for the teacher, regardless of whether differences are seen between both tools. Everything indicates that it has been a problem of interpretation of the analysis request.

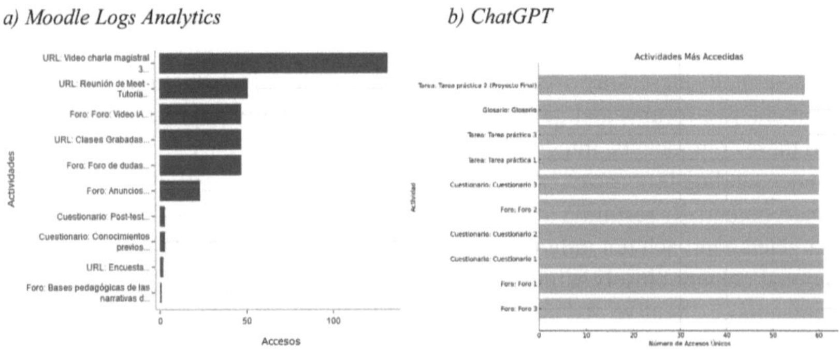

Fig. 4. Most Accessed Activities

The horizontal bar chart provides a clear visualization of the most accessed activities, which can be very informative for course design and improvement. By understanding which specific activities attract the most student attention, educators can identify the elements of the course that are most effective and engaging [5]. This knowledge allows for more strategic allocation of resources and a more precise instructional focus. For example, if certain reading materials are among the most accessed activities, instructors might consider expanding these elements or integrating similar activities into other parts of the course. Additionally, analyzing why certain activities receive less engagement can lead to valuable revisions or improvements, ensuring that all components of the course are optimized for student interaction. This level of detailed analysis supports a more adaptive and responsive teaching approach, ultimately contributing to better educational outcomes and increased student satisfaction.

In the case of the last graph to be generated (Fig. 5), type mundi, of accesses by country, technical limitations arose that prevented the direct creation of the graph in ChatGPT. The tools and libraries available in the current environment did not allow the graph mundi to be generated and displayed effectively.

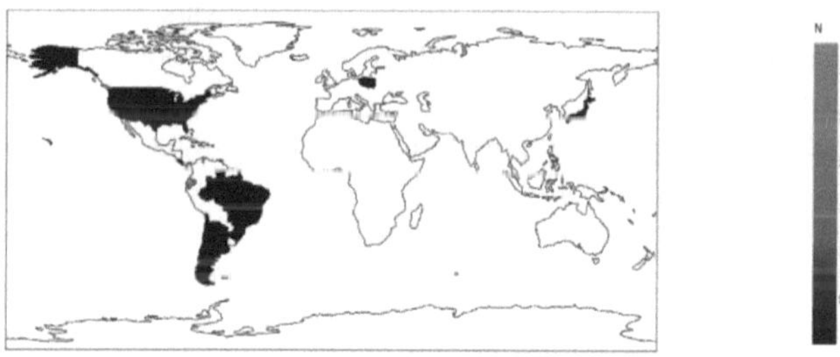

Fig. 5. Mundi map

Despite the technical limitations encountered in generating the global map of accesses by country, which will surely be resolved in future versions of ChatGPT, these types of visualizations have great potential for understanding global participation patterns in online courses. These maps can provide valuable information about the geographic distribution of students, helping educators and administrators identify regions with higher or lower participation. This information is important for tailoring support services and marketing strategies to specific areas. Additionally, understanding the global reach of a course can inform decisions about language support, cultural considerations in content delivery, and scheduling live sessions to accommodate different time zones. Overcoming these technical challenges and successfully implementing such visualizations in future analyses would improve the ability to make data-driven decisions that foster inclusive and effective online learning environments.

4 Conclusions

The importance of this work lies in the exploration of the use of generative artificial intelligence models, specifically GPT-4o, for the analysis of Moodle logs. In an educational context where data is abundant but its effective interpretation can be challenging, the use of advanced technologies such as GPT-4o can offer new ways to understand and improve student interaction with educational resources. The ability to transform raw data into actionable insights enables educators to make informed decisions that can improve course design and delivery.

During this study, a validation of a limited set of results generated by GPT-4o was carried out against those produced by Moodle Logs Analytics. GPT-4o was found to be able to generate detailed reports and graphs that are comparable to those provided by MLA. However, the validation showed that although GPT-4o is effective for many types of analysis, there are still certain areas where specialized tools such as MLA have an advantage, especially in creating complex geographic visualizations. At the same time, GPT-4o produced some graphs that were more informative than those generated by MLA. In addition, as a variant, GPT-4o provided all the code needed to create the graphs in a Python programming environment.

Among the limitations encountered, GPT-4o's inability to generate global access graphs by country effectively within the current environment stands out. Available tools and libraries did not allow overcoming these technical limitations, which underlines the importance of specialized tools in certain areas of data analysis. Furthermore, the need for basic technical knowledge to prepare and process data before using it with GPT-4o may be a barrier for some users.

Despite these limitations, future possibilities for integrating generative AI models into learning analytics are promising. With the continued development of these technologies, it is possible that future versions of GPT-4o and other similar tools may overcome the current limitations and provide a more comprehensive solution for educational analytics. Integrating generative AI with educational data analytics platforms has the potential to revolutionize how educators and administrators interpret and use data to improve teaching and learning.

References

1. Avello Martínez, R., Fernández Álvarez, D., Cortés Iglesias, M.: Covid19 y plataformas de tele-formación. Impacto de políticas públicas. Rev. Univ. Soc. **14**, 655–662 (2022)
2. Marticorena-Sánchez, R., López-Nozal, C., Ji, Y.P., Pardo-Aguilar, C., Arnaiz-González, Á.: UBUMonitor: an open-source desktop application for Visual E-Learning analysis with moodle. Electronics **11**, 954 (2022). https://doi.org/10.3390/electronics11060954
3. Anggraeni, D.M., Sole, F.B.: Identification of digital literacy skill of STKIP Weetebula students in Moodle based online learning. In: Samsudin A., et al. (eds.) AIP Conference Proceedings American Institute of Physics Inc. (2022). https://doi.org/10.1063/5.0104066
4. van Dis, E.A.M., Bollen, J., Zuidema, W., van Rooij, R., Bockting, C.L.: ChatGPT: five priorities for research. Nature **614**, 224–226 (2023). https://doi.org/10.1038/d41586-023-00288-7
5. Marticorena-Sánchez, R., López-Nozal, C., Serrano-Mamolar, A., Olivares-Gil, A.: UBU-Monitor: desktop application for visual e-learning student clustering with Moodle. SoftwareX **26**, 101727 (2024). https://doi.org/10.1016/j.softx.2024.101727
6. Mazza, R., Milani, C.: GISMO: a graphical interactive student monitoring tool for course management systems. Presented at the International Conference on Technology Enhanced Learning, Milan, Italia (2004)
7. Mazza, R., Bettoni, M., Faré, M., Mazzola, L.: MOCLog – monitoring online courses with log data. Presented at the 1st Moodle Research Conference, Heraklion, Crete-Greece (2012)

8. Avello-Martínez, R., Fernández-Álvarez, D., Rodríguez, V.G.G.: Moodle Logs Analytics: an open web application to monitor student activity. Univ. Soc. **15**, 715–721 (2023)
9. Dai, Y., Liu, A., Lim, C.P.: Reconceptualizing ChatGPT and generative AI as a student-driven innovation in higher education. Procedia CIRP **119**, 84–90 (2023). https://doi.org/10.1016/j.procir.2023.05.002
10. Susnjak, T.: Beyond predictive learning analytics modelling and onto explainable artificial intelligence with prescriptive analytics and ChatGPT. Int. J. Artif. Intell. Educ. (2023). https://doi.org/10.1007/s40593-023-00336-3
11. Liu, Z.-Q., Tseng, H.-T., Lu, O.H.T.: The feasibility of utilizing ChatGPT in learning analytics for the identification of at-risk students. In: Joint Proceedings of LAK 2024 Workshops. , Kyoto, Japan (2024)
12. Amo-Filva, D., Beby, B.D., Garcia-Penalvo, F.J., Chen, J.: Towards an ethical data literacy proficiency: a Moodle logs analytical tool. In: Villalba-Condori, K.O., et al. (eds.) Proc. - JICV : International Conference on Virtual Campus. Institute of Electrical and Electronics Engineers Inc. (2022). https://doi.org/10.1109/JICV56113.2022.9934790
13. Yan, L., Martinez-Maldonado, R., Gasevic, D.: Generative artificial intelligence in learning analytics: contextualising opportunities and challenges through the learning analytics cycle. In: Proceedings of the 14th Learning Analytics and Knowledge Conference. pp. 101–111. Association for Computing Machinery, New York, NY, USA (2024). https://doi.org/10.1145/3636555.3636856

AI for Vocational Education and Training - Overview of Developments, Foci and Gaps Within 34 German Funding Projects

Insa Reichow(✉), Sheikh Faisal Rashid, and Berit Blanc

Educational Technology Lab, German Research Center for Artificial Intelligence, Alt-Moabit 91c, 10559 Berlin, Germany
insa.reichow@dfki.de

Abstract. This paper provides an overview of the learning technologies developed within the context of the German funding programme "INVITE" in the field of vocational education and training (VET). INVITE, with a budget of 88 million euros over four years, supports 34 multi-stakeholder projects aimed at enhancing digital learning platforms for VET. Based on self-descriptions and websites from these projects, we categorize the technologies developed along four key phases of the learning process. The results highlight the predominance of applications targeting and supporting individual learning processes, such as recommender systems to find matching learning resources, adaptive learning pathways, and virtual learning companions, which aim to tailor educational experiences to individual needs. Additionally, the paper identifies gaps in the current project work, including the need for greater attention to accessibility to diverse learner groups, a focus on educators and facilitating cooperative learning forms. By sharing these insights we seek to contribute to the EU-wide discourse on AI in and for VET. We particularly encourage international collaboration with the objective of advancing the development of knowledge representations for a range of VET domains and standardised certifications. This will enhance the effectiveness and reach of AI-driven VET applications across Europe.

Keywords: vocational education and training · digital learning · recommender systems

1 Introduction

Just like any other educational domain, the field of vocational education and training (VET) sees large advancements in the field of developing and providing digital learning opportunities. The field benefits from various AI-based technologies - both those that have been explicitly designed for learning (e.g. learning platforms or applications) and general-purpose AI applications, such as text-generating systems. Unlike higher education, VET still remains a rather national endeavour, routed in the peculiarities of national education regulations

F. Bellas and O. Fontenla-Romero (Eds.): AIEER 2024, CCIS 2519, pp. 118–128, 2025.
https://doi.org/10.1007/978-3-031-93409-4_11

and cultural conventions and a far lower amount of international publications that introduce new applications and trends (see e.g. [15]). At the same time, the freedom of movement within the EU leads to an increasingly interconnected, permeable labour market. AI-based learning platforms hold immense potential for equipping learners with the necessary skills to work within this dynamic market. We argue that thinking about AI-based education for VET should extend beyond national boundaries and embrace a European perspective. We want to strengthen a EU-wide discussion and share the status quo on AI in VET in Germany - based on insights from a large public funding programme.

1.1 The German Funding Programme "INVITE"

The German Federal Ministry of Education and Research (BMBF) seeks to facilitate the development of an innovative, digital educational space that supports VET and life-long learning. As part of this mission the BMBF is funding 35 projects with a total of 88 million euros between 2021 and 2025 with the contest "Innovationswettbewerb INVITE". The aim of INVITE is the connection and further developing of platforms for VET and the common use of standards, e.g. for metadata or for AI [10]. The German Federal Institute for Vocational Education and Training (BIBB) has been commissioned to provide technical and administrative support for the programme. One of the 35 projects acts as a meta-project ("INVITE-Meta") that seeks to accompany research and community building processes of the 34 developing projects. As part of its monitoring function, INVITE-Meta has an insight into the project developments that will be the focus of this submission.

1.2 Goal of This Contribution

The goal of this contribution is to give a structured overview of the technological developments of the INVITE funding period and its 34 projects. We want to work out what the core foci of these developments are and highlight some of the gaps or blind spots that should be addressed in subsequent projects.

2 Questions and Methods

Research Questions. Central questions this contribution seeks to answer are: (1) Which (AI-based) technology types and applications are developed within the German INVITE programme by the 34 developing projects? And (2) Which foci and gaps can we identify among these project developments?

Data Basis. Recent project self-descriptions (2.5 years into the project), project websites and public sections of the mandatory interim reports from 2023 were viewed to gather type and number of the application types. The findings were coded and re-checked by two authors along a coding scheme.

Projects. The 34 participating projects of the INVITE funding line are all multistakeholder projects with an average of $M = 5.2$ project partners. 16 projects had a specific domain focus (e.g. learning offers in the domain of elderly care), 18 projects were domain-general. For more information on the participating projects see Table 1.

Table 1. Characteristics of the 34 INVITE projects

Number of Projects	34 Multistakeholder projects
Number of Partners	$M = 5.2$; $min = 2$, $max = 10$
Types of Partners	Research centers, universities, industry partners, training providers, platform operators
Domain-Specific Projects	16 projects
Domains-Specific Projects	Social/health/care sector: 5 projects Handicraft: 3 projects Plastics industry: 2 projects Manufacturing/mech. engineering: 2 projects Public transport: 1 project Logistics: 1 project Retail trade: 1 project Energy technology: 1 project
Domain-General Projects	18 projects
Project Focus	Connecting existing platforms: 17 projects Developing single platforms: 17 projects

3 Results

The results will be structured along a phase model of the learning process. A prototypical learning process on a learning platform within VET encompasses four main phases (see Fig. 1, based on [12]). The phases and central technologies are described as part of this results section.

3.1 Phase 1: Training Demands and Resources

The first phase of a VET process is characterised by an analysis of the needs and resources of learners on the one hand and those of companies and training providers on the other. For example, the prior knowledge, motivation and time availability of those interested in VET could be assessed, as well as the budget and specific skills requirements of companies, in order to later identify appropriate learning resources.

The target group of 18 INVITE projects are professionals from the specific domains addressed (e.g. health care; see above), another 15 projects address the

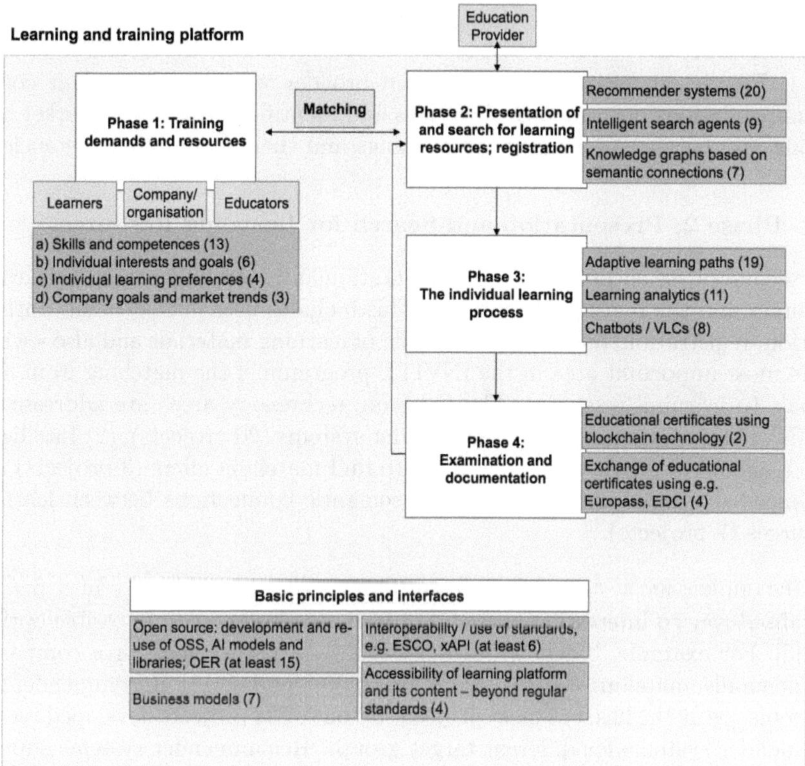

Fig. 1. Results of the analysis are depicted in a phase model of the digital learning process based on [12]. Number of projects (out of 34) with a focus on respective technologies are noted in brackets.

general public interested in VET. 8 projects are additionally aimed at those wishing to change careers and 6 projects each are (also) aimed at managers and continuing education providers. Only 3 projects explicitly focus on VET educators.

The vast majority of projects are dedicated to either searching for and matching suitable VET (22) and/or adapting the learning process to individual needs (17). The main focus is therefore on learners.

Courses and learning paths are recommended based on the assessment of four central parameters: (1) learner skills and competences, (2) learner interests and goals, (3) learning preferences, and (4) company goals and market trends.

(1) Personal and job-related skills, qualifications and competences are most frequently included in the matching process. When assessing prior knowledge and existing competences, 13 projects rely on existing competence models such as ESCO, DQR, EQF, OECD, HQR, EUROPASS and Bloom's Taxonomy.

(2)+(3) In addition to competences, at least 6 projects take into account individual thematic interests and personal and professional goals, and (at least)

4 projects include learning strategy types, preferences and conditions in the matching process.

(4) Finally, at least 3 projects take a broader view and base their course recommendations on company objectives and identified trends and market conditions, e.g. by viewing current job openings and their required competencies.

3.2 Phase 2: Presentation and Search for Learning Resources

The second phase encompasses the presentation and search for available learning resources and the registration process. This includes user management, authentication, registration, and the presentation of learning materials and also - which is the most important area in the INVITE programme: the matching from individuals to learning resources. The following technology areas are addressed in the INVITE programme: (1) Recommender systems (20 projects), (2) Intelligent search agents (9 projects) and chatbots to find matching offers (3 projects) and (3) knowledge representation based on semantic connections between learning resources (7 projects).

(1) Recommender systems are software systems that guide users in a personalised way to interesting or useful objects in a large field of possible options [3]. For example, based on learners' interests, career goals or a company's demands, matching course options are recommended [11]. Recommender systems are at the heart of most projects: 20 out of 34 projects developed recommender systems for different target groups. Recommender systems support users in their selection of suitable continuing education offers. The support is provided in terms of automated recommendations and personalised guidance based on the measurements described in Phase 1 results: learners skills, competences, interests, goals, and learning preferences, and demands of the market. In addition, recommender systems also be used for adaptive or personalised learning by providing adaptive learning paths based on individual learning activity data [11].
(2) Another direction is the implementation of an "intelligent search function" to find suitable learning offers and/or learning resources. 9 INVITE projects developed intelligent search functions in varying contexts. Intelligent search employs both traditional rule-based algorithms and advanced AI methods such as natural language processing and deep learning methods to enable semantic and contextual search. 3 INVITE projects coupled the intelligent search function and recommender systems with chatbots to help users find suitable learning offers or resources. Chatbots not only provide a means of dialogue-based filtering for the content recommendation but they are also used for "light assessments" (low threshold skills tests) by some of the projects.
(3) Knowledge representation and ontologies: An ontology is a machine-readable representation and organisation of knowledge in a domain. Terms, concepts and their relationships are depicted in an ontology. Thereby, relevant information can be structured and used for implementing services on learning

platforms [14]. For example, an ontology of different concepts and learning content in a domain can be used to recommend helpful resources in the learning process. 7 out of 34 INVITE projects developed strategies for representing knowledge in machine-readable form [1]. For example, one of the projects is developing a multimodal knowledge representation, in which semantic relationships are created based on descriptions of courses, topics, and learning material. This machine-readable knowledge representation is crucial for intelligent search and course recommendations.

3.3 Phase 3: The Individual Learning Process

The third phase concerns applications aimed at supporting the individual learning process. Within INVITE there are three main application types that can be assigned to this phase: (1) adaptive learning pathways, (2) learning analytics and (3) virtual learning companions.

(1) Adaptive learning pathways are a central part of adaptive learning systems and aim at the personalisation of learning and adapt e.g. the learning content, the sequence and difficulty of tasks and time of feedback in real time to the users [7]. This is achieved by ongoing analysis of individual learner characteristics (e.g. progress, prior knowledge, learning objectives). Often, adaptive learning systems additionally encourage learners to monitor their learning journeys by providing feedback or visualisations of their progress. In INVITE, 19 of the 34 projects implement adaptive learning pathways to facilitate learning processes tailored to the needs of the learners, e.g. based on individual preferences and prior knowledge.

(2) Learning analytics (LA) refers to the processing and analysis of data produced implicitly or explicitly by learners (e.g. click behaviour on learning platforms). The aim is to measure, present and predict learning progress and learning behaviour in order to optimise digital learning processes [4]. LA is based on large amounts of data and statistical or algorithmic methods to analyse them. In INVITE, 11 of the 34 projects employ LA on their platforms, to adapt the learning process to the learner, e.g. by evaluating the cognitive and emotional strain on the learner. One project uses LA across different learning platforms to ensure that all available data on a learner is used.

(3) Chatbots and virtual learning companions (VLC) support learners during their learning processes [8,16]. They can fulfil a range of didactic functions, such as conveying learning content or strategies, learning in a dialogical or playful way, supporting time management, motivating or providing emotional support. VLCs communicate with learners in dialogue, either text-based (in the form of chatbots) or voice-based (such as Alexa or Siri). They are designed to appear human and support learners in a friendly, interactive way. Chatbots and VLCs were implemented by 8 INVITE projects. The advances in the field of large language models (LLM) influenced the set-up and functionality of the chatbots. Most projects used LLM-based

chatbots, which, in contrast to traditional chatbots, allow a higher degree of personalisation and the simple re-use of user interactions for other courses (new dialogue trees do not have to be created). The majority of chatbots is used to support the search for matching learning resource, e.g. by asking for interests, specific constraints and including light assessments on prior knowledge. Chatbots are seen as a way of providing better matches and improving the usability of the learning platforms. 2 projects additionally use chatbots during the learning process. Learners can use these chatbots to ask content-related or administrative questions. 1 project has an explicit focus on the development of a friendly and helpful VLC, depicted by an avatar. The VLC can create quiz questions, provide individual feedback on the answers and strengthen the overall motivation in self-regulated learning processes.

While almost all projects aim at supporting, self-regulated, individual learning processes, 4 projects have a focus on facilitating cooperative learning processes. 1 project e.g. implements a module that supports finding a peer and then guides the learning process in such a way that cooperative and learning-effective activities are carried out, e.g. peers providing each other with feedback on a task.

An additional measure to make the learning process more interactive is to integrate game-based learning. 1 project specifically focuses serious games for VET and at least 3 other projects employ gamification elements to motivate learners. Additionally, there is 1 project that uses virtual reality to facilitate interactive learning experiences.

3.4 Phase 4: Examination and Documentation

The fourth phase includes all processes and applications related to the assessment and documentation of learning outcomes, e.g. assessments and the issuing of digital educational certificates. Machine-readable, standardised and comparable educational certificates for VET aim at improving comparability and interoperability between different educational sectors [2]. A standardized way for creating digital educational certificates would contribute to the connectivity and interoperability of digital platforms - a key objective of INVITE. Nevertheless, only 4 INVITE projects use standards such as EUROPASS and EDCI to exchange digital educational certificates. For these projects, offering forgery-proof and identity-proof certificates is a main focus supported by the use of distributed ledger technology. Some projects also work on the integration of open educational certificates like open badges.

3.5 Overarching Aspects

Additionally, there are some overarching, fundamental principles such as interoperability and accessibility that need to be considered when designing digital learning platforms. Due to the set-up of the funding line, the INVITE projects have an emphasis on interoperability and the use of standards. Other important issues concern using and offering open source applications and models, ensuring a high level of accessibility and developing sustainable business models such that project outcomes can proliferate after the funding period ends. In particular, finding solutions for the sustainable operation of the learning platforms and applications developed, and accessibility are issues that affect all projects. Some projects have devoted distinct working packages to these aspects:

Interoperability and use of standards: Interoperability is of crucial importance, for example, to exchange learning resources, data on learning activities and smart functions between different learning applications. This is facilitated by the use of standards, e.g. the ESCO standard to describe competences and learning resources (at least 7 projects; see also [5]) or standards to exchange content like xAPI (6 projects).

Open Source: 15 projects explicitly focus on the development and re-usage of open source software and AI models and libraries. 3 projects focus on the development and use of Open Educational Resources (OER), e.g. in the domain of care.

Accessibility: Accessibility refers to the design and development of educational technologies that are inclusive and usable by all individuals, regardless of their physical, cognitive, or socio-economic backgrounds. This includes ensuring that platforms are compatible with assistive technologies, providing content in multiple formats (e.g., text, audio, video), and designing intuitive interfaces that accommodate users with disabilities. 4 projects have an explicit focus on the accessibility of their learning platform and its content - beyond regular standards.

Business models: A difficulty in public funded projects is the need to develop a business model that allows to sustainably continue to offer and refine the developed services after the funding period ends. 7 projects have an explicit focus on this and systematically seek possible solutions (e.g. licenses) for this problem.

4 Discussion

The INVITE funding line supports 34 projects, that develop diverse learning technologies and applications for a range of learning contexts and subject domains of VET. Overall, the analysis shows that different AI methods can be used to support various didactical functions along the whole learning process. The most important foci and gaps of the work performed in the INVITE projects include:

Most of the INVITE projects aim their services at learners, however barely at educators. A mere 3 projects are oriented towards educators. These include training programmes designed to enhance digital competencies and the development of modular toolkits that empower educators to construct their own instructional materials. Nevertheless, increasingly powerful adaptive learning platforms will undoubtedly have an impact on the role of educators in the field of VET. The question of how educators might use AI to augment their tasks and the preparation required for this is yet to be thoroughly discussed (see e.g. [9]).

Among the projects there is a gap concerning granting accessibility for individuals with disabilities or specific target groups. Nearly all of the learning applications developed thus far are primarily designed for able-bodied learners with a strong proficiency in the German language. To effectively serve the diverse learner groups present in VET, greater effort must be dedicated to developing these learning opportunities. This gap highlights that we are still in the early stages of this endeavor. Designing digital learning platforms that effectively serve able learners is challenging in itself, and addressing the needs of a broader range of learners requires even more focused attention and innovation.

A number of different recommender systems have been developed to ensure that learners find appropriate learning opportunities. There is however a lack of generic recommender systems that function also across platforms, e.g. to integrate resources from different learning platforms to build individual learning pathes. Also, the design of machine-readable knowledge, e.g. in the form of ontologies, is still in its infancy and will require more resources and time to enable a wider range of functionalities.

Phase 3 was concerned with technologies aimed at the learning process itself. Most of the applications developed aim to improve individualised, interactive and thus motivating learning experiences through various measures to increase participation in further education. Most of the learning focused on in the participating projects is individual, self-directed learning. Facilitating cooperative learning remains a gap - only one project seeks to find ways of promoting computer-supported collaborative learning which might be a promising direction for VET [13].

Further general observations of the project developments include a growing number of AI-based support functions. Due to the advances in the field of LLMs, new and "unplanned" functions were integrated, e.g. the LLM-based enrichment of course descriptions with metadata [6].

Additionally, almost all projects focus on formal learning contexts, but barely on informal learning (only 4 projects) and learning at the work place. Another observation that became apparent in the course of developments, especially during INVITE-Meta's accompanying workshops and network events, is the importance of an interdisciplinary discourse. To develop meaningful learning opportunities didactical theories (e.g. on types of meaningful feedback) or competence models need to be made machine-readable.

To gather the work foci of the 34 projects, we analysed official documentations of the projects. However, these documents do not capture everything that was worked on. From informal conversations, we know there are many more sub-areas addressed in the projects that are not yet captured by official documentation and thus did not make its way into this paper. In addition, we accessed only self-reported data, which may have introduced a bias towards presenting the project in a more favourable light. We should also mention that although the INVITE programme includes lots of important stakeholders, such as large training providers and well-known research institutes, it is however not representative of the whole learning technology landscape in VET in Germany.

To conclude, we think this paper gives a good account of the recent developments on AI in VET in Germany. The projects' developments indicate the potential future direction of this field, while also underscoring that we are still in the early stages. The work provides a glimpse into what is likely to become standard practice in the coming years: learning and working in person will be enriched by personalised digital learning pathways for numerous VET domains and learners.

To present the work that is being conducted at the national level is a crucial step in strengthening the international discourse on the utilisation of AI for VET and facilitate international collaboration. It would be advantageous for the field to benefit from mutual developments, for example, the implementation of internationally accepted competence models (such as ESCO) and the respective standardised certifications that are accepted EU-wide. Another potential benefit of international collaboration is the development of ontologies for the various subject areas of VET. This could facilitate the creation of ontology-based adaptive learning pathways, which could then be adapted to suit national contexts if necessary. We hope that this publication will contribute to such an EU-wide discourse on AI for VET.

Acknowledgments. This study was funded by the German Federal Ministry of Education and Research (grant number: 21INVI1703).

Disclosure of Interests. The authors declare no conflict of interest.

References

1. Abu-Rasheed, H., Dornhöfer, M., Weber, C., Kismihók, G., Buchmann, U., Fathi, M.: Building contextual knowledge graphs for personalized learning recommendations using text mining and semantic graph completion. In: 2023 IEEE International Conference on Advanced Learning Technologies (ICALT), pp. 36–40. IEEE (2023). https://doi.org/10.1109/ICALT58122.2023.00016
2. Camilleri, A., Muramatsu, B., Schmidt, P.: Credentials to employment: the last mile (2022). https://digitalcredentials.mit.edu/docs/Credentials-to-Employment-The-Last-Mile.pdf
3. Drachsler, H., Verbert, K., Santos, O.C., Manouselis, N.: Panorama of recommender systems to support learning. In: Ricci, F., Rokach, L., Shapira, B. (eds.) Recommender Systems Handbook, pp. 421–451. Springer, Boston, MA (2015). https://doi.org/10.1007/978-1-4899-7637-6_12
4. Gedrimiene, E., Silvola, A., Pursiainen, J., Rusanen, J., Muukkonen, H.: Learning analytics in education: literature review and case examples from vocational education. Scand. J. Educ. Res. **64**(7), 1105–1119 (2020). https://doi.org/10.1080/00313831.2019.1649718
5. Goertz, L., Rashid, S.F., Vogel-Adham, E., Vogt, A., Wilhelm-Weidner, A.: Metadata standards in the German funding program "Innovationswettbewerb INVITE". Which standards are used for which purpose? mmb Institut GmbH, Essen (2023). https://doi.org/10.25656/01:27697

6. Hübsch, T., Vogel-Adham, E., Vogt, A., Wilhelm-Weidner, A.: Articulating tomorrow: large language models in the service of professional training. A contribution by the Digitalbegleitung (technological monitoring and research) within the framework of the German funding program “Innovationswettbewerb INVITE”. VDI/VDE Innovation + Technik GmbH, Berlin (2024). https://doi.org/10.25656/01:29036
7. Kabudi, T., Pappas, I., Olsen, D.: Ai-enabled adaptive learning systems: a systematic mapping of the literature. Comput. Educ.: Artif. Intell. (CAEAI) **2**(12) (2021). https://doi.org/10.1016/j.caeai.2021.100017
8. Khosrawi-Rad, B., Schlimbach, R., Strohmann, T., Robra-Bissantz, S.: Design knowledge for virtual learning companions. In: Proceedings of the 2022 AIS SIGED International Conference on Information Systems Education and Research (2022). https://aisel.aisnet.org/siged2022/6
9. Molenaar, I.: Towards hybrid human-AI learning technologies. Eur. J. Educ. **57**(4), 632–645 (2022). https://doi.org/10.1111/ejed.12527
10. Rashid, S.F., Reichow, I., Blanc, B.: Standards für Künstliche Intelligenz im Bildungsbereich. Ein Dossier im Rahmen des INVITE-Wettbewerbs. Deutsches Forschungszentrum für Künstliche Intelligenz, Berlin (2023). https://doi.org/10.25656/01:26921
11. Reichow, I., Buntins, K., Paaßen, B., Abu-Rasheed, H., Weber, C., Dornhöfer, M.: Recommendersysteme in der beruflichen Weiterbildung. Grundlagen, Herausforderungen und Handlungsempfehlungen. Ein Dossier im Rahmen des INVITE-Wettbewerbs. Deutsches Forschungszentrum für Künstliche Intelligenz, Berlin (2022). https://doi.org/10.25656/01:24517
12. Reichow, I., Hochbauer, M., Goertz, L.: Standards und Empfehlungen zur Umsetzung digitaler Weiterbildungsplattformen in der beruflichen Bildung: ein Dossier im Rahmen des INVITE-Wettbewerbs. Bundesinstitut für Berufsbildung, Bonn (2021). https://lit.bibb.de/vufind/Record/DS-779586
13. Schwendimann, B.A., de Wever, B., Hämäläinen, R., Cattaneo, A.A.P.: CSCL and vocational education: a bond worthy of investigation? In: Smith, B.K., Borge, M., Mercier, E., Yon, K.Y.K. (eds.) Making a Difference: Prioritizing Equity and Access in CSCL, pp. 557–560. International Society of the Learning Sciences, Philadelphia (2017). https://repository.isls.org/handle/1/282
14. Villegas-Ch, W., García-Ortiz, J.: Enhancing learning personalization in educational environments through ontology-based knowledge representation. Computers **12**(10), 199 (2023). https://doi.org/10.3390/computers12100199
15. Windelband, L.: Artificial intelligence and assistance systems for technical vocational education and training – opportunities and risks. In: Shajek, A., Hartmann, E. (eds.) New Digital Work, pp. 195–213. Springer, Cham (2023). https://doi.org/10.1007/978-3-031-26490-0_12
16. Wollny, S., Schneider, J., Di Mitri, D., Weidlich, J., Rittberger, M., Drachsler, H.: Are we there yet? A systematic literature review on chatbots in education. Front. Artif. Intell. **4**, 654924 (2021). https://doi.org/10.3389/frai.2021.654924

VET Teacher Training for AI in Specific Sectors in Spain

Fátima María García Doval(✉) and María Concepción Fernández Munín

Consellería de Educación, Universidades y Formación Profesional. Xunta de Galicia, San Caetano, Ciencia s/n 15781, Santiago de Compostela, Spain
fmgdoval@edu.xunta.gal

Abstract. The purpose of this paper is to discuss the lack of functional AI knowledge in both, students who have undergone a basic level VET cycle in Spain without completing compulsory secondary education, as well as those who have studied an intermediate level cycle, the majority of whom have not completed baccalaureate studies. It also puts forward the lack of digital competence in AI and the complete absence of initial VET teacher training on the subject, particularly for those who have not undergone university degrees. As a result of this situation almost a fifth of the professionals accessing labor force in the near future in Spain will be AI illiterates and poor AI users in industrial and business environments. We draw awareness of the urgent need to tackle both problems by designing specific programs for students during their VET cycles but, also, for teachers during their compulsory initial teaching and education training.

Keywords: Vocational training · Artificial intelligence · education

1 Introduction

When we think of the impact of AI (Artificial Intelligence) on the educational area, and therefore on the professional world, we often focus our attention on university students, as they are the future high-level specialists accessing labor market. Although university curricula are not renewed and updated quickly, especially in technical branches, where degree programs are already designed with maximum flexibility to accommodate innovations, the development of basic competences in the use of intelligent systems for professional practice has been progressively introduced in recent years, with better or worse fortune, all things considered. This means that, for university graduates we might expect some AI basic knowledge and even the development of initial competences on the matter.

Moreover, the vast majority of Spanish university students have gone through compulsory secondary education and a baccalaureate with updated curricula that include various approaches to AI, however imperfect they may be. All of them are based on the European framework for digital competences in education, DigCompEdu [1], which reflects the challenges, potentials and threats of intelligent systems. In many cases,

F. Bellas and O. Fontenla-Romero (Eds.): AIEER 2024, CCIS 2519, pp. 129–135, 2025.
https://doi.org/10.1007/978-3-031-93409-4_12

specific subjects have been developed and, in others, the training is included in a cross-curricular manner, with a special emphasis in the contents of various technological areas of the compulsory and upper secondary education.

In contrast, the attention required by vocational training students in this respect has always been comparatively modest. The educational provision of vocational training in Spain is governed by a basic state regulation, which takes its fundamental precepts from the European Qualifications Framework [2]. This basic ruling is then particularized by each region, with minor adjustments to their context. Thus, nationwide three training levels are offered [3]:

1. Basic level cycles: aimed at students at risk of dropping out of school before completing compulsory secondary education.
2. Intermediate level cycles: for students who have completed either a basic level cycle or compulsory secondary education.
3. Higher level cycles: for students who have completed either an intermediate level cycle or baccalaureate.

In addition, specialization courses are offered to complete this training. These are aimed to provide some specialization either for intermediate or higher level cycle graduates.

2 AI Competence in Basic and Intermediate Level VET Cycles

It is, somehow, surprising to see the lack of attention paid in education policies to the AI training of those students following a basic or intermediate cycle. The vast majority of these students have not completed the baccalaureate and sometimes not even compulsory secondary education in its entirety. Therefore, they have been deprived of access to the entry level training in digital competences for the use of AI, which we tend to judge as universal.

Specifically, in Spain in the academic year 2022/2023, there were 78.674 students [4] in Basic Vocational Training, which means that they did not complete part of Compulsory Secondary Education. For many of them, there will be no further training in the education system, others will continue their pathway in intermediate and higher cycles. As far as intermediate cycles are concerned, in the aforementioned academic year, there were 436.438 students [4], an overwhelming majority of whom did not come from or go to baccalaureate studies.

It is also important to note that many of these pupils belong to a medium-low socio-economic level, which means that they are likely to have very limited non-formal and informal opportunities to acquire these competences outside schooling.

Finally, it should be noted that in vocational training in Spain among the professional families available, there is no-one dedicated to AI, and that the only possible training in this matter is to complete a specialization courses in AI and Big Data for qualified technicians (Computer systems, Web and multiplatform applications, Telecommunications or Mechatronics, automation and industrial robotics).

If we take into account that in Spain in the 2022/2023 academic year there were 1,353,347 students [5] at university level and 1,080,963 students in the various levels of

VET [4] (of which almost half a million have not completed the Baccalaureate and some have not completed the last years of Compulsory Secondary Education), we can get an idea of the magnitude of the issue. Around half a million students, just over 20% of all future professionals in a country like Spain, depend almost entirely on the teachers of their vocational modules to acquire basic digital competences in AI before entering the labor market.

3 Target Group of Affected Teachers

Ilkka Tuomi, in his publication The Impact of Artificial Intelligence on Learning, Teaching, and Education [6], highlights the potential impact of AI for learning, teaching and education, defining it as the next "electricity"; with a gradual transformative impact, where society will reinvent itself in the use of new technologies, especially in the world of education. In fact, the term "Fourth Industrial Revolution" (also "4IR" or "Industry 4.0") has been recently coined to refer to the deep industrial changes that come from extreme digitalization and automation, particularly from high-tech cutting-edge technologies [7] such as AI, Virtual Reality (VR), big data processing, etc.

All those professionals previously mentioned will have contact with smart technologies through digital tools and any VET student will be affected by the use of AI in their different jobs. Big changes are foreseen in the human-machine relationship where experiential knowledge will be successful if professionals are sufficiently qualified and can implement their new knowledge in their daily work.

In order to provide the teaching foreseen in the different levels mentioned in the previous section, Spain currently has professionals assigned mainly to two different professional categories [8]: secondary education teachers and teachers specialized in specific sectors of Vocational Training. Of all the professionals with teaching responsibilities in Vocational Education and Training, these are the only ones who have a specific training requirements for teaching at ordinary education levels.

The former are teachers who have completed a university degree, followed by the corresponding qualifying master's degree. The latter are those who teach applied and practical modules that do not have a directly related university degree and who, therefore, enter the teaching profession from a higher cycle. This is the case of car mechanics, metallic construction workers, carpenters, cooks, hairdressers and make-up artist, among others. These teachers must have the pedagogical and didactic training equivalent to a master's degree for teaching purposes.

In Table 1, it can be seen, side by side, a comparison [9, 10] of both, the qualifying master's degree and the equivalent course for those with a higher level cycle in the above-mentioned VET areas.

In both trainings we can observe three similar modules but differing in their content, duration and certification in hours. None of the modules is linked to AI and human-computer interaction, their possibilities and challenges, their risks, ethical implications or any other current issue that we regard urgent to address. In fact, neither the master's degree nor the equivalent course include any clear specific mention to technology applied to the future professional; not even to it as a pedagogical resource to deploy in the classroom.

Table 1. Comparison of the training modules in secondary and other initial VET teacher training courses.

Teachers specialized in specific sectors of vocational training	Secondary education teachers
Generic (10–16 ECTS) Learning and personality development Educational processes and contexts Society, family and education	**Generic (12 ECTS)** Learning and personality development Educational processes and contexts Society, family and education
Specific (15 a 22 ECTS) Vocational Orientation Learning and teaching (subject) Teaching innovation and initiation to educational research	**Specific (24 ECTS)** Complements for disciplinary training Learning and teaching (subject) Teaching innovation and initiation to educational research
Practicum (15 a 22 ECTS) Practicum of the specialty End-of-Studies Final Project	**Practicum (16 ECTS)** Practicum of the specialty End-of-Studies Final Project

As it is easy to see, in the not so distant future, AI will affect a large number of jobs that have never received specific and basic training, such as for example, personal image and hairdressing, transport and vehicle maintenance, design and graphic arts. hospitality, etc.

All of them need basic working knowledge of AI, not in mastering programming or system administration skills, but in adequate, relevant, effective and ethical use of software and tools that can use AI. This would be the case, for example, of the popular simulators for testing different make-ups on customers' faces or tools and apps capable of changing the color and hairstyle of clients.

In other words, they all need to develop digital compentences directly related to AI and its use in their area of expertise from a practical point of view. This includes skills but also conceptual knowledge and, what is most important and frequently overseen, a set of values and ethical references.

4 Challenges in Initial Teacher Training

In view of this situation, we now explore the position of political stakeholders and administrations in Spain, always bearing in mind SDG 4 [11]. Europe recommends the local development of intelligent technologies in the field of education, promoting innovation and encouraging synergies with research groups with a future focused on the human being, not on technology. The human being must always be the axis of technological development from which the whole fabric of learning is articulated. In this line, there is a UNESCO recommendation to create adequate resources for target groups to strengthen the progress of AI that could be applied in Spain [12, 13].

In the definition of the target groups for AI training, both from an official perspective and in practice, as we have mentioned, secondary education students are clearly identified, both at compulsory and baccalaureate level, and it is hoped that, in some way, the university will also respond to the professional needs in the use of AI through its programs.

Continuing vocational training is also the subject of attention in terms of concerns about the introduction of AI. However, initial vocational training is not as much of a focus as it should be, especially in the case of basic and intermediate training cycles, taking into account the possibility that a significant number of the students who attend them have not completed the compulsory secondary education that lays the foundations for training in and for AI.

The worst situation, though, is that of the students in the professional families taught by teachers specialized in specific sectors, being those:

1. Cookery and Patisserie.
2. Hairdressing and personal image.
3. Carpentry and furniture manufacture and installation.
4. Vehicle maintenance.
5. Machining and machine maintenance.
6. Pattern making and dressmaking.
7. Graphic arts production.
8. Hospitality and catering services.
9. Welding.

Above all, in this work we would like to draw attention to the significant challenge of the training of such who, neither in their professional studies nor in their initial teacher training, have received dedicated instruction in this respect and who will be responsible for educating students who lack the slightest basis in all aspects of AI due to their own academic background.

So, this professional group should be of special interest in AI education and training for use in professional environments and, therefore, specific initial and continuous training programs should be designed to provide them with the pedagogical and didactical, but also ethical and regulatory tools that will enable them to teach from, by and for a professional environment that already makes extensive use of intelligent systems. We must bear in mind that initial teacher training is the appropriate moment to provide them with the key aspects and competences they will need to pass onto students because it is the only dedicated compulsory training they all must accredit before entering the classrooms.

It should also be pointed out that these sectors are key due to their massive social presence, which makes them a huge weak flank in protecting citizens from inappropriate or abusive uses of AI. These are also the sectors that are not of public concern when thinking about AI risks. Anybody can see the importance of training sanitary workers on AI ethics forgetting that a humble hairdresser might accidentally feed an AI with hundreds of even thousands of faces by using insecure systems. A graphic arts producer must incidentally give away the art of his clients by using enhancement software that do not comply with author's rights. Or, the car mechanic might pose a risk by confidently installing assistive AI software in a car without the owner knowing or consenting, thus tracking detailed information of their whereabouts.

In contrast to specific AI training programs for professionals in IT systems management or telecommunications, we put forward the need to develop programs aimed at these unique sectors, with special emphasis on the teachers who provide this training.

5 Future Perspectives and Conclusions

The 18th century Scottish philosopher Thomas Reid said that a chain is only as strong as its weakest link. And our weakest social link may be the one that is most ubiquitous and that, unfortunately, we are forgetting.

In this brief presentation we have aimed to determine that there is a large pool of low and mid-level technical professionals who do not have any public access to training in an area as important and demanded as artificial intelligence. The OECD (Organization for Economic Co-operation and Development) highlights in its publication Opportunities and drawbacks of using artificial intelligence for training [14] that AI will be a great catalyst for training, especially in underrepresented groups, reducing barriers and increasing motivation to learn and train.

It would be advisable to design, pilot and evaluate a master plan for the use of AI in Vocational Education and Training, which can fully guarantee the inclusive and equitable use of AI in this education area.

Such plan should involve a greater incidence in sectors that have so far been neglected, most of them invisible everyday workers that do not come to mind when thinking of the use of AI. It should start at the university level, within the required initial teacher training but, because of the slow pace in implementing changes in university curricula and, also, because of the rapid changes this domain experiments, parallel in-service training should be also put into practice as an urgent issue.

This AI training should be explicit and contextualized in the vocational area of interest, as an opportunity to boost the employability of VET graduates and their job mobility (either necessity or desire driven). But, also, it should include specific content and AI as a pedagogical resource from a deontological perspective. Aspects related to human-computer interaction (HCI), ethics, data protection, user experience (UX) and computing thinking, should be the fundamentals of this dedicated training. This does not necessarily mean a specific module should be designed. This training might well be transdisciplinary and cross-curricular yet explicit and deliberate.

We certainly need AI-trained computer system experts, laboratory technicians and industrial refrigeration experts. But, above all, we want make-up and hairdressing experts who know how to make ethical and responsible use of our personal image, clothing or cooking professionals who know how to use our body measures, allergies and other health data without exposing us, or mechanics who know the limits of AI access to our vehicles (and therefore to a myriad of personal data).

A secure use of data and a solid transparency of the system that is able to promote the development of skills for the improvement of professional life in the above-mentioned fields should always be valued and kept in mind.

Acknowledgements. We would like to thank the referees for their comments, which helped improve this paper considerably.

References

1. European Commission Homepage: Digital Competence Framework for Educators (DigCompEdu). https://joint-research-centre.ec.europa.eu/digcompedu_en. Accessed 1 Nov 2024
2. Comisión Europea: Marco Europeo de las Cualificaciones, Oficina de Publicaciones de la Unión Europea, Luxemburgo (2019). https://europass.europa.eu/system/files/2020-05/EQF%20Brochure-ES.pdf
3. Consellería de Educación: Ciencia, Formación Profesional y Universidades (Xunta de Galicia) Homepage, Normativa. https://www.edu.xunta.gal/fp/normativa. Accessed 1 Nov 2024
4. Ministerio de Educación: Formación Profesional y Deportes (Gobierno de España) Homepage, Estadística del alumnado de Formación Profesional. Curso 2022–2023. https://www.educacionfpydeportes.gob.es/dam/jcr:153d5f6f-9091-405b-a493-cb2c5a3b7fe8/nota-2022-2023.pdf Accessed 30 Oct 2024
5. Ministerio de Ciencia: Innovación y Universidades (Gobierno de España) Homepage: Catálogo de datos. Estadística de estudiantes. Número de estudiantes en las universidades españolas. https://www.universidades.gob.es/estadistica-de-estudiantes/. Accessed 30 Oct 2024
6. Tuomi, I.: The impact of artificial intelligence on learning, teaching, and education. In: Cabrera Giraldez, M., Vuorikari, M., Punie,Y. (eds.) Publications Office of the European Union, Luxembourg (2018). https://publications.jrc.ec.europa.eu/repository/handle/JRC113226
7. Schwab, K.: The fourth industrial revolution, World Economic Forum, Geneva (2016). https://law.unimelb.edu.au/__data/assets/pdf_file/0005/3385454/Schwab-The_Fourth_Industrial_Revolution_Klaus_S.pdf
8. Ministerio de Educación: Formación Profesional y Deportes (Gobierno de España) Homepage, TodoFP. Acceso a la función docente. https://todofp.es/comunidad-docente/acceso-funcion-publica-docente.html#cla-0-05. Accessed 30 Oct 2024
9. Orden EDU/2645/2011: de 23 de septiembre, por la que se establece la formación equivalente a la formación pedagógica y didáctica exigida para aquellas personas que estando en posesión de una titulación declarada equivalente a efectos de docencia no pueden realizar los estudios de máster. https://www.boe.es/buscar/act.php?id=BOE-A-2011-15628
10. Orden ECI/3858/2007: de 27 de diciembre, por la que se establecen los requisitos para la verificación de los títulos universitarios oficiales que habiliten para el ejercicio de las profesiones de Profesor de Educación Secundaria Obligatoria y Bachillerato, Formación Profesional y Enseñanzas de Idiomas. https://www.boe.es/buscar/pdf/2007/BOE-A-2007-22450-consolidado.pdf
11. Miao, F., Holmes, W., Huang, X., Zhang, H.: Inteligencia artificial y educación: guía para las personas a cargo de formular políticas, UNESCO, Paris (2021). https://unesdoc.unesco.org/ark:/48223/pf0000379376
12. OECD: Governing with Artificial Intelligence: Are governments ready? OECD Artificial Intelligence Papers, 20, Paris (2024). https://doi.org/10.1787/26324bc2-en
13. Prud'homme, B., Régis, C., Farnadi, G., Dreier, V., Rubel, S. D'Oultremont, C.: Missing links in AI governance, UNESCO, Paris (2023). https://unesdoc.unesco.org/ark:/48223/pf0000384787
14. Verhagen, A.: Opportunities and drawbacks of using artificial intelligence for training, OECD Social, Employment and Migration Working Papers, 266, Paris (2021) https://doi.org/10.1787/22729bd6-en

Personalized Learning of Programming Fundamentals Through Robotic Simulations

Antonio Leis(✉), Alma Mallo, Sara Guerreiro-Santalla, Alejandro Paz-López, and Francisco Bellas

GII, CITIC Research Center, University of A Coruña, A Coruña, Spain
{antonio.leis,alma.mallo,sara.guerreiro,alejandro.paz.lopez, francisco.bellas}@udc.es

Abstract. Personalized learning is one of the main targets of the Artificial Intelligence in Education (AIEd) community. The potentiality of Artificial Intelligence (AI) techniques in student profiling could be very beneficial to support teachers when using technology in their classes. This way, each student could follow a learning path adapted to his/her progress, allowing the teacher to focus on those who require special attention. The current work is focused on this scope, and it presents the initial version of ProgTutor, an intelligent tutoring system designed to teach fundamental programming principles to high school and university students in a personalized manner. ProgTutor employs an interactive educational approach focused on solving realistic challenges with the assistance of a robot. The system uses a 3D simulator developed in Unity to take full advantage of the motivational and customization capabilities that this interface offers students. The current paper focuses on the conceptual and functional design of ProgTutor, presenting initial application results with high school students, and some interesting conclusions obtained from the teachers.

Keywords: Personalized learning · Intelligent Tutoring System · Autonomous robotics · User profiling

1 Introduction

An Intelligent Tutoring System (ITS) is a software tool designed to provide immediate and personalized content, instructions, and feedback to students without requiring human teacher intervention [9]. An ITS can employ various computational techniques for personalized teaching, ranging from simple rules derived from expert teachers to machine learning models trained on large datasets from real interactions, as is the case of this study.

The ITS presented in this work is called ProgTutor, aimed at providing personalized instruction on the fundamentals of computer programming to high school and university students. ProgTutor follows a hands-on educational approach focused on solving realistic challenges with the assistance of a robot. This

F. Bellas and O. Fontenla-Romero (Eds.): AIEER 2024, CCIS 2519, pp. 136–148, 2025.
https://doi.org/10.1007/978-3-031-93409-4_13

approach emphasizes not only problem analysis, algorithm creation, and coding stages but particularly the final validation stage in practical scenarios. To achieve this goal, challenges are addressed within a robotic simulator created using the Unity game development tool [18], exploiting its capabilities for motivating and customizing the learning experience for students.

Most ITSs for teaching programming have been proposed in the context of university courses and typically address a limited number of concepts [4]. Some focus only on programming tasks, while others include multiple-choice questions and planning exercises. The personalized tutoring process can generally be categorized into two main areas: providing feedback on students' produced programs, suggestions for the next steps, and debugging assistance [16], as well as offering customized task programming, resource allocation, and methods for visualizing learning progress and next steps.

In this context, notable work includes the Bayesian Intelligent Tutorial System based on Games (OGITS) presented by Hooshyar et al. [6], aimed at enhancing programming skills and online information search through board games. Another relevant study is by Wang et al. [20], proposing an ITS based on the classical Knowledge Tracing (KT) model. Regarding ITSs specifically focused on robotic programming, similar works are rare. There are various approaches utilizing robots as tutors in education, categorized under Intelligent Tutoring Robots (ITR) [12,21]. ,arily utilize real robots as interfaces with students, involving considerations beyond the scope of this project.

Conversely, in educational contexts utilizing robotic simulation environments, several initiatives stand out. Constructsim [17] offers materials and exercises with online simulations targeting experienced robotics developers and graduate students. Blockly Games [2] provides a simple graphical programming environment aimed at teaching programming, including the option to use robots. Coderz [3] and OpenRoberta [11] offer straightforward graphical programming environments for programming the behavior of real and simulated robots in 2D or 3D. Robotbenchmark [15] provides interactive challenges with realistic 3D robot simulations for students to solve by programming robot behavior in Python. While these initiatives combine programming and robotic simulations, none integrate an ITS for autonomous learning.

The following sections will elaborate on the conceptual and functional design of the initial version of ProgTutor. This version was developed to collect real data using a simple exercise difficulty adaptation rule, which will subsequently inform the development of models for more personalized teaching in a future iteration of ProgTutor. Data collection was conducted over an entire academic year with two groups of first-year high school students, focusing on their interaction with the tool during program execution and their acquired programming knowledge.

2 The ProgTutor ITS

ProgTutor utilizes the educational robot Robobo [1] as a fundamental tool to achieve the practical programming approach it aims for. This robot consists of a mobile base with a smartphone attachment, providing advanced technological capabilities such as a camera, microphone, speaker, touchscreen display, and a powerful CPU. ProgTutor is specifically designed for learning programming through the Python language, currently the most popular for various professional and educational developments. Robobo supports a Python library and tailored documentation for easy adoption. It's important to note that in ProgTutor, students do not program the real robot directly; instead, they use the proprietary 3D simulator RoboboSim [14], developed in Unity, as the main interface.

2.1 Conceptual Architecture

ProgTutor has been designed following the classical architecture of ITS [5], based on 4 modules or components, depicted in pink in Fig. 1: Interface, Tutor, Student, and Domain. Additionally, there are 5 other components (shown in black in the figure) that provide basic functionalities to these modules. Figure 1 also includes a series of arrows indicating relationships between elements.

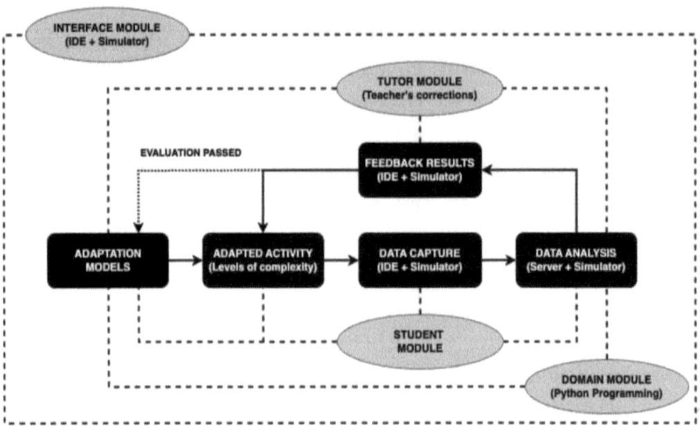

Fig. 1. ProgTutor flowchart and basic building blocks

Starting with the Domain Module, it encompasses specific knowledge about Python programming intended to be to be covered through the tool. In this initial version of ProgTutor, theoretical knowledge about the language is not included but provided externally as documentation; instead, the module focuses on programming exercises. Specifically, it contains exercise statements organized into thematic blocks (detailed in Sect. 3) and difficulty levels. Initially, 3 levels have been established, with Level 1 being the simplest and Level 3 the most complex. It is crucial to note that ProgTutor aims to teach the fundamentals of Python programming assuming no prior knowledge in this subject.

Moving on to the Interface Module, it connects students bidirectionally with the tutoring system. In ProgTutor, this module consists of two independent tools: the Integrated Development Environment (IDE) Visual Studio Code (VSC) [19],

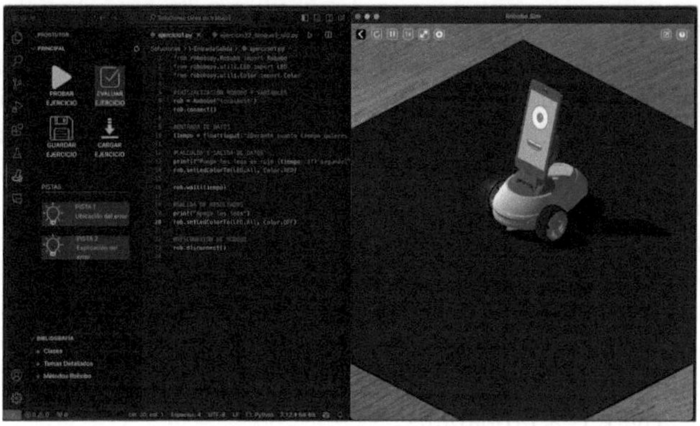

Fig. 2. Left: VSC extension for ProgTutor. Right: RoboboSim simulator

where students write their programs, and the 3D simulator RoboboSim in which they test them, as shown in Fig. 2.

In the case of VSC (Fig. 2, left), a specific extension has been created containing the following functionalities: (1) MAIN: this section includes buttons to test the exercise, evaluate it, save it and load the latest version. As will be explained in the following sections, these functionalities are necessary to be able to manage the interaction flow through the database that stores the interactions; (2) HINTS: provides feedback on errors in the student's code, which are displayed above the line with the error. The texts used contain simplified explanations of those provided by the Python interpreter, and translated into Spanish in order to facilitate understanding in the initial stages of learning; (3) BIBLIOGRAPHY: includes access to the documentation of the Python methods associated with the specific exercise, Jupyter notebooks with an introduction to each thematic block, as well as the documentation of the Robobo library; (4) TEACHER: contains only a button for the teacher to indicate whether he/she has actively helped the student with the exercise.

On the other hand, RoboboSim has been developed in Unity (Fig. 2, right), taking advantage of all functionalities and flexibility typical of video game interfaces. This setup serves as the primary element to enhance student attention and motivation. Within this simulation window, students can verify the functionality of their programs, requiring them to learn basic interaction with RoboboSim. While direct interaction with the real robot is possible, it would sacrifice the level of customization and interaction facilitated by the Unity interface.

The Tutor Module integrates the teacher's expertise, manifesting in feedback provided to students on programming errors, documentation of specific Python and Robobo methods for solving each exercise, and evaluation criteria. This module conducts automatic evaluation of student activity, comparing their solution against predefined assessment criteria.

The Student Module contains student identification data within the system, including enrolled courses, groups, and assigned exercises. For each exercise,

ProgTutor collects six basic real-time metrics: (1) Python code submissions, (2) number of failed evaluations, (3) instances of teacher assistance requested, (4) types of coding errors made, (5) time taken to complete the activity, and (6) interactions with the tool. These data points will be utilized in future development stages to build models for profiling student types and providing more tailored learning paths.

Turning to the functional blocks shown in gray in Fig. 1, the Adaptation Models module performs the primary task of an ITS, which is to personalize learning based on student characteristics and progress. In this version of ProgTutor, new exercises are assigned to students based on the following rule:

Once a student successfully completes a level $n \in \{1, 2, 3\}$ exercise from topic $t \in \{1, \dots, T\}$, there is a probability:

- $1 - \epsilon_t$ that the system proposes a level $n+1$ exercise (or moves to topic $t+1$ if $n = 3$)
- ϵ_t that the system proposes a new exercise of level n (up to a maximum of 3 times),

where:

$$\epsilon_t = \max\left(0.05, \min\left(0.95, \alpha_t m_a + \beta_t m_e\right)\right), \quad \alpha_t = 0.2/\sqrt{t} \quad \text{and} \quad \beta_t = 0.1/\sqrt{t}$$

$$m_a = \text{number of teacher assists}, \qquad m_e = \text{number of failed evaluations}$$

As observed, this rule is based on two variables, m_a and m_e, to determine whether the student should remain on an exercise at the same level or progress to the next level (these variables correspond to metrics (2) and (3) mentioned earlier). The goal is to automatically assign exercises to students based on a logical and straightforward criterion, leveraging the interaction data explained previously, and thus train machine learning models.

Once an exercise is selected, the Adapted Activity block is executed, representing the period during which the student programs their solution. During this stage, the Data Capture block is active, capturing information through the student's interaction with ProgTutor's graphical interface. Upon completing the exercise, the student voluntarily submits it for evaluation, as detailed in Sect. 2.3. This automatic evaluation occurs in the Data Analysis block, where the student's solution runs in the simulator with different use cases.

This block considers the following criteria for marking an evaluation as not passed: (d1) failure to meet evaluation criteria in the commands specified by the teacher, (d2) Python code generates an error, (d3) execution time exceeds the maximum specified by the teacher, (d4) the robot's number of collisions in the environment exceeds the maximum specified by the teacher, (d5) the final position of the robot does not match the position specified by the teacher.

Finally, the Feedback block is executed, providing personalized information to the student through the simulator interface. At this point, if the student has not passed the activity, the feedback will assist them in improving their program (see Sect. 2.3.). If they have passed, a new challenge will be assigned to them based on the rule established in the Adaptation Models block.

2.2 Software Architecture

To implement the ProgTutor system, we adopted a client-server architecture as illustrated in Fig. 3. Users authenticate using a combination of username and password (fully anonymized), which upon validation returns a unique identification token. The client includes a customized version of RoboboSim with an internal REST API, enabling other local components to communicate with the simulator and access user identification tokens. Additionally, the client utilizes the Visual Studio Code (VSC) IDE with a specific extension developed to interact with both the server and simulator.

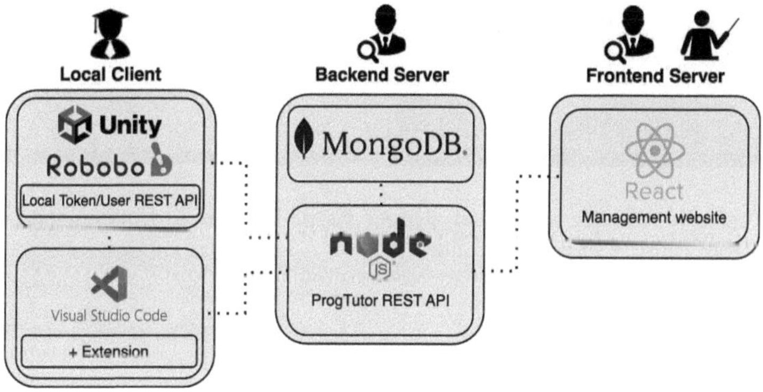

Fig. 3. ProgTutor software architecture diagram

On the server side, we implemented a NoSQL database using MongoDB [7] to store all system data. This database houses information on offered courses organized into thematic blocks containing exercises that students are required to complete. Each exercise includes a statement and three different use cases that serve as examples for running the program with varied input data, and these use cases are also used for automated evaluation. Each use case provides a specific environment in RoboboSim where the program must function, along with a video or image illustrating the expected solution. Furthermore, exercises assigned to each student and associated performance metrics are logged.

To facilitate interaction with the database, we developed a Node.js [10] REST API on the server. This API models MongoDB data using Mongoose [8] and provides CRUD (Create, Read, Update, Delete) methods for secure communication over HTTPS. Both the simulator and Visual Studio Code extension access MongoDB data through this interface.

Finally, a web tool was developed in React [13] to enable teachers to manage exercises within the database. This web tool offers an intuitive interface for editing, creating, deleting, and modifying exercises, as well as uploading associated files such as Python solutions, custom JSON environments, and visual materials illustrating exercise solutions.

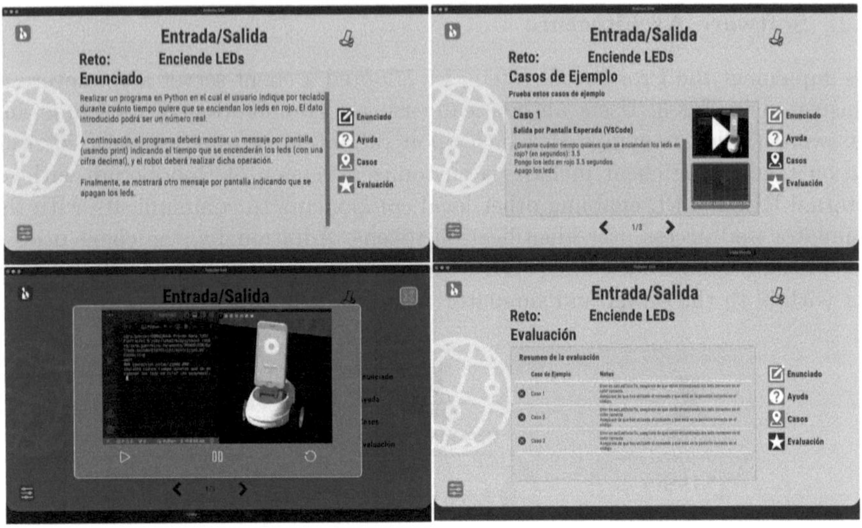

Fig. 4. Top left: Activity statement. Upper right: Use cases. Bottom left: Example video. Bottom right: Evaluation results

2.3 Operation

ProgTutor has been designed as an educational tool intended for classroom use, with a teacher overseeing students' progress. Prior to its use, it is assumed that Visual Studio Code (VSC) IDE along with the ProgTutor extension, and RoboboSim have been installed, and the teacher has explained their basic usage to the students. The computer can run on Windows, MacOS, or Linux and must have internet access to communicate with the database.

Starting from a specific thematic block, it is also assumed that the teacher has explained the theoretical concepts to all students in the course. For this purpose, teachers can utilize Jupyter notebooks accessible through ProgTutor or their own materials. ProgTutor's usage follows these steps:

1. *Challenge presentation:* Once the simulator is launched, as depicted in the upper left image of Fig. 4, the student has access to the challenge statement tailored to the current theme. In this window, there is also a Help button describing the necessary Robobo methods for resolution. Just below, there is another button called Cases, which displays the use cases where their program should work (upper right image of Fig. 4). Each use case includes the input data used, the expected output, and a video demonstrating the expected response in the robot (see lower left image in Fig. 4).
2. *Programming:* Once the challenge objective is understood, the student proceeds to program their solution. They select one of the use cases in the window shown in the upper right image of Fig. 4, which opens the associated environment in RoboboSim. At this point, they have a layout similar to that shown in

Fig. 2. In the VSC interface, there is a Test Exercise button that allows them to execute their code in the simulator. The student can test their solution in all three use cases by returning to the Cases screen.

3. *Evaluation:* When the student believes they have solved the challenge for the use cases, and provided there are no syntax or runtime errors in Python, they can submit their program for evaluation using a specific button in the VSC extension. As explained, ProgTutor performs automated evaluation by running the student's code on the use cases defined by the teacher. This evaluation runs in the background. If successful, the student is notified of their success, and the statement for the next activity is displayed. If unsuccessful, the Evaluation window appears (lower right image of Fig. 4), providing feedback on errors in each use case and how to address them.
4. *Continuous Work:* The system allows students to resume their activity at any time. When ProgTutor is first launched, a unique code is assigned to the user. This code can be used if the application is closed, so when the user returns, they continue from where they left off.

3 Educational Contents

The programming challenges involving robot programming form the core content for learning Python programming and have been designed to facilitate gradual learning for students. These challenges are structured into different thematic blocks based on the programming concepts intended to be taught in each block. Additionally, since these challenges are executed using a robotic simulator, there is a gradual introduction of Robobo operational concepts necessary to solve these challenges.

Table 1 illustrates the division into thematic blocks based on programming topics and the concepts related to Robobo usage. It is important to note that while each block introduces new concepts, the learning process is incremental, with concepts from previous blocks also incorporated into the challenges of subsequent blocks.

As previously explained, within each block, three levels of complexity have been established. When students initially engage with ProgTutor, they begin with Block 1 at Level 1. As they progress, the system automatically assigns the level of the next challenge based on their current progress. For instance, upon completing a Level 3 exercise in a specific block and as per the rule not to repeat the same level, the student proceeds to a Level 1 exercise in the subsequent block. At this point, the system notifies the teacher of the topic change, allowing them to decide when to explain the corresponding theory as deemed appropriate.

The exercises have been designed by professors of programming and robotics from the Universidade da Coruña, who have many years of experience teaching these subjects at various levels. The sequence chosen for introducing new concepts in each block, and the type of exercise used at each level, is based on their extensive teaching experience. While the primary goal is programming learning, priority has been given to these concepts, using the robot as a tool to motivate this learning, while also ensuring that the exercises make practical sense.

Table 1. Activity blocks.

Block	Introduced knowledge	
	Programming	Robot use
1	Input/Output	Move wheels (basic), say text, turn on LEDs
2	Conditionals	Move head, change facial expression
3	Loops	Move wheels (advanced), distance sensors, orientation, color detection
4	Functions	Sensors for QR code detection, bject detection
5	Lists	Accelerometer

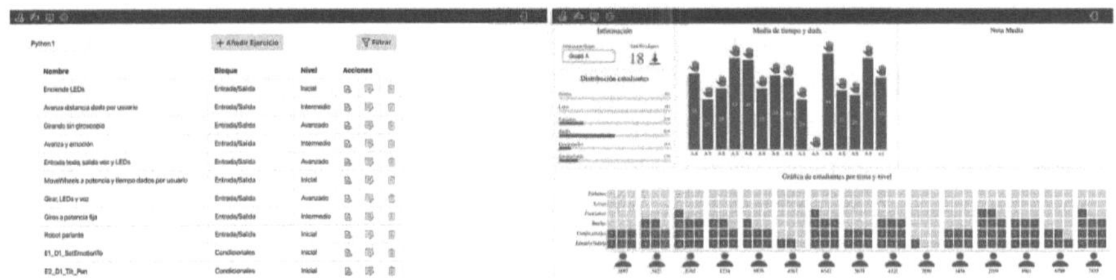

Fig. 5. Left: Exercise management screen. Right: Teacher's control panel

To add exercises into the system, the professors have access to a web-based tool, which is still under development but currently allows them to add, modify, and delete exercises in the system. Figure 5 (left) shows the screen where teachers can manage the different blocks of exercises. On the other hand, Fig. 5 (right) shows the teacher's control panel where he/she can see information regarding the progress and results of the students.

4 Test with Students

The validation of this first version of the ITS ProgTutor, as well as the initial data collection, is being carried out at the Sofia Casanova Secondary Education Institute in Ferrol during the academic year 2023–2024. The study has been organized into two groups of first-year high school TIC (Information and Communication Technology) students: a group of 36 students using ProgTutor and its associated methodology, and a control group of 33 students following a traditional methodology. The control group relies on theoretical explanations from teachers, teacher assistance for problem-solving, and the use of exercises with data output through a terminal, following a traditional scheme for introductory programming courses.

Before the start of the Python programming classes, questionnaires were conducted to determine the interest in these types of contents and the prior knowledge among students in both groups. In Table 2, the obtained responses show a significant difference in the initial level of motivation for the subject, which may be related to a higher number of students in the ProgTutor group who have had some previous exposure to programming.

Table 2. Initial questionnaire responses on students' interests and profile.

Question	ProgTutor Group % positive	Control Group % positive
Do you have a high or very high level of motivation to learn in this subject?	68.0	41.0
Are you interested in learning how to program computers, cell phones, etc.?	51.0	37.0
Have you ever programmed a computer?	22.0	10.0
Are you interested in computer related topics?	27.0	18.0

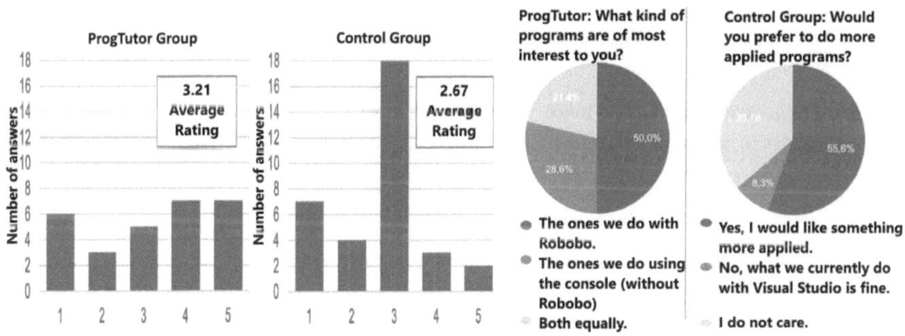

Fig. 6. Left: Satisfaction with Python programming. Right: Preferred program type.

After the first academic year of work, students in both groups have completed four content blocks: input/output, conditionals, loops, and functions. However, it's important to note that progress in the ProgTutor group is not homogeneous and is determined by the dynamics of the ITS itself. At this point, new questionnaires were presented to the students, evaluating two aspects:

1. Whether students find learning to program in Python satisfactory.
2. Whether students value positively the ability to solve seemingly more complex problems with richer interaction using the Robobo robot simulator, compared to programming more abstract algorithms that involve only simple interaction through a text terminal.

In Fig. 6, we can see the results obtained for both questions of the questionnaire. Regarding the first question, a more positive perception towards Python programming is observed among the students of the ProgTutor group. However, of greater interest for this line of study are the answers to the second question, where there is a marked preference among the students of both groups for working on more applied problems, as the ProgTutor group is doing with the use of a robotic simulation environment.

Table 3. Final responses to the questionnaire on the interests of the ProgTutor group.

Question	ProgTutor Group % positive
Are you finding it easy to learn to program with ProgTutor?	61.0
Do you find the help ProgTutor gives you when you have an error in your program useful?	45.0
Is it good that ProgTutor evaluates your exercises automatically?	52.0
Do you like that ProgTutor assigns a level to the exercises?	58.0
Now that we have finished the course, do you think ProgTutor has provided you with exercises that match your progress?	79.0
Would you use ProgTutor next year to continue learning to program?	75.0

For the ProgTutor group, information was also gathered about the students' interaction with the ITS on a day-to-day basis in their programming classes (see Table 3). It can be observed that, overwhelmingly, they do not identify any special difficulty in the process of starting to program with the ITS, and they are reasonably aligned with the experience of ProgTutor automatically assigning a level based on the exercises completed, which positively influences their motivation to improve. Another important aspect of the ITS is its capability to perform initial automatic evaluation of exercises without teacher intervention, and in this regard, although to a lesser extent, some students (21%) express concern because they do not know in detail the criteria that have been applied. However, we believe that this latter assessment may vary significantly over time if students repeatedly observe that evaluations are consistent and coherent with their performance. Additionally, future versions of the system will incorporate an information panel for students.

5 Conclusions

ProgTutor provides a personalized learning path to students on the learning of programming fundamentals, according to their progress. This initial version is fully functional and has been tested during a course with students to gather interaction data for upcoming machine learning modeling.

Hence, the current version does not include model-based profiling to perform the learning path adaptation, but a simple rule established by experienced teachers. Consequently, although the personalization level is low, is has allowed us to get the student feedback about the use of this type of personalized tool in classes, as a support for traditional teaching. In addition, we received positive feedback regarding the use of robotic simulations for programming.

It must be pointed out that the teachers that were involved in the validation highlighted how ProgTutor promoted the creation of different progress levels in the classroom, with clear differences between them. Thus, some students advanced autonomously and finished all the exercises soon, while others required much more time. Therefore, teachers could focus their attention on this last group and, in contrast with traditional methodologies, the most advanced students were not limited by the average level.

Acknowledgments. This work was supported by grant TED2021-131172B-I00, funded by MCIN/AEI/10.13039/501100011033 and by the EU NextGenerationEU/PRTR.

References

1. Bellas, F., et al.: The Robobo project: bringing educational robotics closer to real world applications. In: Lepuschitz, W., Merdan, M., Koppensteiner, G., Balogh, R., Obdržálek, D. (eds.) RiE 2017. AISC, vol. 630, pp. 226–237. Springer, Cham (2018). https://doi.org/10.1007/978-3-319-62875-2_20
2. Blockly Games. https://blockly.games. Accessed 14 June 2024
3. CoderZ. https://gocoderz.com. Accessed 14 June 2024
4. Crow, T., Luxton-Reilly, A., Wuensche, B.: Intelligent tutoring systems for programming education: a systematic review. In: Proceedings of the 20th Australasian Computing Education Conference, pp. 53–62. Association for Computing Machinery, New York (2018)
5. Holmes, W.: Artificial intelligence in education. In: Tatnall, A. (ed.) Encyclopedia of Education and Information Technologies. Springer (2019)
6. Hooshyar, D., Ahmad, R.B., Wang, M., Yousefi, M., Fathi, M., Lim, H.: Development and evaluation of a game-based Bayesian intelligent tutoring system for teaching programming. J. Educ. Comput. Res. **56**(6), 775–801 (2018). https://doi.org/10.1177/0735633117731872
7. MongoDB. https://mongodb.com. Accessed 14 June 2024
8. Mongoose. https://mongoosejs.com. Accessed 14 June 2024
9. Mousavinasab, E., Zarifsanaiey, N., Kalhori, S.N., Rakhshan, M., Keikha, L., Ghazi Saeedi, M.: Intelligent tutoring systems: a systematic review of characteristics, applications, and evaluation methods. Interact. Learn. Environ. **29**(1), 142–163 (2021). https://doi.org/10.1080/10494820.2018.1558257
10. Node.js. https://nodejs.org. Accessed 14 June 2024
11. Open Roberta Lab. https://lab.open-roberta.org. Accessed 14 June 2024
12. Ramachandran, A., Sebo, S.S., Scassellati, B.: Personalized robot tutoring using the assistive tutor POMDP (AT-POMDP). In: Proceedings of the AAAI Conference on Artificial Intelligence, vol. 33, no. 01, pp. 8050–8057 (2019). https://doi.org/10.1609/aaai.v33i01.33018050
13. React. https://reactjs.org. Accessed 14 June 2024

14. RoboboSim simulator. https://github.com/mintforpeople/robobo-programming/wiki/Unity. Accessed 14 June 2024
15. Robotbenchmark. https://robotbenchmark.net. Accessed 14 June 2024
16. Sharma, P., Harkishan, M.: Designing an intelligent tutoring system for computer programming in the Pacific. Educ. Inf. Technol. (2022). https://doi.org/10.1007/s10639-021-10882-9
17. The Constructsim. https://www.theconstructsim.com. Accessed 14 June 2024
18. Unity. https://unity.com. Accessed 14 June 2024
19. Visual Studio Code. https://code.visualstudio.com/. Accessed 14 June 2024
20. Wang, M., Wu, W., Liang, Y.: A novel intelligent tutoring system for learning programming. In: 2020 International Conference on Development and Application Systems (DAS), pp. 162–168 (2020). https://doi.org/10.1109/DAS49615.2020.9108925
21. Yang, J., Zhang, B.: Artificial intelligence in intelligent tutoring robots: a systematic review and design guidelines. Appl. Sci. **9**, 2078 (2019). https://doi.org/10.3390/app9102078

Evaluating the Impact of Advanced LLM Techniques on AI Lecture Tutors for a Robotics Course

Sebastian Kahl[1], Felix Löffler[2], Martin Maciol[2], Fabian Ridder[2], Marius Schmitz[2], Jennifer Spanagel[2], Jens Wienkamp[2], Christopher Burgahn[1], and Malte Schilling[2(✉)]

[1] fronyx GmbH, Rüttenscheider Str. 120, 45131 Essen, Germany
[2] Autonomous Intelligent Systems Group, University of Münster, Münster, Germany
malte.schilling@uni-muenster.de

Abstract. This study evaluates the performance of Large Language Models (LLMs) as an Artificial Intelligence-based tutor for a university course. In particular, different advanced techniques are utilized, such as prompt engineering, Retrieval-Augmented-Generation (RAG), and fine-tuning. We assessed the different models and applied techniques using common similarity metrics like BLEU-4, ROUGE, and BERTScore, complemented by a small human evaluation of helpfulness and trustworthiness. Our findings indicate that RAG combined with prompt engineering significantly enhances model responses and produces better factual answers. In the context of education, RAG appears as an ideal technique as it is based on enriching the input of the model with additional information and material which usually is already present for a university course. Fine-tuning, on the other hand, can produce quite small, still strong expert models, but poses the danger of overfitting. Our study further asks how we measure performance of LLMs and how well current measurements represent correctness or relevance? We find high correlation on similarity metrics and a bias of most of these metrics towards shorter responses. Overall, our research points to both the potential and challenges of integrating LLMs in educational settings, suggesting a need for balanced training approaches and advanced evaluation frameworks (An extended report is released as a preprint at https://arxiv.org/abs/2408.04645).

1 Introduction

Large Language Models have become popular with the introduction of ChatGPT. In particular, the novel dialogue capabilities of these Assistant Models [17] have stimulated an interest as these provide a flexibility that allows to apply LLMs in various sectors, including education. These Large Language Models (LLMs) are Transformer-based neural networks [23] that were trained on massive text corpora and that exhibit impressive abilities to comprehend, process, and generate human-like language. Originally, Large Language Models—now

F. Bellas and O. Fontenla-Romero (Eds.): AIEER 2024, CCIS 2519, pp. 149–160, 2025.
https://doi.org/10.1007/978-3-031-93409-4_14

often called Foundation Models—were trained with the goal to predict the following text token, taking into account long and diverse relationships of the given previous input. The models learnt from this to perform well on a large number of different tasks across a variety of topics. Importantly, early work on GPT-2 already demonstrated the flexibility of these models as these models can be explicitly directed to execute a specified language task simply through prompting these models accordingly [19]. Early-on, these models had difficulties staying on track for a given task and often their responses lingered or drifted away from a topic. As a consequence, the earliest application were in specific and narrowly defined tasks as translation. In such a task the model could continuously be forced to follow the original input sequence. The work by Ouyang et al. [17] changed this, as they further trained models to better imitate human behavior which lead to the emergence of Assistant Models as ChatGPT. These demonstrated for the first time the ability to provide a–to a certain degree–consistent partner for dialogue which can be engaged in a conversation. Modern models are now able to understand and generate language with remarkable fluency and coherence. The success of such models has now spread and there is a growing number of models similar to ChatGPT that are further improving at a rapid pace (e.g., Meta's LLaMA-2 as an open-source model [22]; for an overview on the current landscape of LLMs see [16]). LLMs present now valuable opportunities to design and develop innovative assistant systems.

In the area of education, the early debate on the impact of powerful LLMs has sadly mostly focused on negative consequences, e.g., how this might allow students to cheat as these models are capable of generating written course work—as currently used to test learning capabilities—or even parts or a full thesis work. But LLMs can also be beneficial in education and teaching: LLMs as an assistant can be utilized to provide individualized teaching for every student. In particular, the possibility to prompt them to answer in a certain role—e.g., as a primary or high school teacher—and addressing a specific audience—e.g., a fourth grader or a grad student—offers novel possibilities for better adapted teaching that takes the need of the individual learner into account [4]. This has lead to the idea of introducing LLMs as tutors for courses or lectures. There are already quite a number of different nice examples. One particular area is the area of coding assistants (see [15] and for a systematic overview [13]). Other examples include assistants in language learning. Khan Academy's assistant Khanmigo [9] is an early example in this area as they started to develop this in cooperation with OpenAI before the official release of ChatGPT. In general, Khan Academy has embraced LLMs as powerful tools for education and their founder has detailed a positive outlook how this not only can help to provide better teaching—in the sense of more individualized tutoring that supports learning—, but as well more engaging learning experiences [8]. Following such a route, we are seeing an increasing number of LLM-based systems acting as tutors in university courses (as one example, see [3]; for a broad review see [5]).

A significant challenge in deploying LLMs are hallucinations. Hallucinations in LLMs refer to cases in which the model generates plausible-sounding, but incorrect or nonsensical responses [14]. It is assumed that this occurs because the model relies solely on patterns in textual data it was trained on without any understanding of factual correctness [7]. Detecting hallucinations has proven difficult, but different techniques and metrics have been proposed (for a comprehensive review see [7] which outlines principles, a taxonomy, and open questions regarding hallucinations in LLMs, while as well providing insights on developing effective detection and mitigation strategies). The risk of hallucinations is particularly concerning for an educational setting and has to be addressed in such an area that demands factual correctness.

One major focus in utilizing LLMs in education as a tutoring system is, therefore, in how to prevent hallucinations and restrict answers to the specific course [2,4]. Our work is directed in this direction, as we aim for an LLM as a tutor for learning and in teaching of a University course on robotics. This LLM-powered tutor was envisioned as a supplementary resource, providing tailored assistance and facilitating personalized learning paths for participants. The explicit goal of the presented work was to develop a tutor-like system that is utilizing the flexibility of Assistant Models. By this, we want to address two main research questions: First, LLMs can show the tendency to provide wrong or hallucinated responses. We wanted to analyze how different—currently widely proposed—advanced techniques for LLMs can improve the responses of LLMs in a specific knowledge domain? Do such extended LLMs hallucinate less and provide more factual answers? Secondly, evaluation of the performance of LLMs has shown to be difficult and lead to inconsistent results. Therefore, we want to address how can we measure performance of LLMs and how good do currently applied measurements represent factuality? In particular, we are interested in how do different metrics relate to each other or overlap? Furthermore, can we identify biases that affect these measurements?

In this paper, we want to summarize our experience with current State-of-the-Art techniques in the area of LLMs and demonstrate how these differentially impact the behavior of the lecture tutoring system. Therefore, the paper covers current methods all applied in the area of a lecture tutor for an introductory robotics course. First, simply using an of-the-shelf LLM that is purely put to the task through prompt engineering. Secondly, enriching the input by course material through Retrieval-Augmented-Generation in which content from slides and the annotations of the lecture videos were also provided to the model. Third, an LLM. was fine-tuned for the specific task on a generated set of question-answer pairs. The article is organized in the following way: We first provide a detailed overview of our AI lecture tutor, explaining the design requirements, the different applied LLM extension techniques and how they are realized, the selected LLMs, as well as details on dataset and preparation. Then we present our results on an introduced test data set specific to the robotics course. One crucial aspect of our work is the evaluation of LLMs which still appears in its infancy. We describe our multi-faceted approach, combining automated benchmarks to quantify performance and a human-centered evaluation using questionnaires to garner qualitative insights into student interaction with the AI Lecture Tutor. Finally, we conclude with a critical reflection of our findings and highlighting potential avenues for future research in the domain of AI-powered educational technologies.

2 Methods: Large Language Model as an AI Tutor

The proposed AI tutor will be integrated into the learning platform of the lecture and is designed as a chatbot that allows students to communicate via written messages. Regarding its function, the tutor system should consistently respond in a polite and helpful way, as a human tutor would do. It needs to be able to understand questions given in natural language and to generate answers that are both syntactically and semantically accurate. Most importantly, the answers should be consistent with the lecture which means, answers are, first, correct and the system should not tell falsehoods. Easy and general questions should be answerable based on the pre-trained model. Secondly, as the tutor should support the student in learning the concepts, the answers should relate to the content of the lecture as well as the way it is taught, e.g., picking up examples or providing references to content as the slides. Therefore, slides of the lecture as well as the transcripts of the recordings should be taken into account.

These requirements guide the realization of the tutor system and we applied different advanced techniques for LLMs in the tutoring system[1]. We are interested in comparing how well an LLM can work as a lecture tutor. This requires an experimental setup in which different variations of the tutor are questioned in a systematic way and evaluated. In the following, we will introduce the necessary parts for such an evaluation and comparison. We will briefly describe the preprocessing of the lecture material and, secondly, how we derived a test data set for evaluation and a data set for training. Afterwards, we will briefly provide details on the used models and the fine-tuning process. Last, we introduce different evaluation metrics for the comparison.

2.1 Preprocessing of Lecture Material

Integration of lecture material into the query process using RAG or deriving training data from it, requires significant preprocessing of the available information. First, the information has to be extracted, in our case from slides which consist of written text that could be directly extracted from the original files (based on PDFs of the lecture slides). In addition, graphical information and images from the slides were extracted and transferred to textual descriptions using multimodal Large Language Models. The visual information was fed into an LLM (GPT-4) that was tasked with briefly describing the figure. Secondly,

[1] These techniques are explained in detail in the extended report at https://arxiv.org/abs/2408.04645.

original audio was taken from lecture videos in which the slides were explained and discussed in more detail. This requires transcribing the audio (realized using OpenAI's Whisper framework) and aligning the oral explanations with the content presented visually on the slides. The audio showed important providing complementing information and more detailed explanations. As a result of this process, we end up with a vast amount of data for eleven lectures (each one 90 minutes long, roughly around 45 slides per lecture) that is available to the system. During operation, the AI tutor should focus solely on relevant parts from the lecture and, therefore, needs an understanding of which different parts of the lecture and transcripts are necessary to answer the question. As an additional requirement, the AI tutor should provide information on its sources, e.g., pointing out which slides were used for a given answer (for example: "@10-slam-deck Slide 11"). This allows the user to check slides and verify the given answer.

2.2 Test and Fine-Tuning Dataset

Evaluation of the different LLM techniques and models was done on the test data set. This data set consisted of chats (overall 478) which each included a dialogue consisting of the question and a possible answer. Questions in the test set (and similarly in the training data set described below) were targeted for the specific robotics course and based on the material covered. In case of the test set, two lectures (on the topic of SLAM and navigation in robotics, lecture nine and ten) were used. Three students worked through the material of these lectures and generated by hand questions for the covered material which was then used again by the human writers to formulate an answer.

For fine-tuning a training data set for the robotics course was generated. It explicitly excluded the topics covered in the test set for which there where humanly written chats. For generating the test set, a LLM was used which was advised through a prompt to generate question-answer pairs for specific slides. In addition, an example question-answer pair written by a human was given in a form of one-shot learning. The generated chats were afterwards read and checked by humans and were found to be generally of sufficient quality. This produced overall 2791 chats for training that did not overlap with the test data set.

2.3 Models and Fine-Tuning

There are many LLMs openly available which are accessible through specific APIs and even more so through standard libraries and frameworks like Huggingface or their APIs. For our tutor system, we focussed, first, on GPT-3.5 which is accessible through OpenAI and for which we used the OpenAI API for access (model can be queried through simple python function calls).

For RAG, the AI Tutor uses a PostgreSQL database equipped with the PGVector plugin. This database configuration allows to store original text chunks alongside their respective embedding vectors in a distinct vector column[2]. The

[2] PGVector: https://github.com/pgvector/pgvector (Accessed: 28.02.2024).

embedding vectors are derived using an OpenAI embedding model[3]. The vector storage can be used to retrieve useful information during the query stage.

One significant drawback of OpenAI's models is the fact, that they are close-sourced and operated by OpenAI which might pose privacy issues and, at least early-on in the project, excluded the possibility of further training on specific data as envisioned in our project. In our case, we therefore used as an additional model Llama-2-13B from Meta as it is openly accessible and can be further trained locally [21,22]. Meta's LLaMA series of models was trained only on publicly available data (overall around 1.25 trillion tokens, the majority of data is gained from CommonCrawl with about 850 billion tokens). This model was used in different setups: a baseline approach in which the model was directly queried and, again, a setup in which the prompt was enriched using the system message as well as RAG (prompt engineering and RAG are identical to the approach used with GPT-3.5).

As one further step, LLaMA-2 was used in a fine-tuned version. The model was hosted and trained locally (we used a workstation equipped with a NVIDIA RTX A6000 with 48 GB of RAM on the graphics card). Therefore, we decided to use the mid-size LLaMA for all our experiments (with 13 billion parameters) as this still allowed to train and fine-tune the model when using quantization and LoRA [6].

2.4 Evaluation of LLMs in Question-Answering

Measuring question-answering is difficult because for many questions there are multiple correct answers. This makes comparison to a ground truth difficult. There are different approaches for question-answering and quite a large number of metrics have been proposed. A couple of these focus on overlap between the model's output and the ground truth response provided by a human. BLEU-4 is widely used as such a metric [18] providing values in the range of 0 to 1. Furthermore, we also use ROUGE-1 [11] and METEOR [1] for evaluation which have been found to best correlate with human evaluation [10].

It is currently assumed that such metrics by itself are not sufficient to analyze LLMs [14]. Therefore, human evaluations are still used as a gold standard for assessing the capabilities. As a first step, we setup a web-based framework that present a question together with an answer to a user. The user is tasked with judging how helpful and how correct the given answer is. There is additional information provided for each question (the original slide for which we generated the question, plus a context of neighboring slides). This human evaluation has only been tested with two teaching assistants for the given robotics course which can be considered domain experts. We will run this evaluation in the upcoming semester inside the robotics course.

Using another LLM—and often a more capable one with larger parameter counts—is currently an active area of research. Approaches as LLMEval [12] use

[3] OpenAIEmbedding: https://platform.openai.com/docs/guides/embeddings (Accessed: 28.02.2024).

an LLM for similarity rating itself, often using an elaborate prompt that guides the model to mimic a human-like evaluation. In general, LLMEval showed some promising results, but appears difficult to directly apply in our approach. In our case, the integration of RAG lead to quite long context inputs which has shown problematic for LLMEval. Therefore, we adapted their general approach and prompted an LLM (GPT-3.5) as an evaluator which was provided with the original question, the generated answer, and the ground truth answer. In particular, we developed three different prompts that addressed different parts of our evaluation. First, 'GPTSimilarity' is an evaluation of the similarity between the generated response and the ground-truth response in the test set. Secondly, for the metrics of the human evaluation, we introduced 'GPTRater' which evaluated independently trustworthiness and helpfulness on the same scale as given to human evaluators (details see below).

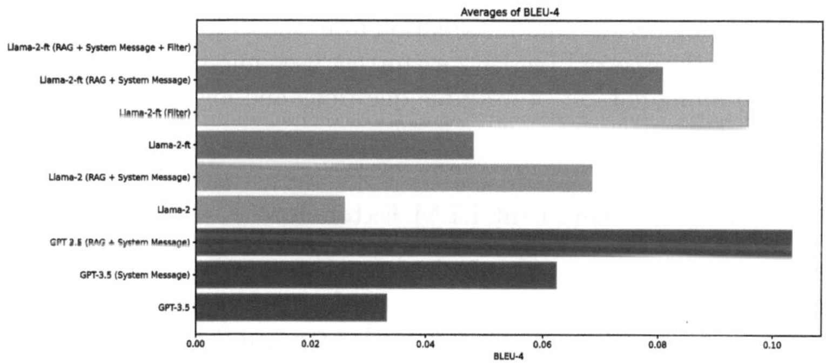

(a) BLEU-4 Score

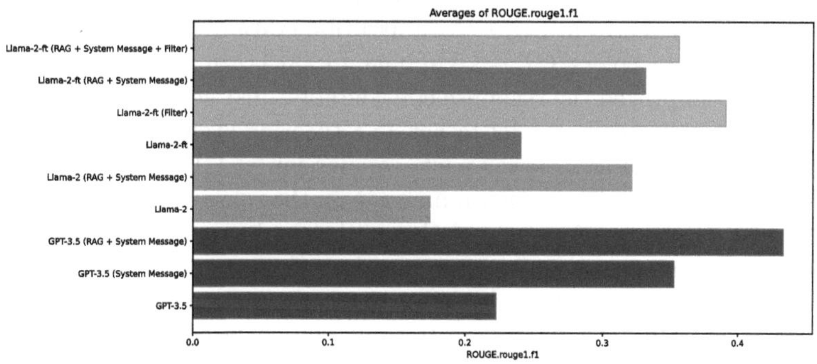

(b) ROUGE Score

Fig. 1. Evaluation of Large Language Models: (a) BLEU-4 score which measures the precision of n-grams (here 4-grams) in the generated text compared to the ground truth text, while (b) ROUGE evaluates recall, measuring the overlap of n-grams between the generated and reference texts.

3 Results

We tested the different LLM versions and different applied techniques in a question answering task with the questions tailored to the robotics course from the test set. As a first model, we used ChatGPT (GPT-3.5) as a standard high-performing and well-known general model. For GPT-3.5 we could apply prompt engineering and RAG as we accessed the model through OpenAI's API and simply enriched the prompt. As we considered fine-tuning as a third step, we also evaluated an open model in LLaMA-2. This lead to multiple different setups and different groupings: On the one hand, we used two different models of quite different size (GPT-3.5 has around 175 billion parameters, LLaMA-2 in the midsize version of around 13 billion parameters). On the other hand, we used different input versions for both models: Simply providing a question as an input, prompt engineering using an optimized prompt that provides context on the use case, and, in addition, Retrieval-Augmented-Generation in which the input was further enriched using background information from the lecture as additional input to the model. In the case of LLaMA-2 we further used fine-tuning and trained the model on a training dataset of example questions and answers for the robotics course.

3.1 Comparison of Different LLM Extension

As a first research question, we are interested in how well do different models perform and how do the different extension techniques affect the performance. Therefore, we evaluated these models on our test dataset. The different metrics compare the provided ground truth answer from the test set with the answer given by the model on the particular question. Given are the BLEU-4 and ROUGE similarity scores in Fig. 1. As a first observation, for both generic LLM models (indicated by colors: GPT-3.5 in blue, LLaMA-2 in orange) extending the prompt always improved the response considerably. Just adding a simple system message that instructs the model to act as a tutoring system showed a considerable improvement (Fig. 1, lower part, comparison of GPT-3.5 with GPT-3.5 (System Message) in which a general message on the role and topic was provided to the model). Retrieval-Augmented-Generation and prompt engineering show a further improvement and quite large positive effect.

For the fine-tuned LLaMA-2 (shown in darker green and lighter green) these results differ slightly: Importantly, in training on our specific dataset the model was fine-tuned on a specific interaction structure that further included additional keywords, e.g., start and stop symbols. After learning these, the model tended to overproduce some of such tags which could be easily cleaned up as these were not fitting to the predefined structure. For example, when the model produced an end-tag but still continued to produce output, the text following that end tag could be dropped. Therefore, we filtered the output of the fine-tuned model (the filtered and cleaned-up responses are shown in the figures in light green). This improved the similarity scores dramatically which might be partially explained as the texts were significantly shortened (for the fine-tuned LLaMA-2 model output length dropped from 413 ± 153 words to 109 ± 81 words after filtering; when integrating RAG output length dropped from 246 ± 181 words to 173 ± 109 words after filtering). There is an assumed bias of such similarity metrics for shorter answers (see below our analysis and comparison on relation between the different metrics). One curious observation after filtering was that RAG and prompt engineering did not show an advantage for the fine-tuned version. This might be due to the training dataset to which the model fitted its interactions which did not include RAG.

When considering fine-tuning, we compare different versions of the LLaMA-2 model (all with 13 billion parameters), i.e., shown in orange and the fine-tuned version in green. Fine-tuning improved the results considerably, in particular when filtering the results afterwards. Last, when comparing the results of the fine-tuned model with GPT-3.5 (which is much larger with 175 billion parameters), we observed that a fine-tuned LLaMA-2 (with filtering) without additional prompting techniques performed considerably better as GPT-3.5. Adding RAG and prompting techniques (see above) improved GPT-3.5 by a huge margin and this model setup was the best we found in evaluation. But the margin towards fine-tuned LLaMA was slim and our fine-tuning training data appeared to have a detrimental effect to RAG which should be further analyzed (see note above).

3.2 Analysis of Evaluation Metrics

Evaluation of LLMs and their responses is difficult and there are multiple metrics and different approaches have been proposed. We further analyzed some of these metrics: First, we considered how the different metrics correlate with each other in order to understand better what these represent and how they might capture similar characteristics. In addition, we computed correlations to other characteristic features of the given responses. As one example, we considered the length of the response as it has often be assumed that there is a bias for shorter answers in some of the more traditional metrics.

We observed (Fig. 2) that the traditionally computed similarity metrics as BLEU, ROUGE, and BERTScore (to a slightly lesser extend) are highly correlated. Interestingly, all these metrics showed a negative correlation with the token count. In our case, we found the assumption confirmed that shorter sentences are preferred by these metrics. METEOR also showed a positive—but smaller—correlation with the metrics above. It appeared nearly uncorrelated with the token counter (only a very small negative correlation). GPTSimilarity, as a measurement that prompts an LLM to evaluate similarity, did not show any large correlation with the more traditional similarity metrics, but surprisingly has a positive correlation with the token count, meaning in our evaluation longer answers were usually favored (this should be further analyzed).[4]

[4] We further conducted a human evaluation, but that included only two subjects. First results are given in the extended report at https://arxiv.org/abs/2408.04645.

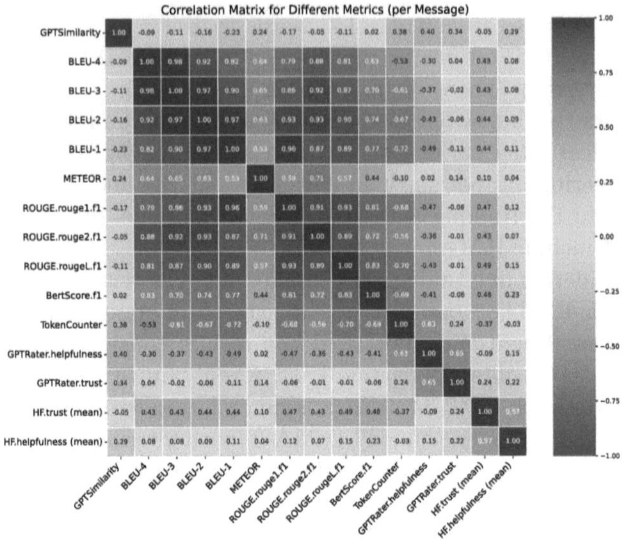

Fig. 2. Correlation Matrix of Evaluation Metrics: The color-coded matrix represents correlations between evaluation metrics used to assess the performance of LLMs (measured on our test set). Each cell in the matrix indicates the correlation coefficient between two metrics, with color intensity (from blue to red) reflecting the strength of the correlation. Metrics include traditional similarity scores like BLEU and ROUGE, as well as newer ones like BERTScore, and their relationships with model output features, e.g., token count and human evaluation scores on trustworthiness or helpfulness. (Color figure online)

4 Discussion and Conclusion

The evaluation of a Large Language Model-based tutoring system for a University robotics course highlighted several insights into the application of advanced LLM techniques and the resulting performance in an educational setting. First, our findings underscored the positive impact of Retrieval-Augmented-Generation (RAG) and prompt engineering, which consistently improved model performance across similarity metrics. Particularly, the use of RAG demonstrated a considerable enhancement in providing factual answers and is consistent with the general belief that RAG is reducing hallucinations [20]. Therefore, RAG appears as a very valuable technique that should be—together with some form of prompt engineering—considered first. As further advantages, in our experience RAG is quite straight forward to realize, in particular in a course setting in which well-curated background material is readily available. Furthermore, from a teaching point of view a tutor should stick to the lecture material, e.g., when going over a concept the tutoring system should carefully choose examples and ideally stick—or at least start—with the ones provided in the lecture. This should positively affect the learning of students.

Fine-tuning has to be considered as a more involved technique. It requires additional effort in setting up a data set for training. As an advantage, in our case we saw that already quite a small fine-tuned model (13 billion parameters) consistently performed on the same level—or better—as GPT-3.5 (175 billion parameters) when used without RAG. Fine-tuning produced a much more efficient expert which showed as quite capable. But, on the downside, the process of fine-tuning appeared as more delicate. In our data, we observed a curious drop-off when adding RAG to the fine-tuned model which was unexpected and would contradict our and others' experience with RAG. As an explanation, fine-tuning aims to specialize a model to a specific task and a specific type of interaction. A fine-tuned model might loose some of its general flexibility. As a consequence, when interacting very differently with the model, the model might produce worse results or even behave erratically. The introduction of RAG drastically changes the input to a model and this change appears as problematic when RAG is introduced after fine-tuning. Therefore, the combination of techniques should be considered carefully beforehand. In the future, we want to further test how fine-tuning on interactions that include RAG affect the result which, unfortunately, requires a different data set.

We further compared different metrics to evaluate question answering in LLMs and found a high correlation between BLEU-4, ROUGE, and BERTScore. The analysis of these metrics revealed an inherent preference for shorter responses, suggesting that these metrics might be biased against lengthier, albeit potentially more informative, answers. This observation is crucial for designing future LLM evaluation frameworks, as it challenges the effectiveness of current automated metrics in truly capturing response quality in educational settings. LLM-based evaluations still appear difficult as we could not demonstrate a large correlation of a similarity evaluation with the more conventional metrics.

References

1. Banerjee, S., Lavie, A.: METEOR: an automatic metric for MT evaluation with improved correlation with human judgments. In: Proceedings of the ACL Workshop on Intrinsic and Extrinsic Evaluation Measures for Machine Translation and/or Summarization, pp. 65–72 (2005)
2. Dong, C.: How to build an AI tutor that can adapt to any course and provide accurate answers using large language model and retrieval-augmented generation. arXiv preprint arXiv:2311.17696 (2023). https://arxiv.org/abs/2311.17696
3. of Education, B.S.: Leveraging AI to improve adaptive tutoring systems (2023). https://bse.berkeley.edu/leveraging-ai-improve-adaptive-tutoring-systems
4. Extance, A.: ChatGPT has entered the classroom: how LLMs could transform education. Nature **623**(7987), 474–477 (2023)
5. García-Méndez, S., de Arriba-Pérez, F., Somoza-López, M.D.C.: A review on the use of large language models as virtual tutors. Sci. Educ. 1–16 (2024)
6. Hu, E.J., et al.: LoRA: low-rank adaptation of large language models. arXiv preprint arXiv:2106.09685 (2021)
7. Huang, L., et al.: A survey on hallucination in large language models: principles, taxonomy, challenges, and open questions. arXiv preprint arXiv:2311.05232 (2023)

8. Khan, S.: Brave New Words: How AI Will Revolutionize Education (and Why That's a Good Thing). Viking, New York (2024)
9. Khan Academy: Khanmigo: Khan academy's AI-powered teaching assistant (2023). https://www.khanmigo.ai. Accessed 16 June 2024
10. Kim, S., Eric, M., Gopalakrishnan, K., Hedayatnia, B., Liu, Y., Hakkani-Tur, D.: Beyond domain APIs: task-oriented conversational modeling with unstructured knowledge access. arXiv preprint arXiv:2006.03533 (2020)
11. Lin, C.Y.: ROUGE: a package for automatic evaluation of summaries. In: Text Summarization Branches Out, pp. 74–81 (2004)
12. Lin, Y.T., Chen, Y.N.: LLM-eval: unified multi-dimensional automatic evaluation for open-domain conversations with large language models. arXiv preprint arXiv:2305.13711 (2023)
13. Liu, Q., Wang, B., Zhang, Y., Zhou, Q., Li, Y., Huang, X.: Large language models for software engineering: a systematic literature review. arXiv preprint arXiv:2308.10620 (2023). https://arxiv.org/abs/2308.10620. Accessed 16 June 2024.
14. Maynez, J., Narayan, S., Bohnet, B., McDonald, R.: On faithfulness and factuality in abstractive summarization. In: Jurafsky, D., Chai, J., Schluter, N., Tetreault, J. (eds.) Proceedings of the 58th Annual Meeting of the Association for Computational Linguistics, pp. 1906–1919. Association for Computational Linguistics, Online (2020). https://doi.org/10.18653/v1/2020.acl-main.173, https://aclanthology.org/2020.acl-main.173
15. Mehta, A., Gupta, N., Kumar, D., Jalote, P., et al.: Can chatGPT play the role of a teaching assistant in an introductory programming course? arXiv preprint arXiv:2312.07343 (2023)
16. Naveed, H., et al.: A comprehensive overview of large language models. arXiv preprint arXiv:2307.06435 (2024)
17. Ouyang, L., et al.: Training language models to follow instructions with human feedback. In: Advances in Neural Information Processing Systems, vol. 35, pp. 27730–27744 (2022)
18. Papineni, K., Roukos, S., Ward, T., Zhu, W.J.: BLEU: a method for automatic evaluation of machine translation. In: Proceedings of the 40th Annual Meeting of the Association for Computational Linguistics, pp. 311–318 (2002)
19. Radford, A., Wu, J., Child, R., Luan, D., Amodei, D., Sutskever, I., et al.: Language models are unsupervised multitask learners. OpenAI blog **1**(8), 9 (2019)
20. Shuster, K., Poff, S., Chen, M., Kiela, D., Weston, J.: Retrieval augmentation reduces hallucination in conversation. In: Moens, M.F., Huang, X., Specia, L., Yih, S.W.T. (eds.) Findings of the Association for Computational Linguistics: EMNLP 2021, pp. 3784–3803. Association for Computational Linguistics, Punta Cana (2021). https://doi.org/10.18653/v1/2021.findings-emnlp.320, https://aclanthology.org/2021.findings-emnlp.320
21. Touvron, H., t al.: LLaMA: open and efficient foundation language models. arXiv preprint arXiv:2302.13971 (2023)
22. Touvron, H., et al.: LLaMA 2: open foundation and fine-tuned chat models. arXiv preprint arXiv:2307.09288 (2023)
23. Vaswani, A., et al.: Attention is all you need. In: Advances in Neural Information Processing Systems, vol. 30 (2017)

A Computerized Adaptive Competency-Based Placement Test to Determine the Optimal Entry Point in Online Courses

Kim Alexa Schwarz[1(✉)], Sylvio Rüdian[1,2], and Christian Kellermann[1,3]

[1] German Research Center for Artificial Intelligence (DFKI), Berlin, Germany
kim_alexa.schwarz@dfki.de
[2] Humboldt University of Berlin, Berlin, Germany
[3] University of Labour, Frankfurt am Main, Germany

Abstract. Personalization in online learning can be found in several domains, such as language learning, chemistry, or math education. Going beyond these domains is rarely seen. Due to fixed learning progressions, learners enrolled must complete the entire course to succeed. Learners' prior knowledge is often not considered. This can lead to disengagement as learners are not challenged appropriately if task difficulty levels do not align with their skills. To allow a flexible course entry, we introduce a placement test to estimate learners' competency levels employing the item response theory and implement a computerized competency-based adaptive placement test in real-world online courses of the KI-Campus. We illustrate the challenges of applying item response theory with multiple competencies in a real-world setting and demonstrate how to identify a domain-independent, optimal course entry point tailored to the learner. This application promises to optimize the learning time considering learners' prior knowledge, which in turn, can reduce drop-out rates.

Keywords: Personalization · Online Learning · Item Response Theory · Computerized Adaptive Test · Placement Test

1 Introduction

Learning is a life-long process, allowing learners to enhance competencies and skills. While the motivation to learn can be manifold in adult education [25], lack of time is often a concern that prevents individuals from expanding their knowledge. It is important that the topic taught aligns with the learners' interests and learning goals [33], while the difficulty level should meet learners' abilities [12]. Learners can choose from various available courses, but courses are often designed to suit most learners by following a one-size-fits-all approach [7], which causes dropouts if the course and learner are not properly matched [28]. If a

F. Bellas and O. Fontenla-Romero (Eds.): AIEER 2024, CCIS 2519, pp. 161–174, 2025.
https://doi.org/10.1007/978-3-031-93409-4_15

course is too difficult, learners may become frustrated and give up, while courses that are too easy fail to provide new knowledge [20]. Subsequently, there must be an optimal fitting to keep learners engaged [12].

In this paper we conduct a placement test to assess learners' skills, aiming to suggest the optimal entry point within a course and allowing them to skip content that they already know. This approach enables learners to make better use of their time and, as a result can reduce the high dropout rates caused by course items that are "too easy" or already familiar.

The tool is developed for the KI-Campus, which is a MOOC learning platform for AI skills and offers courses to understand, scrutinize and shape AI professionally. The platform is a project funded by the German Federal Ministry of Science and Research and will run until the end of 2024. KI-Campus originals are produced especially for the KI-Campus. The online courses impart fundamental knowledge as well as specialized skills. Course completions are certified through badges, micro-degrees and as part of embedding in degree programs. Focus groups are (1) universities and students to integrate the courses into degree programs and continuing education and to support teachers, (2) companies and professionals so that HR departments can offer AI courses, and (3) the general public to increase their general understanding of AI fundamentals. As of May 2024, approximately 50,000 profiles are registered on the platform and are taking AI Campus courses.

2 Related Work

Placement tests enable learners to estimate their proficiency level and have often been applied in language learning [19]. Such computerized tests can be adaptive to employ a small number of tasks for estimating the latent variable of learner knowledge, skills, or abilities [10,21,44].

In language acquisition, they have successfully been utilized in language learning application like "Duolingo" [41], due to a well-defined classification of learning content in the Common European Framework of Reference for Languages (CEFR) [11]. This framework defines proficiency levels based on topics, vocabulary lists, and grammar skills [31]. Subsequently, learners can demonstrate their existing skills within a fixed set of learning content.

Four decades ago, Weiss and Kingsbury [45] introduced computerized adaptive testing (CAT) in education for different purposes, including determining whether the learner mastered a topic, adaptive grading, and testing for knowledge increase. Frey et al. [18] employ computerized adaptive testing to estimate ability levels for competencies. The study proposes an approach that integrates item response theory for ability testing, though its validity is limited to simulations.

Researchers question the importance of item selection or ability estimation, but without utilizing real-world data and scenarios, it cannot be determined whether the approach can be successfully operationalized. More recent studies like that of Zhuang et al. [46] propose neural computerized adaptive testing, utilizing reinforcement learning to estimate learners' proficiency levels. The performance of that approach is comparable to the item response theory but at the cost of interpretability. However, a technology-enhanced solution for adjusting the learning path to allow a personalized starting point within courses is still missing. This paper aims to bridge that gap.

3 Methodology

To identify and recommend an optimal entry point for a KI-Campus course chosen by the learner, we apply CAT combined with the item response theory (IRT) [29].

Online courses include several tasks, some consisting of questions. We extract questions from real-world courses that require specific skills and use them to employ CAT. In the context of IRT, these questions are referred to as items. As students have already completed courses used within this paper, a great resource of learner performance data exists, that can be analyzed with IRT.

Unlike static paper-and-pencil tests, CAT iteratively selects questions most suited for the test taker based on previous responses. Meaning, only items whose difficulty best matches the test taker's estimated ability are chosen. This results in a more relevant and tailored testing experience, which can decrease test length while simultaneously maximizing measurement efficiency. Subsequently, learner abilities can be estimated with a small number of items [45].

The iterative CAT procedure consists of six main components: The IRT model (Sect. 3.2), an item pool (Sect. 3.3), an ability estimation algorithm (Sect. 3.4), an entry level, an item selection method and a termination policy (Sect. 3.5) [22,45].

3.1 The Learner's Perspective

Before we describe the components and their assembly, we will give a brief overview of the testing tool from the learner's perspective.

Once the learner has selected a course, the system prompts the user to choose the subject they want to study, e.g. "Machine Learning". The system then designs a test with questions relevant to the subject and tailored to the user. Upon completing the test, the ability is computed in the background. Finally, based on the ability score, the system recommends a course entry point to the learner. The learner can then decide to follow the recommendation or disregard the test results and begin the course from the beginning.

3.2 The IRT Model

IRT is a method commonly used in psychometrics. It models the relationship between a test taker's response pattern and their underlying latent ability θ [15].

A variety of models exists within IRT. We opted for the two-parameter logistic (2-PL) IRT model that assumes that an item k can be described by two parameters: The item difficulty b_k, representing the ability level needed to answer an item correctly with a probability of 50%, and the discrimination a_k [35], which expresses how well an item discriminates between individuals with high and low ability scores, i.e. the slope of the function.

Given the item parameters and the latent ability θ_i of individual i the probability Y of a correct response is given as [30]:

$$P(Y_{ik} = 1|\theta_i, b_k, a_k) = \frac{exp(a_k(\theta_i - b_k))}{1 + exp(a_k(\theta_i - b_k))} \tag{1}$$

The item parameters have historically been estimated using marginal maximum likelihood (MML) and the Expectation-Maximization (EM) algorithm [5]. However, this traditional approach has limitations when dealing with small samples, extreme response patterns, and non-normal ability distributions, which can potentially be overcome with variational Bayesian Interference (VB) [30]. Unlike MML, which provides a point estimates of the item parameters, VB assumes that the item parameters follow a prior Gaussian distribution to estimate the entire posterior distribution [27,30].

3.3 The Item Pool

We create a distinct item pool for each KI-Campus course and every subject within each course. To do this, we extract all multiple-choice questions from the courses and categorize them based on the 28 subcategories of "artificial intelligence" in the Computer Science Ontology (CSO) [40], which was automatically generated by analyzing research publications in the field of Computer Science. A 2-PL model [13] is then trained for each item pool with VB.

3.4 Ability Estimation

After the item parameters have been approximated and fixed, the examinee's underlying ability θ_i is assessed based on the correctness of their responses to a set of items. This process is commonly known as "scoring" [16].

Various approaches are available to estimate θ, such as the maximum likelihood method, which returns the maximum of the likelihood function L as the test-taker's ability score. Here, L represents the likelihood of each possible θ based on the test-taker's responses [3]. However, the maximum likelihood estimation may not converge if the test-taker has provided only correct or only incorrect responses [3]. As a result, Bayesian methods are sometimes preferred [23]. One such method is the Bayesian Expectation A Posteriori (EAP) [5] measurement, in which we first multiply L with an assumed distribution and then return the average of the resulting function as the approximated θ. Furthermore, EAP accounts for asymmetric likelihood functions [23]. Hence, why we opted for EAP as our scoring method.

Let $\mathbf{x_i} := [x_{i0}, x_{i1}, x_{i2}, ..., x_{iK}]$ be the response vector of individual i where x_{ik} is the binary score for an item k as defined below [6]:

$$x_{ik} = \begin{cases} 1 & \text{if response correct} \\ 0 & \text{else} \end{cases} \tag{2}$$

Addtionally, let $P(x_{ik} = 1|\theta_i, b_k, a_k)$ be the probability that $x_{ik} = 1$ given θ_i as defined in Eq. 1. With that L of θ_i at the Kth trial in an adaptive test is given as [6]:

$$L_K(\theta_i) = \prod_{k=0}^{K} [P(x_{ik} = 1|\theta_i, b_k, a_k)]^{x_{ik}} \\ [1 - P(x_k = 1|\theta_i, b_k, a_k)]^{1-x_{ik}} \tag{3}$$

The EAP in the Kth trial approximates the mean of the distribution of θ by using the Gaussian quadrature as follows [6]:

$$EAP_K = \frac{\sum_{j=0}^{q} X_j L_K(X_j) \cdot W(X_j)}{\sum_{j=0}^{q} L_K(X_j) \cdot w(X_j)} \tag{4}$$

where q is the number of quadrature points X_j and $W(X_j)$ the associated weight with $\sum_{j=0}^{q} W(X_j) = 1$. Furthermore, $W(X_j)$ is defined as the probability of the assumed distribution at point X_j [6].

3.5 Test Assembly

After training our models, establishing item pools, and defining the scoring method, we can create an adaptive test.

Before starting the test, the user selects a course and chooses a subject from the ontology. Based on this selection, we pick the corresponding item pool. The first question every user receives in the adaptive test is the item with the overall highest information. The item information $I_k(\theta)$ for an item k and a given θ can be calculated as follows [2,9]:

$$I_k(\theta) = a_k^2 P(x_{ik} = 1|\theta, b_k, a_k)(1 - P(x_{ik} = 1|\theta, b_k, a_k)) \tag{5}$$

After the user answers the question, the ability score is calculated as described in Sect. 3.4. We then select the next item based on which item provides the highest information for test-takers with the new ability score. The user answers the question, and the procedure is repeated until a stopping criterion is reached.

We define the stopping criteria as either the test exceeding a predefined length or having a high certainty of the approximated ability score closely reflecting the user's actual ability. The reliability of the estimation can be computed via the standard error (SE) [2]:

$$SE(\theta) = \frac{1}{\sqrt{D^2 \sum_{k=0}^{K} I_k(\theta)}} \tag{6}$$

where $D = 1.7$ is a scaling constant, scaling the logistic discrimination coefficient a to the normal metric [8].

3.6 Placement

Once the adaptive test is completed, the user will receive a recommended starting point in the course based on their final ability score. We organize the items in the item pool by their corresponding sections in the course and arrange them based on their occurrence. Subsequently, we calculate the average probability of correctly answering all items in a section given the user's ability score. If the probability is lower than a predefined threshold, we recommend the user to start in this section. If the probability consistently exceeds the threshold, the user is advised to start in the section with the lowest probability.

4 Experiments

We attempted to apply IRT to 116 KI-Campus courses with data from previous users. The first step was to create the item pools. But, to ensure their reliability, we applied a set of filters. First, we removed questions with fewer than 40 responses, as well as questions where the probability of being answered correctly decreases as the ability score increases. This could indicate labeling errors or noisy data [2]. Subsequently, we eliminated item pools with fewer than a total of 500 responses. Furthermore, item pools with fewer than ten items have been removed as such small number of items would limit the employment of the adaptive test. Finally, after applying these filters, we were left with 18 courses for which we could estimate the IRT parameters to administer tests.

We trained the IRT model with VB and hierarchical priors for $10,000$ epochs and a learning rate of 0.1 with a learning decay rate of 0.9999. We stop the adaptive test if the SE drops below 0.5 or a test length of ten questions is reached. EAP is estimated with 41 quadrature points and bounds -4 and 4.

The minimum number of required examinees to estimate the required parameters to utilise the IRT differs in the literature. While DeMars recommends using at least 1,000 samples [14], Thissen & Wainer used 500 samples and received robust results [42]. Şahin et al. [39] lists a range between 200 and 1,000 samples required to estimate parameters. However, there is no definite answer and the required sample size also depends on the model's complexity and on how well items and data adhere to the IRT assumptions. Depending on their quality, sample size requirements may differ [15]. Generally speaking, the standard error decreases with a growing sample, making the estimations more reliable, but it is reasonable to start with smaller samples for first tests [9].

To measure learning progress, the individual tasks are linked to learning objective competencies that build on each other in a linear fashion. The more interdisciplinary a course is designed, the more prerequisite the link to learning objective competencies is. At the same time, however, it is precisely the progression of learning objective competencies across tasks that makes it possible to measure learning progress in modules with complex content in the first place. The majority of MOOCS on the KI-Campus are task-based and follow a linear learning progression.

5 Results

In this section, we present the results of our testing tool by taking the course "Data Literacy - Daten interpretieren durch Data Mining" and the subject "Machine Learning" as an example.

5.1 Data

During our experiments, we also looked closely at the underlying data since a meaningful data set is the foundation for a good IRT model.

As described in Sect. 4, 98 out of 116 courses had to be removed due to an insufficient amount of data. Additionally, our example course, "Data Literacy - Daten interpretieren durch Data Mining"", only had a limited item pool that lacks more difficult questions to distinguish learners with higher abilities.

Figure 1 illustrates the average number of responses for each section in the course. Notably, the average amount of responses significantly drops with the progression of the course. Similar results can be seen for the most popular KI-Campus course, "Einführung in die KI", as depicted in Fig. 1. While the average amount of responses generally is higher than for the data literacy course, they still drop with course progression. However, this dropout pattern is typical and can be observed in online courses in general [32].

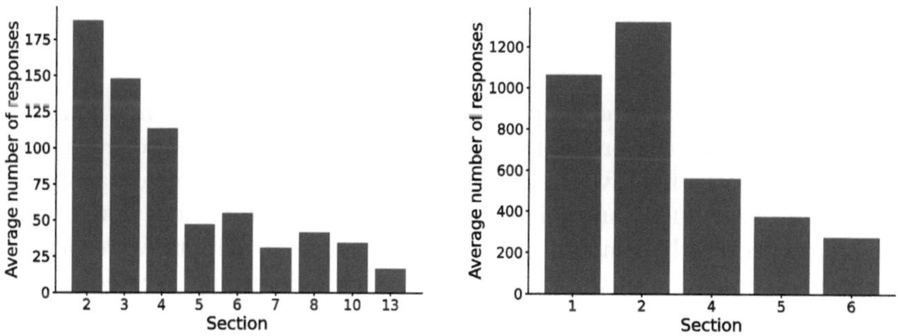

Fig. 1. Average number of responses for each section in courses "Data Literacy - Daten interpretieren durch Data Mining" (left), and "Einführung in die KI" (right).

5.2 Applying IRT

Figure 2 illustrates the item characteristic curves (ICC) for each item of the pool. ICC describes the probability of correctly answering a question in relation to the learner's ability as defined in Eq. 1, respectively [37]. If we focus on the point where the probability of a correct response is 50%, we observe that, on average, most questions have a relatively low difficulty level, thus they are easy to solve.

Additionally, the discrimination, represented by the steepness of the slope, is rather similar for most items. This raises the question of how informative the items truly are. To investigate, we will create item information curves (IIC) using the information function in Eq. 5 as depicted in Fig. 2. Most IIC peak between an ability score of −2 and 2, some for ability scores lower than −6, whereas there is very little information for higher scores.

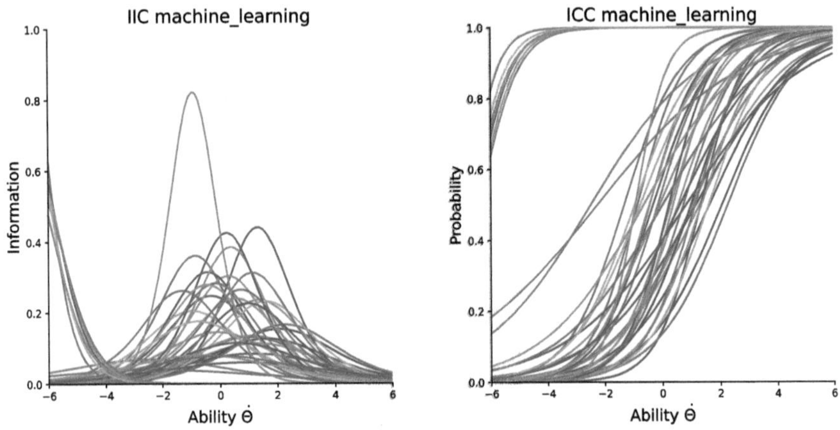

Fig. 2. IIC (left) and ICC (right) of all items covering the subject "machine learning" in the course "Data Literacy - Daten interpretieren durch Data Mining" after filtering.

Nevertheless, we can provide placement recommendations as shown in Fig. 3, which shows the average probability of correctly answering all questions within a test section correctly given a certain ability score. The horizontal red line represents a pre-defined threshold of 0.65. This threshold decides how high the probability of correctly completing a section should be to skip it. We recommend a range of 0.5 and 1.0, but the exact value has to be determined experimentally. The first time a learner's probability given a certain ability falls below the threshold, they are recommended to start in the corresponding section. For learners with an ability between −3 and 1, that would be Sect. 3; learners with ability 2, however, should start in Sect. 5. If a learner's ability is greater than or equal to 3, they never fall below the threshold. In this case, they are recommended to start with the section in which they have the lowest probability of completing. So, learners with an ability 3 are also recommended to start in Sect. 5. Learners with an ability less than or equal to −3 should not skip any sections and start at the beginning.

6 Discussion

Like most models requiring training, the performance of IRT highly depends on the availability of adequate training data. Our experiments have demonstrated

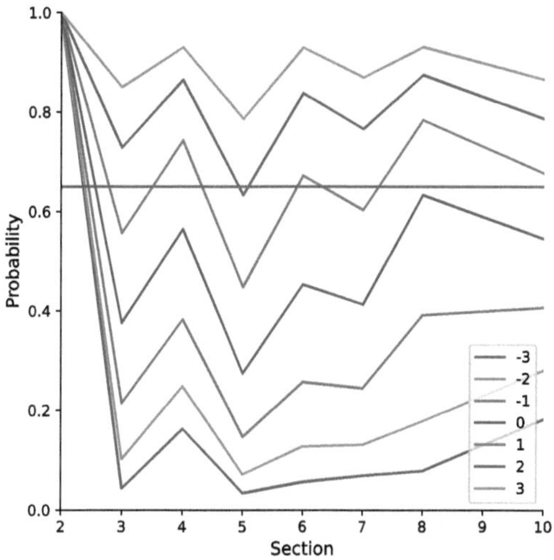

Fig. 3. Average probability of answering all items in a section of "Data Literacy - Daten interpretieren durch Data Mining" correctly with a given ability θ. The horizontal red line at 0.65 represents a threshold. A learner whose ability drops below that threshold is recommended to start in the corresponding section. (Color figure online)

that acquiring data to construct the item pools can be difficult. We need a sufficient number of participants from whom we can gather trace data to derive robust measures. In some cases, certain courses lacked the required number of learners, leading to their exclusion from model training. However, for the remaining courses, we could effectively apply IRT.

Currently, our item pools consist of multiple-choice questions, which allow for automated assessment. Additionally, most questions have a low difficulty and give little information about learners with a high ability. This is due to the natural dropout that happens as the course progresses [32]. As a result, we lack challenging questions in the adaptive test, as more complex questions are typically asked in later sections [34], where we may not have enough data due to high dropout rates. This effect is further enhanced by the task-based learning approach of the courses [43]. Since such tasks are part of the learning process, they are designed to be solved correctly by most learners. While these are potentially too easy and lack discrimination, selecting discriminating questions is crucial for the expressiveness of the test results to represent learners with a wide ability range. However, since we directly source our items from the courses, the difficulty of item pools also represents the difficulty of the course itself. Admittedly, the recommendations for learners with high abilities are not as accurate as recommendations for learners with lower abilities. But, it is more important not to discourage lower-achieving learners by placing them in an advanced section, as opposed to having higher-achieving learners repeat material they have already mastered.

Another challenge arises with the structure of the courses. While many courses follow a linear structure, allowing sections to be easily skipped based on recommendations, others are interdisciplinary, covering multiple subjects simultaneously. Although a learner might be advanced in one subject, they may still need more practice in the other and thus, they should not skip these sections.

In general, there may be potential conflicts between teachers' expectations and personalization. While learners are constrained by time, teachers may want them to complete all sections without skipping due to the pre-defined learning progression. Additionally, some sections must be completed and cannot be skipped if certification is desired. Moreover, curated courses often require a preset learning time, where credit points are proportional to timely effort. In contrast, for lifelong learning, parallel to working or daily life, optimizing learning time can be highly beneficial. Furthermore, if learners can choose the competencies they want to enrich, they might not be aware of their decisions due to a lack of meta-cognitive skills [26]. Thus, learners may not know which skill they want to train and should be able to skip the selection if they need further assistance.

This emphasizes the importance of close collaboration between teachers and developers and an interdisciplinary discourse between educational and computer science. Developers must consider teachers' and learners' expectations and map tasks with competencies and skill levels supported by educational theory. We need to fix a set of competencies before training the model and ensure that tasks and competencies are correctly matched to provide reliable labels. IRT is designed to measure a single latent variable, so it is vital to ensure that the items in an item pool all address the same variable, otherwise, the parameters become uncorrelated to the ability we want to access [15]. In real-world settings, however, we often have to estimate more than one competency. Furthermore, tasks may require a set of competencies to succeed. Subsequently, it remains challenging to estimate competency levels.

For example, in language learning, sets of competencies are merged into proficiency levels, from which the most fitting one is estimated for the learner. However, combining different skill sets (like known vocabulary or grammar skills) to proficiency levels results in a complex estimation process, which may only be utilizable if the learning progression follows the same path. If learners do not consume learning material that has been designed based on the CEFR [11], it is challenging to estimate their proficiency level. In such a setting, competencies must be estimated separately to be able to recommend the most suitable learning material that bridges knowledge gaps. This abstraction level can also be transferred to the estimation of AI competencies. An adaptive test cannot assume that there is a fixed and pre-defined learning progression which all teachers and learners follow. Due to the highly diverse knowledge background, skill levels must be estimated separately to derive a learner competency model, which is the base to predict the optimal course entry point. From the practical perspective, it can be beneficial to define proficiency levels for AI competencies, which are then estimated for learners. Such a definition may reduce the complexity of building competency models, and it can also support the process of designing a curriculum based on AI competencies.

These findings highlight the importance of integrating knowledge from educational theory into development to ensure that applications can be successfully deployed in real-world settings. Additionally, it should not be forgotten that most people, learners and teachers, do not have a deep understanding of computational models [24] and generally view them as a black box. Thus, entry-point recommendations made by an algorithm may not be as trustworthy as those made by teachers and other experts. To increase trustworthiness, models need to be transparent and easy to understand. So, rather than developing more complex and obscure models, we should focus on making them more comprehensible, as well as making their assumptions and outputs justifiable by educational experts [24]. This is why IRT is an excellent foundation for our testing tool. It has a long history in medical and psychological testing [2,36], and its parameters and assumptions can be easily interpreted. We can further improve transparency and reliability by clearly defining competencies and skill levels in advance. To conclude, integrating educational theory into application development and using transparent, easily interpretable models is essential for ensuring the trustworthiness and effectiveness of educational tools in real-world settings.

7 Conclusion and Future Work

We have developed an adaptive testing tool that enables learners to determine the best entry point for an online course aiming to decrease dropout rates. By guiding learners to focus on the most relevant content, the tool can reduce learning time and improve integration into their daily lives.

Learning target competencies lay the ground for adaptive tools and need to be interlinked with the corresponding content, which in itself varies alongside the context complexities of knowledge. The limits of representing complex knowledge in adaptive tests must be addressed by the course development team by linking isolated learning units to learning target competencies. While an adaptive test alone can't fully replace the dramaturgy of complex learning, it can support and enhance the probability of a successful learning experience.

The current effectiveness of the adaptive tool is constrained by data limitations and requires further research to investigate real-world performance. Future work should focus on understanding how well learners adapt to the tool, whether they follow its recommendations, and if dropout rates decrease as a result, or if an adaptive test prior to the course will lead to drop-outs even before they begin. However, as more learners participate in the courses and use the tool, the database becomes more diverse, potentially enhancing the quality of estimations. Lastly, expanding the application of the adaptive testing tool beyond the KI-Campus to other learning platforms and subject areas could further validate its effectiveness and generalizability.

Our ongoing work includes gathering more diverse and up-to-date data for further testing and refining the tool. Additionally, we are relabeling tasks with learning goals and competencies defined by educational experts, based on Bloom's Taxonomy [1,4], to further enhance the tool's accuracy and relevance.

Nevertheless, the ability for a flexible course entry is just a subset of a personalized learning experience, applied to static courses with fixed progression. In a broader scope, placement tests can be used to derive learner competency models. If courses are planned as micro-learning units, the competency model could identify knowledge gaps for which a personalized learning path can be built. Then, selecting and arranging learning materials according to learner needs and their goals can be operationalized as the next step to optimize the learning time. The technology exists [38], that must be combined with appropriate competency models and micro-learning units, for which the KI-Campus has built the foundations [17]. Its combination is part of future work.

Acknowledgments. This work was supported by the German Federal Ministry of Education and Research (BMBF), grant number 16DHBQP058 (KI-Campus 2.0).

Disclosure of Interests. The authors have no competing interests to declare that are relevant to the content of this article.

References

1. Anderson, L.W., Krathwohl, D.R.: A Taxonomy for Learning, Teaching, and Assessing: A Revision of Bloom's Taxonomy of Educational Objectives. Longman (2001). google-Books-ID: EMQlAQAAIAAJ
2. Baker, F.B.: The Basics of Item Response Theory, 2nd edn. ERIC Publications (2001). https://eric.ed.gov/?id=ED458219
3. Baker, F.B., Kim, S.H.: The Basics of Item Response Theory Using R. Statistics for Social and Behavioral Sciences, 1st edn., 2017 edn. Springer (2017). https://doi.org/10.1007/978-3-319-54205-8
4. Bloom, B.S.: Taxonomy of Educational Objectives: The Classification of Educational Goals, 1st edn. Longman Group, Harlow, Essex (1956)
5. Bock, R.D., Aitkin, M.: Marginal maximum likelihood estimation of item parameters: application of an EM algorithm. Psychometrika **46**(4), 443–459 (1981). https://doi.org/10.1007/BF02293801
6. Bock, R.D., Mislevy, R.J.: Adaptive EAP estimation of ability in a microcomputer environment. Appl. Psychol. Meas. **6**(4), 431–444 (1982). https://doi.org/10.1177/014662168200600405
7. Brusilovsky, P., Millán, E.: User models for adaptive hypermedia and adaptive educational systems. In: The Adaptive Web: Methods and Strategies of Web Personalization, pp. 3–53. Springer (2007)
8. Camilli, G.: The scaling constant d in item response theory. Open J. Stat. **7**(5), 780–785 (2017). https://doi.org/10.4236/ojs.2017.75055
9. Cappelleri, J.C., Jason Lundy, J., Hays, R.D.: Overview of classical test theory and item response theory for the quantitative assessment of items in developing patient-reported outcomes measures. Clin. Ther. **36**(5), 648–662 (2014). https://doi.org/10.1016/j.clinthera.2014.04.006
10. Choi, Y., McClenen, C.: Development of adaptive formative assessment system using computerized adaptive testing and dynamic Bayesian networks. Appl. Sci. **10**(22), 8196 (2020). https://doi.org/10.3390/app10228196

11. Council of Europe. Council for Cultural Co-operation. Education Committee. Modern Languages Division: Common European framework of reference for languages: Learning, teaching, assessment. Cambridge University Press (2001)
12. Csikszentmihalyi, M., Csikszentmihalyi, M., Abuhamdeh, S., Nakamura, J.: Flow. Flow and the Foundations of Positive Psychology: The Collected Works of Mihaly Csikszentmihalyi, pp. 227–238 (2014)
13. De Leeuw, J., Verhelst, N.: Maximum likelihood estimation in generalized Rasch models. J. Educ. Stat. **11**(3), 183–196 (1986)
14. DeMars, C.: Item Response Theory. Oxford University Press (2010)
15. Edelen, M.O., Reeve, B.B.: Applying item response theory (IRT) modeling to questionnaire development, evaluation, and refinement. Qual. Life Res. **16**(1), 5–18 (2007). https://doi.org/10.1007/s11136-007-9198-0
16. Ferrando, P.J., Lorenzo-Seva, U.: A note on improving EAP trait estimation in oblique factor-analytic and item response theory models. Psicológica **37**(2), 235–247 (2016)
17. Flasdick, J., Mah, D.K., Bernd, M., Rampelt, F.: Micro-credentials und micro-degrees. In: Aktuelle Entwicklungen und Perspektiven aus der Praxis des KI-Campus, pp. 1–24 (2022)
18. Frey, A., Kroehne, U., Seitz, N.N., Born, S.: Multidimensional adaptive measurement of competencies. In: Competence Assessment in Education: Research, Models and Instruments, pp. 369–387 (2017)
19. Fulcher, G.: Computerizing an English language placement test. ELT J. **53**(4), 289–299 (1999). https://doi.org/10.1093/elt/53.4.289
20. Graesser, A.C., D'Mello, S.: Emotions during the learning of difficult material. In: Psychology of Learning and Motivation, vol. 57, pp. 183–225. Elsevier (2012)
21. Hambleton, R.K., Zaal, J.N., Pieters, J.P.: Computerized adaptive testing: theory, applications, and standards. In: Advances in Educational and Psychological Testing: Theory and Applications, pp. 341–366. Springer (1991)
22. Han, K.: Components of the item selection algorithm in computerized adaptive testing. J. Educ. Eval. Health Prof. **15**, 7 (2018). https://doi.org/10.3352/jeehp.2018.15.7
23. Han, K.T.: Maximum likelihood score estimation method with fences for short-length tests and computerized adaptive tests. Appl. Psychol. Meas. **40**(4), 289–301 (2016). https://doi.org/10.1177/0146621616631317
24. Kerres, M., Buntins, K.: Recommender in AI-enhanced learning: an assessment from the perspective of instructional design. Open Educ. Stud. **2**(1), 101–111 (2020). https://doi.org/10.1515/edu-2020-0119
25. Kim, C., Park, S.W., Cozart, J., Lee, H.: From motivation to engagement: the role of effort regulation of virtual high school students in mathematics courses. J. Educ. Technol. Soc. **18**(4), 261–272 (2015)
26. Kirschner, P.A., van Merriënboer, J.J.: Do learners really know best? Urban legends in education. Educ. Psychol. **48**(3), 169–183 (2013)
27. Lalor, J.P., Wu, H., Yu, H.: Learning latent parameters without human response patterns: item response theory with artificial crowds. In: Proceedings of the Conference on Empirical Methods in Natural Language Processing. Conference on Empirical Methods in Natural Language Processing, vol. 2019, pp. 4240–4250 (2019). https://doi.org/10.18653/v1/D19-1434
28. Lee, Y., Choi, J.: A review of online course dropout research: implications for practice and future research. Educ. Tech. Res. Dev. **59**, 593–618 (2011)
29. Lord, F., Novick, M., Birnbaum, A.: Statistical Theories of Mental Test Scores. Addison-Wesley (1968)

30. Natesan, P., Nandakumar, R., Minka, T., Rubright, J.D.: Bayesian prior choice in IRT estimation using MCMC and variational bayes. Front. Psychol. **7** (2016). https://doi.org/10.3389/fpsyg.2016.01422
31. North, B.: The CEFR levels and descriptor scales. In: Multilingualism and Assessment: achieving transparency, assuring quality, sustaining diversity. In: Proceedings of the ALTE Berlin Conference, pp. 21–66 (2005)
32. Onah, D.F., Sinclair, J., Boyatt, R.: Dropout rates of massive open online courses: behavioural patterns. In: EDULEARN14 proceedings, pp. 5825–5834 (2014)
33. Paechter, M., Maier, B., Macher, D.: Students' expectations of, and experiences in e-learning: their relation to learning achievements and course satisfaction. Comput. Educ. **54**(1), 222–229 (2010)
34. Print, M.: Curriculum Development and Design. Allen & Unwin (1993). https://books.google.de/books?id=0AaeaqKoElEC
35. Pyrczak, F.: Validity of the discrimination index as a measure of item quality 1. J. Educ. Meas. **10**(3), 227–231 (1973)
36. Reise, S.P., Waller, N.G.: Item response theory and clinical measurement. Annu. Rev. Clin. Psychol. **5**(1), 27–48 (2019). https://doi.org/10.1146/annurev.clinpsy.032408.153553
37. Rosenbaum, P.R.: Comparing item characteristic curves. Psychometrika **52**, 217–233 (1987)
38. Rüdian, S., Pinkwart, N.: Generating adaptive and personalized language learning online courses in moodle with individual learning paths using templates. In: 2021 International Conference on Advanced Learning Technologies (ICALT), pp. 53–55. IEEE (2021)
39. Şahin, A., Anıl, D.: The effects of test length and sample size on item parameters in item response theory. Educ. Sci.: Theory Pract. **17**(1) (2017)
40. Salatino, A.A., Thanapalasingam, T., Mannocci, A., Osborne, F., Motta, E.: The computer science ontology: a large-scale taxonomy of research areas. In: Vrandečić, D., et al. (eds.) ISWC 2018. LNCS, vol. 11137, pp. 187–205. Springer, Cham (2018). https://doi.org/10.1007/978-3-030-00668-6_12
41. Teske, K.: Duolingo. CALICO J. **34**(3), 393–401 (2017)
42. Thissen, D., Wainer, H.: Some standard errors in item response theory. Psychometrika **47**(4), 397–412 (1982)
43. Van Marcke, K.: A generic task model for instruction. In: Instructional Models in Computer-Based Learning Environments, pp. 171–194. Springer (1992)
44. Wainer, H., Dorans, N.J., Flaugher, R., Green, B.F., Mislevy, R.J.: Computerized Adaptive Testing: A Primer. Routledge (2000)
45. Weiss, D.J., Kingsbury, G.G.: Application of computerized adaptive testing to educational problems. J. Educ. Meas. **21**(4), 361–375 (1984). https://doi.org/10.1111/j.1745-3984.1984.tb01040.x
46. Zhuang, Y., Liu, Q., Huang, Z., Li, Z., Shen, S., Ma, H.: Fully adaptive framework: neural computerized adaptive testing for online education. In: Proceedings of the AAAI Conference on Artificial Intelligence, vol. 36, pp. 4734–4742 (2022)

Correction to: Automated Essay Scoring with ChatGPT

Sebastian Maidl and Annette Hautli-Janisz

Correction to:
Chapter 7 in: F. Bellas and O. Fontenla-Romero (Eds.):
***AI in Education and Educational Research*, CCIS 2519,**
https://doi.org/10.1007/978-3-031-93409-4_7

The original version of the book was inadvertently published with an error related to author name Sebastian Maidl. It has been corrected.

The updated version of this chapter can be found at
https://doi.org/10.1007/978-3-031-93409-4_7

F. Bellas and O. Fontenla-Romero (Eds.): AIEER 2024, CCIS 2519, p. C1, 2025.
https://doi.org/10.1007/978-3-031-93409-4_16

Author Index

F. Bellas and O. Fontenla-Romero (Eds.): AIEER 2024, CCIS 2519, pp. 175–176, 2025.
https://doi.org/10.1007/978-3-031-93409-4

MIX
Papier aus verantwortungsvollen Quellen
Paper from responsible sources
FSC® C105338

If you have any concerns about our products,
you can contact us on
ProductSafety@springernature.com

In case Publisher is established outside the EU,
the EU authorized representative is:
Springer Nature Customer Service Center GmbH
Europaplatz 3, 69115 Heidelberg, Germany

Printed by Libri Plureos GmbH
in Hamburg, Germany